What Evil Means to Us

What  *Means to Us*

C. FRED ALFORD

Cornell University Press

ITHACA AND LONDON

First published 1997 by Cornell University Press.

Printed in the United States of America

Library of Congress Cataloging-in-Publication Data

Alford, C. Fred.
  What evil means to us / C. Fred Alford.
    p. cm.
  Includes bibliographical references and index.
  ISBN 0-8014-3430-0 (cloth : alk. paper)
    1. Good and evil. I. Title.
BJ1406.A44 1997
111'.84—dc21   97-10437

Cloth printing   10 9 8 7 6 5 4 3 2 1

To all who spoke with me about evil,
above all the inmates at Patuxent Institution
who participated in the Friday-afternoon "evil group"

Contents

Preface

For all things, from the Void
Called forth, deserve to be destroyed. . . .
Destruction,—aught with Evil blent,—
That is my proper element.

— GOETHE, *Faust*, Part I

Sigmund Freud did not write very much about evil, or at least he did not call it that. In *Civilization and Its Discontents* he did, quoting the devil in these lines from *Faust* that equate evil with the *Todestrieb*, the drive toward death. Not just because the *Todestrieb* seeks destruction, but because it seeks the void, nothingness.

I too argue that evil is about nothingness—not just the nothingness we seek but the nothingness we dread. Evil has its origins in nothingness because it is no-thing: the dread of boundlessness and all that goes with it—loss of self, loss of meaning, loss of history, and loss of connection to the world itself.

Though I refer to Freud, among other analysts, and to philosophers, writers, and artists, I more frequently refer to my informants, as I call them: the men and women who talked with me about evil. It is they who defined evil in this way: not as a moral problem, not as a religious problem, not as an intellectual problem, but as an experience of dread almost beyond words. Evil is this experience, and evil is an attempt to master the experience by inflicting it on others.

Explaining evil is not the same as understanding it, an issue to which I return again and again. Even if I succeed in explaining the psychological origins of evil in dread, I shall not have explained the most important aspect of evil: why in the world do we live in a world like this one, a world so filled with evil? One should not, however, cease trying to explain, and understand, evil for this reason. If we can understand evil a little better, we may lessen the amount of evil in the world. Not, probably, by a lot—the understanding I seek is not of the type to bring control or mastery—but a little.

Some argue that we should not try to understand evil because doing so may lead us to forgive evildoers too readily, that to understand all may lead us to forgive all, or so the saying goes. Though that may sometimes be so, humans are often intellectually and emotionally supple enough to do two things at once, to understand and condemn. Not to understand is also filled with moral risk, the risk that we shall fail to recognize evil when we see it. If evil is present in everyday life, if there are little evils as well as large ones, and if they are connected, then the failure to understand evil may blind us to its more subtle manifestations in us all.

My greatest debt, expressed in the dedication, is to all those who spoke to me about evil. In addition, I am indebted to the administration of Patuxent Institution, a state prison. Dr. Henry Richards, Associate Director and Director of Behavioral Sciences, understood why I might want to study the views of inmates confined in a socially designated container of evil. He, together with Debra Kafami, Director of Research, took my proposal to the director, Joseph Henneberry, without whose understanding and support my research at Patuxent Institution would have been impossible.

Inmates are exaggerations of the rest of us. To understand their violence better is to understand our own. Patuxent Institution contributed to this understanding. During the fourteen months I spent there, no attempt was ever made to restrict my access to prisoners, staff, programs, or any other aspect of prison life. On the contrary, the psychological staff and administration seemed generally interested in fostering my learning, so that I might help them think about evil. I hope I did; I know they helped me think about it. About the attitude of the prison administrative staff I can do no better than quote Alexis de Tocqueville, who learned much about our society by talking with prisoners and their wardens. "We have no other interest," the warden of a Philadelphia prison told him, "than that of the truth."

My greatest debt is to Dr. Kevin McCamant, the prison psychologist assigned to work with me. Without his willingness to spend hours (much of it after work) talking with me about the "evil group," as it came to be known, I would not have understood much of what went on in the frequently chaotic sessions. His insight, his warmth, and above all his gift for caring about inmates without overidentifying with them, were an education to me.

At the risk of failing to learn from Dr. McCamant's example regarding overidentification, I wish to express my regret that the topic of this book does not allow me to present the rich humanity of the inmates more sympathetically. Each is more, and better, than the worst thing he or she has done. First they told me this; then they convinced me it is true.

Rex Bloomstein, producer of dozens of documentaries on torture, prison, and other dreadful things, invited me to work with him on a documentary about evil. Although I was at first reluctant, and although I have not seen the result, I appreciate his seriousness, and I think he appreciated my imagination. Chapter 9, particularly, reflects our conversations.

My wife, Elaine Feder Alford, and my father, Starley Alford, listened to my stories and theories about evil for hours, and so helped me weave my narrative.

C. FRED ALFORD

Seoul, Korea

What Evil Means to Us

ONE   *"I Felt Evil"*

Do average—and not-so-average—people think Evil exists and, if so, what do they think it is? Would they tell? Do they even know? Do people have depths of knowledge about things like evil, depths they are unaware of, depths the right questions might tap? Plato thought so. Everything we shall ever learn, possibly everything humans can learn, we already know. It just takes the right questions to bring the knowledge forth.[1] Could it be this way with evil?

Wait just a minute, you might reply. This approach gets it wrong from the beginning. Going around asking people about evil is not going to tell you what evil is, only what people think it is. They are not the same. Even if one arrived at a coherent definition of evil from asking people about it, that is all one would have—a definition. A definition is just a name. It does not help us understand the concept, the experience, the reality of evil.

There would be some truth in such an objection, but only some. People use terms like "evil" in ways they are unaware of. Their definitions contradict their examples. It is into this space between definition and example that my research was directed. My goal was to discover not so much how people define evil, but how they experience it—in themselves, in others, in the world. Or rather, my goal was to see how experience affects definition.

"I never knew I believed these things about evil, I don't know where half the things I said came from." Half a dozen informants made similar statements. Some things that people think about evil are buried deeply in the unconscious; other things people know as surely as they know their name. Most things people think and feel about evil fall somewhere in between, connotations falling outside the penumbra of everyday use but by no means inaccessible to reflection. It is reflection that my interviews, many hours long, encouraged.

Were the men who made the Holocaust evil, or do we better understand them as human, all too human—obedient to a fault? Does Hannah Arendt's concept of the banality of evil make sense, or is it an apology for evil, a refusal to look? Is radical evil best seen in terms of Kant's concerns about self-serving morality, or in terms of the enormity of the deed?

These are the formulations of the problem of evil most academics would recognize, evil as a moral problem. I did not expect my informants to express their understanding of evil in these terms. I did expect their responses to reflect these questions in a general way, to address popular variants such as the question of when it is evil to take a human life. In addition, I expected religious informants to be struggling with the issue of theodicy, the justice of God. How could an all-good and all-powerful God allow the suffering of innocents? Is that not evil?

These are not, however, the categories formulated by most informants, not even religious ones. Instead, most informants approached evil as an experience of dread. From this perspective evil is not a moral or theological problem. It is a problem of life, more practical than theoretical: how to know and live with an uncanny presentiment of disaster which sneaks up on one from time to time. For some, this problem is part of all the evil in the world, the evil on the television news. Evil has a human face, and for many it is that of the predatory violent criminal. But most informants did not equate criminal violence with evil, reserving the term "evil" for an experience of dread whose locus was unclear.

Asking about Evil

Almost every question I asked was pretested on the computer Internet, which has a bulletin board on evil. It was there that I first became aware of the widespread tendency to define evil as an uncanny experience of discomfort and anxiety. One might hold that this is an odd way to think about the experience of evil. In fact, it is an experience as old as history. In *The Symbolism of Evil*, Paul Ricoeur characterizes the primordial experience of evil in terms of dread. *Kakía*, the New Testament term we translate as "evil," has a similar sense, as Elaine Pagels argues in *The Gnostic Gospels*.[2] Dread is not the whole of evil, possibly not even its most important part, but it is its ground: the dread of being human, vulnerable, alone in the universe, and doomed to die.

Evil is an experience of dread. *Doing* evil is an attempt to evacuate this experience by inflicting it on others, making them feel dreadful by hurting them. Doing evil is an attempt to transform the terrible passivity and helplessness of suffering into activity. This is how I eventually came to interpret how most of my informants saw the relationship between the experience of dread and the concept of evil. Viewed from this perspective, informants are not so much defining evil as presenting a *theory* about it, where it comes from, and where it goes. Or rather, informants tacitly assume that a definition of such an important concept as evil must be more than a definition, a definition-cum-explanation. It is not a bad assumption.

Not that most put it just this way. Most did not even use the term "dread." This is the interpretation that made sense of the stories they told me. In some cases their interpretation was the same, but not always. This is my narrative as much as theirs: my story about their stories, my narrative that renders dozens of their narratives (but not all) commensurable, stories with a common theme. This method disqualifies my work as a rigorous empirical study (though one might argue that listening carefully to what people say is the most rigorous empirical approach of all). But it is hard to imagine that one could approach the problem in any other way.

One reason so many informants talk about evil in terms of dread, one might argue, is that they are responding to the emotional power of the term "evil," not the concept of evil, which is presumably more abstract —a class, not an instance. It is the emotional power that makes their responses so extreme. This is not a useful distinction, and following Ludwig Wittgenstein (see Appendix 1) I do not make it. My questions are designed to capture the use of the term in a variety of situations. This pattern is equivalent to an informant's concept of evil.

I proceed this way not because my perspective is that of a grammatical behavioralist, in which we know all about a term by knowing its use. Instead, my approach is "solving for x," examining the use of the term in a variety of settings, so that we may know something of the principles by which it is applied. The result is an informant's function for evil: the rules he or she follows to generate the term. Call this the informant's concept of evil if you will, but it is a distinction that makes no difference.

My approach raises several difficult philosophical and methodological issues. What does it mean to ask people about the status of a concept? Does this approach not reify the concept, turning it into a thing? What is the relationship between the concept and the reality of evil? Instead of burdening the introductory chapters with an important but possibly distracting issue, I discuss it in Appendix 1, comparing my approach with that of Wittgenstein.

A man with a method is like a baby with a hammer. Everything looks like a nail. I trust I am not this baby, but my method frames the manuscript: not the methodology of questionnaire construction and sampling, but the method of talking with different people about evil.[3] People do not have concepts of evil, or at least that is not the experiential ground. People live an experience of evil, and it lives them. Aspects of this experience can be put into words, especially if people are encouraged to try. No matter how theoretical I was tempted to get, the experience of talking with people about evil brought me back to earth. Whether it happened soon enough only the reader can decide.

Among the informants are eighteen prison inmates, most serving long sentences for murder. Throughout I compare the responses of free citizens and inmates, each a foil to the other. These differences point the way to understanding evil, not because inmates are more evil but because they live closer to it, closer to their dread—so close, in many cases, that they live it instead of speaking it.

More than other informants, the inmates had difficulty putting their experiences of evil into words. It may be that talking about evil is the best, possibly even the only, alternative to doing it. On many questions, inmates and free informants differed little from each other. On a few questions the differences were profound. In finding Adolf Eichmann, who orchestrated the murder of millions of Jews, not evil, almost all free informants argued that he was a cog in the war machine. Very few inmates made this argument. Instead, almost all inmates argued that in war anything goes—there are no bystanders, everyone is either victim or executioner. Focusing on differences like these, trying to explain the differences in terms of the different experiences of evil of the two groups, was the most powerful way I found to understand evil.

"This place recruits exotic crimes," said one inmate about the prison where I conducted my research, a maximum-security institution with a small psychological treatment program. He was just right: exotic crimes, but not exotic criminals. Though the inmates were no random sample of prisoners, they were neither crazy nor, with one exception, psychopathic. Inmates are like the rest of us only more so, as Sigmund Freud said about neurotics.

Informants

I began to recruit informants by placing an advertisement in the campus newspaper, which reaches a community of over sixty thousand people.

TALK ABOUT EVIL

Have you experienced evil? What is it? Can you forgive? Talk with a professor doing research on the topic.

Students, faculty, staff and all others invited. Pays $10.00 for 1–2 hour on-campus interview. Call xxx-xxxx.

Almost a hundred responded, more than could be interviewed. Most cared little for the money. A number refused it, still others thought they had to pay. As I expected, most of the informants were young. To achieve a better age distribution, I placed similar advertisements in a local newspaper and in *Leisure World News*, the organ of a large retirement community. Eventually I interviewed over sixty people, many for several hours.

The "sample" is hardly random, but it is remarkably diverse, including three "races," a dozen religions, and a roughly equal number of men and women aged eighteen to eighty. Appendix 2 characterizes the informants according to the usual variables, as well as addresses the problem of self-selection. Is there any reason to believe that those who volunteered (for a fee) to talk about evil were different in significant ways from those who did not? There is. Those who came to talk about evil may have been more in touch with their dread. In Appendix 2, I argue that this characteristic should not affect the reliability or validity of the results. On the contrary, it may result in our actually understating the dramatic differences between inmates and free informants on some questions.

For most free informants the problem was getting evil off the TV and into the interview room. "I know the TV news has lots to say about evil, but tell me about the worst experience of evil in your *own* life." Repeatedly I found myself saying something like this. I did not have to say it to the eighteen prisoners, whom I usually met with as a group. So convinced were they of their own evil that the problem with them was to get a little distance on the subject. At the first session one of the inmates said, "We're the most evil guys you're ever going to meet. In the most evil place you're ever going to be. If you stay here, we're going to make you evil too." He was wrong on all three counts.

All the inmates in the group, officially called "Popular Concepts of Evil," are serving serious time, two for theft, the rest for crimes of violence which include serial rape, torture, murder (multiple), child murder, infanticide, patricide, matricide, and fratricide. I never learned how the group got its name. One of the prison staff must have a sense of humor. We met for two hours a week for over a year, spending well over one hundred hours talking about evil. Some inmates came and went, but seven of the original members remained after a year. The average size of the group was a dozen members.

Could the fact that I met with inmates in a group, and with free informants individually, have influenced the results? This does not seem to have been the case. In addition to meeting with the inmates in a group, I spoke with several of them individually at length and have corresponded with others about their views of evil (their mail is not routinely censored). Never was there any difference between what they said privately and what they said in the group.

In addition, I was a participant-observer in a psychopathy-identification project at the prison. The prison uses live and taped interviews with inmates deemed to be psychopathic to teach staff how to identify them. For all the horror of their crimes, the members of "Popular Concepts of Evil" are passionate men and women, filled with remorse. The psychopath is not. This is an important distinction, though not decisive for our conceptual understanding of evil. Not because the psychopath is not evil; most are. But because it is too easy to use the psychopath's evil to let the rest of us off the hook. Much evil, I argue, has a psychopathic quality, a quality in which we all participate by virtue of being human.

Presenting the results in numbers (32 hold this, 21 hold that) or percentages does not seem appropriate or useful, because it grants an unwarranted and unnecessary aura of precision. As Aristotle said, "It is the mark of a trained mind to expect no more precision than the subject matter allows" (*N. Ethics* 1094b30). Instead, I have employed the terms "almost all," "most," "many," "some," "few," and "very few" in as precise a manner as seems warranted by the terms themselves, using each to reflect a specific number range of responses outlined in Appendix 2.

References to questions by number in the text refer to the numbered questions in Appendix 2. When it seems especially important, the question, or an abbreviated version, is stated in the text.

Free citizens are referred to by first name and last initial (the initial is dropped in subsequent references in the same section). Prison inmates are referred to as Mr. or Ms. I do this not to patronize, but because the use of surnames is the practice of the prison, the way I came to know the inmates. All surnames are pseudonyms.

All subjects, free citizens and inmates alike, are referred to as informants (a dreaded word among inmates), after the practice of anthropologists. It is how I see my study, as a domestic anthropology of evil. Not "How do a representative group of people define evil?" but "How is a concept like evil active in the culture?" is my concern. This approach requires that the diversity of the culture be adequately represented among informants. It does not require a random sample.

Is Understanding Evil Evil?

Evil is a popular topic these days. Understanding it is not. In "No Excuses," an essay in the *Washington Post*, published shortly after the bombing of the Federal Building in Oklahoma City, David Walsh struggles with whether we should want to understand the motives of the bombers: "The core reality of the Oklahoma bombing is the evil that is hidden within the human heart. All the so-called explanations slip away when we submit them to closer examination. When we think about them, none of them justifies the wanton destruction of upward of 130 innocent human lives."[4] In the course of two sentences, Walsh has slipped from explanation to justification, assuming that they are identical: "By looking for an explanation, we give the murders a justification. But it is precisely the lack of an explanation that makes the actions so evil." Evil loses its power, its explanatory power to make sense of the world, when we try to understand it in terms of ordinary human motives. Yet, after repeatedly saying that we should not try to understand evil, Walsh goes on to give his explanation. The bombers did it because of "the sheer satisfaction of destruction. There is even the delight in doing what is evil, of being really bad. The sobering aspect to this reflection is that we can begin to enter into it because we glimpse the possibility of such radical evil within ourselves." Immediately after this explanation, Walsh does another one-hundred-eighty-degree turn: "The search for explanations is the search only for excuses. Evil itself cannot be explained, and the attempt to do so is both a denial of its reality and a cheapening of the suffering of its victims." This after offering a clear and sobering explanation of evil, the delight in destruction.

Walsh's incoherence is our own, reflecting how difficult it is to come to terms with evil—not so much because evil cannot be explained, but because the explanations seem so inadequate. Unless (and the author hints at this) we let ourselves know the sheer destructiveness in our own hearts, projecting that knowledge into the bombers, so that in a certain sense their act becomes our own. Perhaps it is this that we will not let ourselves do. If so, then our inability to understand evil is a willful failure to know our own hearts.

Why did you do it? "Because I'm evil," replies Mr. Marcus, who is serving a sixty-year sentence for beating a policeman on the head with a hammer. "Yeah!" adds Mr. Albright, who stabbed a man to death. "That's why I did it too. Because I was an evil bastard." For some inmates, being evil *is* the justification. They like it; it gives them a type of power. "If I weren't evil, man, I'd just be shit." More important, defining themselves as evil means they do not have to look inside and grieve for what they find. Being evil covers it all; that is, it provides a cover story.

Imagine that Walsh could speak to them. He might say, "Don't try to understand your evil or explain it by whining about your unhappy childhood. Just admit it." Each would respond, "Sure. That's what I've been doing for years." Each would be right. Pretending to a steely confrontation with evil, Walsh refuses to look. Or, rather, he just peeks. It requires no muscular intelligence to label something as evil. The real trick is to know the human face of evil while still knowing it to be evil. For that you have to look.

Mr. Redeux shot and killed a twelve-year-old girl; within months he hogtied and executed a middle-aged man. "Evil's relative," he says. "My mother beat me. I thought she was evil, but she didn't. Who's to say what's evil?" We are. Relativism is sometimes the problem. More often relativism is a defense against experience, the overwhelming emotional and moral experience of evil. In this regard relativism is not so different from Walsh's strategy of "Let's call it evil and be done with it." Both are a way of not looking, and not feeling. The most relative thing about evil is that it is frequently committed by relatives. Of all the things to be learned about evil, this is possibly the saddest, that love is no stranger to evil.

Evil Is Rooted in Dread

Roughly following the order in which I asked my questions, the book touches on a various topics, from the shocking results of Stanley Milgram's experiments to younger informants' fascination with vampires as icons of evil. Frequently I compare informants' responses to the ideas of the great philosophers and littérateurs of evil, from Augustine to Paul Ricoeur, from John Milton to Thomas Mann.

My book is not, however, a report. *It is a thesis.* The experience of dread which so many call evil stems from what the psychoanalyst Thomas Ogden calls the "formless dread" of our presymbolic, preverbal experience, what he calls the autistic-contiguous position, the fear that the self is dissolving. Doing evil is not just about inflicting this dread on others. Doing evil is also an attempt to shortcut our access to the autistic-contiguous position, a dimension of experience that is a source not only of dread but also a source of vitality and meaning in life.[5] In doing evil, the evildoer seeks vitalizing contact with the autistic-contiguous dimension of experience while avoiding its price, an awareness of human pain, vulnerability, and death. In a word, evil is cheating.

There is a connection between my argument and that of Otto Rank and Ernest Becker. Not only do humans deny the dread that is our doom, our death, but as Rank puts it, "The death fear of the ego is lessened by the killing, the sacrifice, of the other; through the death of the other, one buys oneself free from the penalty of dying, of being killed."[6] One difference between my argument and theirs is that I see dread as rooted more in fear of life than of death, though surely they know this too. Another difference is that I am primarily concerned not with killing but with the thousand ways evil aims to sacrifice the soul of another.

For some informants, the experience of dread swamped all one might ordinarily define as evil. "What's Hitler got to do with evil?" "Murder's bad, so is war, but it's not really evil, is it?" For most, however, dread represented a different dimension of evil, not incompatible with moral evil but belonging to a separate reality. We shall not be as moral as we might be until we can connect the psychological experience with morality. It is the gulf between the experience of dread and moral standards, such as Immanuel Kant's categorical imperative, which makes morality seem so empty to some, such a luxury to others. It is a gulf that cannot be eliminated, but it can be bridged.

By the second interview the dread that defines evil for so many was already apparent. Tell me about your worst experience with evil, I asked?

"It was last year, this feeling I couldn't shake. That I was losing myself, my separate identity, to my boyfriend," Patricia D. responds.

What's *that* got to do with evil, you might ask? Everything. If we can understand why Patricia experienced her fear of losing her identity as evil, we shall have learned one of the most important things about it.

The most common image of evil was the most mundane, the experience of going down into the basement as a kid, the feeling that something dark and dangerous was about. "I felt evil," says Matt C. about this experience.

Do you mean that you felt that you were evil, or that you felt that evil was around you?

The distinction makes no sense to Matt. His experience was prior to such normal, wide-awake distinctions as subject and object, man and world. It is an experience that will be called precategorical, prior to the categories by which we normally know the world.

Spury F. liberated Dachau as a young PFC. He remembers corpses laid out as far as he could see, but his leading example of evil is drowning some kittens as a child. What is it about the concept of evil which produces such private and personal responses? How can we connect this private and inward experience with the shared moral world, so as to respect both: the integrity of private experience and the reality of shared moral experience? These are the leading problems of evil, made so much more difficult by the terror evil evokes, a threat to the self so profound we tend to isolate it deep in the mind. This burial only makes the threat more powerful, and morality more irrelevant, as what we say becomes disconnected from what we feel and do.

A sense of evil is an important constituent of morality. But feeling evil is no barrier to immorality. Frequently feeling oneself to be evil only encourages our doing it, another reason not to "call it evil and be done with it." For months before he raped a relative, Mr. Prior knew that he was going to hell. "I was out of control. I was acting like an animal. I knew it was wrong. But I couldn't stop. The more bad shit I did, killing cats, hurting people, the more evil I felt, and the more evil I did. Finally I took her out of spite. I didn't even want her. I wanted to be a beast. I didn't know any other way to live."

Take the last statement quite literally—not merely that Mr. Prior was ignorant of how to live as a civilized human but that if he did not live like a beast he could not live at all. He became the evil beast in order to be powerful and beastly enough to defeat it. Or rather, he became the evil beast so as not to be devoured by it, as if these were the only choices. When doom overwhelms us, they are.

Only when he went to prison and "went sort of crazy" did he understand. Heavily medicated on Thorazine and other antipsychotics, he could no longer react quickly enough to defend himself. He gave up his shiv, his homemade knife. "Then I realized. The thing that scared me most wasn't the other guy. It was me. When I couldn't defend myself any more, I had to accept being a victim. I don't like it, but it's better than living like an animal, always on the edge." Mr. Prior has learned an important lesson about evil the hard way. So has his victim.

In general, inmates are more controlled and less imaginative than other informants, especially about evil. Not all are. Lou Cipher (Lucifer), as he calls himself, imagines that the devil is whispering in his ear, tempting him to take terrible indecencies with women. But not with every woman. One of the inmates shot her husband dead, and like Socrates' daimon who kept him out of trouble, Lou Cipher's devil tells him to stay away from her. "Man, I wouldn't even skywrite her." Skywriting is how men and women inmates communicate, men standing at the big windows of their tiers, drawing letters in the sky with their fingers for the inmates of the women's prison a hundred yards and a forest of razor wire away.

Of course inmates are less imaginative than others about evil, you might reply. They do their evil, they don't just fancy it. It is an important point, suggesting that the ability to imagine evil, giving it symbolic form, is an alternative to doing it. The impulse to do evil—that is, the impulse to inflict our dread on others rather than know it in ourselves—cannot be eliminated. We live with it by giving it symbolic form. For many inmates, the capacity to symbolize is restricted to the body, their crime a physical acting-out of their dread. If we can learn to express our evil more abstractly, in stories and pictures, we shall be less likely to do it. It is the task of culture to provide symbolic forms by which we may contain and express our evil in ways that do not inflict it on others.

It will not do to draw this distinction too sharply, however, this difference between doing evil and telling a story about it. Doing evil *is* telling a story. Consider Ms. Gans, who shot and killed her lover on Christmas Eve, holding a beloved stuffed animal in her left hand and a gun in her right. Carefully placing his body under the Christmas tree, she placed the stuffed bunny in his folded arms. Then she wrapped him in a crazy quilt: "You know, the kind where the pieces don't fit together right, like there's no pattern." Finally she called the police.

Ms. Gans knows that her crime tells a story. "I know it means something. It's even kind of funny, if you know what I mean. But it's been two years, and I just can't crack the code." When she finally cracks the code she will have done more than figure out the meaning of her act.

She will have entered another conceptual world, in which symbols are more abstract, less embodied and thinglike. Feeling what she is talking about will replace acting it out (or reciting its acting-out, what she was doing in the group). How we tell our stories about evil is as important as what we tell. It is here that Ogden's autistic-contiguous position, a presymbolic state in which bodily experience takes the place of symbols, is useful, explaining not merely the failure of some inmates and others to symbolize their dread, but helping to explain the failure of culture to provide the symbolic forms necessary for them to do so.

What we tell is also important. For younger informants, the vampire has replaced Satan as the leading image of evil. The change is not a good sign. Satan tempts your soul, corrupting you from inside out, exploiting your pride against your will. The vampire just wants to suck your blood; about your soul he knows and cares nothing. Inmates think vampires are childish, silly, not to be taken seriously. Yet, many of their crimes have a vampire-like quality. One calls it "stomping for intimacy," a brutal assault the only way to get really close to someone, blood the sign of true love. It is not a good sign that younger informants and inmates sound more alike than different.

The culture that could provide better and richer narrative forms by which to contain our dread is failing not just inmates and younger informants. It is failing us all. The verbal and imagistic reenactment of evil in all its graphic, bloody detail is not the symbolic containment of evil. It is the imitation of evil, not the same thing. The language of the autistic-contiguous position is mimesis, living out one's ineffable experiences in and on the body of another. Ogden writes of a disturbed young man who mimicked his every gesture. It drove Ogden crazy until he figured out that his patient was trying to live in his body because his own seemed lifeless and dead.[7]

Though movies, television, popular novels, and the rest use a symbolic language, portrayals of evil in these media are frequently not distant enough from the experience of dread to give it containing form. Instead, they imitate it, the "language" of the autistic-contiguous position. The result is an excitement that may in the short run distract us from our doom but in the long run can only desensitize us to evil.

In *After Virtue*, Alasdair MacIntyre imagines that a catastrophe strikes the natural sciences. Laboratories are destroyed, books and journals burned, and scientists killed.[8] Subsequent generations attempt to reconstruct their beliefs, using fragments of charred manuscripts and terms remembered by the children of survivors. They use such terms as "electron," "molecule," and "DNA" but in an arbitrary and meaningless fashion, because this generation had lost both the theoretical context and the everyday practice of science which had given them their meaning.

Such is the state of ethical discourse today, according to MacIntyre. Living tradition, be it Aristotelian or Christian, which once gave ethical discourse meaning is long gone. The terms remain, but they are essentially empty. One might expect the concept of evil to be similarly hollow, the term essentially theological. In the absence of a dominant theological worldview, even among the religious, evil must become an empty term, meaning little more than "bad" or "I don't like it."

About this MacIntyre is mistaken. The term "evil" is neither hollow nor empty. It is filled with doom. What remains after the traditional culture has fallen into tatters is the primordial feelings that culture has helped individuals defend against for ten thousand years. The experience of evil as doom is nothing new. It is, as Ricoeur argues, an experience as old as history. Today this doom is frequently experienced as meaningless victimhood, a mark of an era in which the traditional culture is rent, so that we can finally see through to the flesh beneath. It is an exciting and scary time to be alive.

It is almost impossible for us to approach evil as a moral category, let alone as a moral problem, while we are overwhelmed with a private, premoral terror. The challenge is not how to reconstruct the traditional culture in order to cover up the dread, and patch the rent. The challenge is to discover new ways to help individuals know and creatively transform their dread, so that they can find new connections to moral categories, and moral choices. Humans must come to accept their doom, their frailty and death, lest they continue to use evil as an escape from being merely human.

My explanation of evil draws heavily on psychoanalytic theory, just as my research strategy does, a strategy of listening, not just for the manifest content but for the image, the feeling, and the caesura. This is not, however, because evil is a mental illness. Nor do I hold that psychoanalysis can fully account for or cure evil. Psychoanalysis and evil are separate categories of experience. Evil is not just a state of mind but a state of being—not just in humans, but in the world.

Nevertheless, psychoanalytic theory can be useful in understanding the roots of dread and the ways in which we defend ourselves against unbearable experience by projecting it into others. It also may help us understand the way in which culture may serve as a transitional object, providing a narrative form through which we may know our evil rather than do it. Ogden, Melanie Klein, and D. W. Winnicott are the psychoanalysts I most frequently draw upon.

In *People of the Lie: The Hope for Healing Human Evil*, a popular book on evil, the psychiatrist M. Scott Peck argues that evil is a type of mental illness. My argument is different. The roots of evil in dread can be explored and explained by means of psychoanalytic categories. Then and only then can we begin to make sense of evil as a moral and ethical problem, for only then can we connect what we know and believe with what we feel. The problem of evil, from this perspective, is the way that the term gets disconnected from lived experience. Evil is both a psychological and moral problem.

In "War Criminals like Us," the columnist Richard Cohen writes of Radovan Karadzic, the longtime leader of the Bosnian Serbs. Most of what appears to be evil in this world, Cohen argues, can be explained in psychological or sociological terms. But because Karadzic, a psychiatrist (or at least he practiced as one), is "the very model of the contemporary Western man, he forces us to use a term that . . . should no longer have any application at all: evil."[9] About this Cohen is mistaken.

Evil is not a residual category, a category we turn to when no other explanations seem to fit. Although the topic of evil is not coextensive with religion, philosophy, psychology, and metaphysics, it touches on most of the issues they do. In the end, evil is a discourse about human malevolence, suffering, and loss: why humans are the way they are, and why we live in a world that is this way. Evil is not a residual category but a foundational one.

Among philosophers, Friedrich Nietzsche is the most profound student of evil. From time to time he makes an appearance in this book and then disappears. Only in Chapter 8 do I confront his argument. Nietzsche is perhaps the bravest soul to have known the truth of evil as dread but been unable to accept it, finding in the cultivation of an ideal of evil a defense against dread.

"Evil's Back" says the cover story of *The New York Times Magazine*. Has it been on vacation? More likely the title signifies that the fugitive attention of the literati has turned once again to evil, as though evil's existence depended on our recognition of it. In a way it does, but not the way the story implies.[10] In her recently published and widely reviewed *History of Satan*, Elaine Pagels argues that evil stems from the failure to accept difference and otherness. As though evildoers could do with a course in political correctness. Most could, but evil is about far more than identity politics, as Chapter 4 argues against Pagels.

Why this resurgent interest in evil, an interest that is at once serious and watered down, recognizing the topic as important but not wanting to grant its full horror? Some time ago Karl Popper argued that we shall never agree on the greatest goods; individuals and cultures are too diverse. The late Judith Shklar made a similar point. If there is a *summum bonum*, we shall never agree on it, at least not in a liberal society. Agreement on a *summum malum* seems far more likely: "That evil is cruelty and the fear it inspires, and the very fear of fear itself."[11] Who could disagree? My book suggests that we should extend the list to include ravaging illness or brutal violence suffered by oneself or a loved one; loss of meaning, hope, and belief; and utter despair. Evil is not only the cruelty another intends; it is the human suffering we cannot escape.

Evil grounds us, showing us our common ground, revealing it to be remarkably real. Not necessarily physical, the ground is nonetheless about all the basics, all the things that can be taken from us which make life worthwhile. Evil reminds us of the contingency of life, while having the quality of permanence. As in "Evil's back, and I'm glad. I almost forgot why I hurt so much, and why the world is so damn' lousy."

Well, someone might say, granted that what you call evil is important, calling it evil is being unnecessarily mysterious, obscure, enigmatic. What you are really talking about is human destructiveness, a topic that is readily amenable to normal social-scientific study, as the work of Anthony Storr, among so many others, demonstrates.[12] Here is one more objection to be dealt with, an objection that Cohen's column does not so much refute as reinforce.

There are three reasons not to reduce evil to human destructiveness. Today the Holocaust is the leading image of evil. It was not always so. For over a century, the Lisbon earthquake of 1755 was the paradigm of evil. Tens of thousands perished, Voltaire wrote *Candide*, and the issue of God's justice, theodicy, was debated as never before. Consider how differently they must have understood evil then: not as what humans do, but as what we suffer.

We best understand a concept like evil when we find a discrepancy between definition and example. Were we to define evil as human destructiveness from the beginning, we could not discover, let alone know, the other dimension of evil, the doom that happens to us all. The definition would obscure the problem. The definition would be the solution, one that excludes most of the answer in advance.

Lacking today is an appreciation of evil as suffering and loss, the passive dimension of evil: evil as what we suffer, not what we do, what the Old Testament called *ra*ᶜ. Much evil in the world today is an attempt to avoid the terrible helplessness of passivity, the terror of paralysis in the face of doom. Better to be the evildoer than the victim if one has to choose, as so many feel they must. It is why almost all informants identify with Eichmann, not his victims.

Always a problem, the terror of passivity is made worse by a failure of cultural memory, the sense that to be a victim is to be forgotten forever. Victimhood is meaningless. A focus on human malevolence, rather than on evil, would perpetuate the problem: the terror of passivity and paralysis in the face of doom. It would make the symptom, malevolence as the illusion of controlling one's doom, into the cause. It would get things backward.

There is a second reason not to define evil solely as human destructiveness. If evil stems from an experience of inchoate dread, then its defining quality is its unboundedness: is that experience inside, outside, both? Defining evil prematurely, before we have investigated the experience, would itself be a defense against the experience. It would be a solution —evil *is* human malevolence—that once again would keep us from knowing the problem, knowing not just that our doom is unbounded but that the unbounded quality of the doom is itself an experience of evil.

In "Buddhism and Evil," Martin Southwold makes the good point that "evil is a special quality of badness." It is misleading to translate Buddhist terms such as *dukkha* as "evil," a common rendering. Similarly, it is misleading to equate Mara with Satan, as J. W. Boyd does in *Satan and Mara: Christian and Buddhist Symbols of Evil. Dukkha* refers to suffering that stems from the grasping desire for things and persons. Although Mara is a tempter like Satan, he has more the quality of a pimp than of a destroyer. Whatever evil is, it must refer to more than ordinary human failings and desires if it is to be a meaningful category of experience.[13]

Surely Southwold is correct that anthropologists often use "the word 'evil' . . . with little or no attempt to distinguish its various senses."[14] His solution is, however, troublesome, distinguishing between "descriptive" and "ethical" evil, tantamount to the more familiar distinction between natural and moral evil—that is, between illness and suffering on the one hand and human destructiveness on the other. He calls the latter "radical evil" and argues that it is the only sense in which the term is currently meaningful, the only sense in which the terms of other religions and cultures should be rendered as "evil." From this perspective he concludes that Buddhism lacks a genuine concept of evil.

The problem with this approach is that it guarantees that we shall never learn anything new from other cultures, as we cannot use its categories to challenge and rethink our own.[15] Nor shall we learn anything new about the complexity of our own culture's view of evil, a view in which natural evil, ra^c, was central for 2,500 years. In addition, Southwold vitiates the richness of the Kantian concept of "radical evil," which has little to do with magnitude and a lot to do with the way in which desire may confuse and corrupt our moral categories.[16] The Kantian concept is rich because it suggests something of the confusion and loss of distinctions at the heart of evil. If evil is itself an experience of "formless dread," then Southwold has given it form at the expense of understanding the dread.

It is important to be vigilant against the tendency to define "evil" too loosely. If evil is anything and everything bad, then it is nothing. The solution is not to reduce evil to a particular definition but to consider whether there is a category of experience which might help to render commensurable (not identical, but comparable) such radically diverse experiences as suffering, illness, "falling on evil days," the malevolence of the human heart, the Lisbon earthquake, the Holocaust, murder, going down into a dark basement, and losing oneself to one's boyfriend. Many informants have in effect answered that there is, and their answer is dread. They are not automatically right, for even if meaning = use, use does not automatically equal meaningfulness. Nevertheless, it is an understanding worth pursuing, the task of this book. Not because it will give us a handle on evil, but because it might give us a richer understanding of its complexity.

The third and final reason not to define evil as human destructiveness is that the definition cannot satisfy. When we ask about evil, what we want to know—in the end—is not why so and so did it, but why in the world is the world like this, so filled with evil? The empirical dimension of evil, its roots in human dread, is crucial. If we can understand this about evil, we can lessen it: both the malevolence and the suffering. But it is not the answer to evil. The answer is metaphysical, why in the world . . . I do not have the answer, but it is wise not to close off this dimension of the problem in advance.

The Path of the Narrative

Chapter 2: "Evil Is Pleasure in Hurting and Lack of Remorse." A straightforward and simple definition of evil held by most informants, inmate and free, is contrasted with the tortured definitions of some academics, who seem to want to deny evil. Evil is closely allied to sadism, and sadism to dread.

Chapter 3: "The Ground of Evil Is Dread." The root of evil is the experience of uncontained, undifferentiated dread. We are evil when, instead of knowing our dread, we become it, trying to inflict it on others, as though it were a thing. The psychopath is the extreme example, but we all have psychopathic moments.

Chapter 4: "Suffering Evil, Doing Evil." For over three thousand years, evil has been understood as what men and women suffer, not just what they do. We are in danger of losing this insight, so that we are at greater risk of inflicting evil in the vain hope we might not suffer it.

Chapter 5: "Identifying with Eichmann." In addition to contrasting subtle differences between inmates and free citizens on the question of whether or not Eichmann was evil, I argue that much literature on the Holocaust fails to appreciate the intensity of the dread that lies behind evil.

Chapter 6: "Splatter Movies or Shiva? A Culture of Vampires." Not Satan but the vampire is the leading icon of evil among younger informants. This replacement is a cultural regression, from the One who would tempt your soul to the one who would suck your blood. The shift tells us much about evil in contemporary society. It tells us much about contemporary society.

Chapter 7: "Evil Spelled Backward Is Live." Evil is not just fascinating, it is attractive, about the power to transgress. If we do not understand that evil is cheating at life, an attempt to get the vitality without the dread, we shall not understand it. Artistic creativity is an alternative that may come frighteningly close to evil.

Chapter 8: "Evil Is No-thing." Evil is no-thing, not just the absence of good, but what Søren Kierkegaard calls "the presentiment of something which is nothing," his definition of dread. Though much of my argument is psychological, evil is not a psychological category but a metaphysical one, about why men and women suffer so much. It is not a question psychology alone can answer. Nietzsche's *Beyond Good and Evil* does not help as much as it might. Greek tragedy does.

Chapter 9: "Scales of Evil." What explains the difference between big and little evils? The difference is less than one might suppose.

Appendix 1: "Asking about Evil." If an appendix is something not integral, but added, then Appendix 1 is not truly an appendix, but an organic part of the argument. What does it mean to ask about a concept? What can we learn? What can't we? I consider Wittgenstein's position and partially reject it.

Appendix 2: "Informants and Questions." Who was asked about evil, what are their characteristics, and what was asked are among the methodological issues I address.

TWO   *Evil Is Pleasure in Hurting and Lack of Remorse*

"Evil is pleasure in hurting and a lack of remorse." Not only most prisoners say this; most informants do. But prisoners find more comfort in the description than others, because most inmates believe that they have done evil but do not want to be evil. "I killed this guy, but I didn't get any pleasure in it, you know?"

Evil is not just about hurting. It is about the pleasures of absolute control inherent in the ability to harm another. "For a minute I'm this guy's god" is how Mr. Beaty describes his relationship to the victim who begs him to spare his life. He is an honest man, and his tone betrays neither satisfaction nor guilt, but recognition.

"The evil person wants to crawl inside me and control everything I do. Everything I think, everything I am. He wants to take me over." Rachel B. elaborates, "Evil people don't just want to hurt you, they want to hurt you from the inside, so it's like you're hurting yourself."

At a loss for words, many define evil in terms of a look, an expression. For a few the look is satanic, the appearance of possession, a wild expression in the eyes. For most it is ice cold, not a spark of humanity, a look that could freeze a polar bear. "Cold joy," one calls it, referring to the expression of a stranger he believes deliberately stepped on his hand when he knelt down to pick up a dropped book.

Grace E. talks about the "cold, shivery feeling" she got around her former thesis adviser. "He didn't care about me at all, he used me like food, just to make himself more famous. That's all he cared about. He didn't even want to know me, just what I could do for him. As a person I didn't exist. That's what gave me the chills."

In Thomas Mann's *Doctor Faustus*, the appearance of the devil is associated with a frightful draft, so cold Leverkuhn is overcome with a chill whenever he appears. Recall Dante's Ninth Circle of Hell, as deep as you can go, filled not with fire but with ice, the shades of the most evil of all, traitors, stuck in the ice forever,

> teeth clicking like a stork's
> desperate beating against a marsh's
> early freeze.
> (Canto 32; Deborah Digges, trans.)

As they lie there, their eyes begin to tear, but the tears which had once fallen freely are frozen to their eyelids.

> The very weeping there prevents all weeping,
> and grief, which finds no outlet at the eye,
> turns inward to increase the anguish—
> Because the first tear, as it gathers,
> freezes in the well of the eye and gives the
> face the aspect of a crystal mask.
> (Canto 33; Robert Hass, trans.)

Evil is cold because the tears are frozen, because the evildoer is unable to connect the anguish in his body to signs and symbols that could express it, the inability that is the mark of Ogden's autistic-contiguous position. The evildoer is, in other words, unable to create: "Leave Every Hope Behind You, You Who Enter," the words inscribed above the gate to hell. Creativity is hope, the hope that overcomes despair, that one could create something new and so begin again. Ice is utter hopelessness and despair, fluid movement turned to stone.

Grace E. switched her graduate major to get away from her frigid adviser. "I couldn't work with him, and I couldn't work for him. Hell, after a while I couldn't work period." In such cold she could not create.

Evil is absence of humanity, the failure to understand or appreciate the humanity of the other. It chills because it threatens our existence, like being dead in the eyes of another. It is creepy, like living with robots, a not-uncommon image of evil. J. Reid Meloy defines psychopathy in terms of cold reptilian eyes, the psychopath regarding the other as mere food for his ego, like a snake its prey.[1] Because it is such a central image of evil, it must be considered. At the same time it may be misleading.

In *People of the Lie*, M. Scott Peck diagnoses evil as a form of malignant narcissism. Evil is not what people do, it is how they relate to the world, as though others do not really exist, as though their feelings do not matter. Evil is moral autism, unadulterated selfishness. We know it when we feel ourselves in the presence of someone with whom we can find no human connection, and who so leaves us feeling chilled inside.[2]

"That's crazy," Beth F., a graduate student in psychology, replies. "Peck's a narcissist too. If he can't reach them, they're evil. What sort of conclusion is that? Maybe they just don't want to be reached by him. Or by anybody." Beth is right. That one cannot be reached by another is not evidence of one's evil. Unreachability is evidence of how scary it is to be with people who fail to share human feeling, or value human connection, but it is also evidence of how careful we must be about translating our feelings of evil into evidence of evil. They are not necessarily the same.

The prison staff employs the Hare Psychopathy Checklist (PCL-R), a list of twenty attributes associated with psychopathy. Each item is scored 0 to 2. Items include "glibness and superficial charm," "grandiose sense of self-worth," "pathological lying," "lack of remorse or guilt," "shallow affect," "parasitic lifestyle," and "callous lack of empathy." It might seem as if the checklist itself defines psychopathy. It does not. The cold, creepy feeling the staff member can get with an inmate defines the score on the checklist, every item filled out in the chill aura of creepiness. I heard this interviewer response a dozen times, once like this: "The way he looked at me made my skin crawl, so I busted-out and gave him all 2s." "Busted-out"—it is a great term, what you do when you are imprisoned with a psychopath, as the interviewer was.

The trouble is that cold, creepy feelings mislead, at least in the short run. I now experience the two creepiest men in the group as among the most human—not necessarily the warmest, but the most fully human. Once you experience this shift, you see every item on the checklist differently. Maybe his superficial charm wasn't so superficial after all, you say to yourself, and the inmate loses two points. There is nothing wrong with defining evil as the creepy feeling we get around some people. We just have to remember that the "feeling instrument" is as fallible as any other, a measure of our own coldness as much as theirs, a sign of how terrifying it truly is to find no human connection. What the feeling instrument does not do is tell us where the connection broke down: in the other, in ourselves, or somewhere in between.

Many informants are well aware of the problem. "If I don't rely on my feelings," says Bob G., "then I will become too intellectual about evil, too academic." He sneaks a look at me and continues. "But my feelings aren't guaranteed either. Anything can be rationalized, anything at all." Warming to his insight, he concludes that "self-deception is the root of all evil."

Kant defines radical evil as "man's inclination to corrupt the imperatives of morality so that they may become a screen for the expression of self-love." [3] Today the term "radical evil" is usually applied to acts such as the Holocaust, evil that goes beyond the bounds of everyday malignancy by virtue of its scale, meaninglessness, or brutality. Kant's insight remains important, however. Evil may be radical not in terms of its scale but because of how evil corrupts the evildoer, transforming every feeling and experience into a justification for maliciousness and a legitimation of cruelty.

The first and most important step in coming to terms with evil is to recognize its potential within, not just that you could *do* evil but that it could corrupt your judgment, your soul. Soon you would see the entire world in terms of how you might exploit it. Even worse, after a while you would not even know that you were doing so. Seeing the world this way would become as natural as breathing. Here is where culture comes in, its task being to remind us of the potential for evil to appear as good, or at least, the way things have always been.

Experimenting with Evil

What if the problem of evil were quite simple? Not the problem of solving it, but the problem of what in the world evil is? People like to hurt other people. They get pleasure in it. That is why they do it. Not unadulterated pleasure, not pleasure per se, but satisfaction, even comfort. "I like it," says Matt C. "I like the feeling that I can hurt someone bad. That's what really scares me. That I could come to like it a lot. That I'd forget to feel guilty." Matt is worried about radical evil, the corruption of his soul.

What if Matt is right, and several famous social psychologists, such as Stanley Milgram and Philip Zimbardo, are wrong? What if Matt recognizes something simple but important they have forgotten, or deny?

The Milgram experiments are now almost thirty years old, yet they remain as challenging as ever. A recent edition of the *Journal of Social Issues* was devoted to reviewing and updating the famous study. Although several of the authors use the term "evil," as Milgram does, like Milgram none seriously considers the possibility that the subjects might have enjoyed shocking the victim.[4]

It may help to rehearse Milgram's method. Subjects, called teachers, believe that they are delivering electrical shocks to a learner, who is actually a confederate of Milgram's. The learner is always the same man, a mild-mannered, vulnerable-looking, middle-aged fellow with a heart condition. Or so he tells each teacher. The learner is to receive the shocks when he fails to memorize word pairs. The shocks are administered from a shock generator that runs from 15 to 450 volts, the higher levels labeled in big letters "Strong Shock," "Very Strong Shock," "Intense Shock," "Extreme Intensity Shock," "Danger Severe Shock," and "X X X." Each teacher gets a sample shock of 45 volts, so he or she knows it is real.

Strapped into his chair with thick leather straps, electrodes attached to his wrist, the learner is ready to learn. The teacher can hear the learner scream, yell, kick the door, demand to be let out, complain of chest pain, and finally fall silent. Before Milgram began the experiment, he asked some psychiatrists to predict the percentage of teachers who would actually deliver the complete sequence of thirty-three shocks, including three at 450 volts. A tiny percentage, the psychiatrists replied, no more than a few disturbed, sadistic individuals. In fact, over 62 percent delivered the full battery of shocks.

The statistics are shocking, the transcripts disturbing, the films of the experiment overwhelming. The teachers do not appear to like their job.

They ask the experimenter not to go on, they talk about how worried they are about the learner. They smoke too much, and sweat furiously. Some jump out of their chairs and act as if they are going to walk out the door. Most do not. They complain, they hesitate, they refuse to take responsibility, but nonetheless most of the teachers continue, 15 volts, 30 volts, 45 volts, 60 volts, up the line of switches on the way to 450 volts. All they have to do, of course, is just say no, and mean it. Less than half do.

Interviewed after the experiment, many of the teachers talk as if they did not really deliver the shocks. They talk as if they had refused to go on. "I just knew it wasn't the right thing to do," "You can't order someone to do something like that," "A person would have to be completely callous to go on with the experiment." Comments like these are from teachers who delivered the full array of shocks.

Milgram argues that the experiment has nothing to do with sadism and everything with obedience: the teachers do not want to deliver the shocks, appear not to enjoy it, frequently ask, even plead not to, then talk as if they refused. It is obedience that is being displayed, man's potential for slavish groupishness.

This interpretation is possible, of course. But if you look at the films long enough you will be struck by something else, the grotesque nervous laughter, the giggling fits at the shock generator. Not all show this behavior, but it is common. Sometimes it is subtle, frequently not. One teacher appears to have a seizure of laughter. What if these men are giggling in embarrassed pleasure at being given permission to inflict great pain and suffering on an innocent and vulnerable man? Milgram rejects this interpretation but offers no reason.

What if what the teachers really want, what they long for, what satisfies, is permission to hurt someone. Permission does not just mean someone's saying, "Go ahead. It's okay." The teachers have a conscience; they know it is not. They have to be virtually forced to do it, compelled by authority. But not really. The structure of the Milgram experiment protects them from knowledge of their own sadism, while allowing them to express it. That is what they want, that is what they do, and that is what they get pleasure from—embarrassed pleasure, guilty pleasure, but it is still pleasure.

It is a situation (actually a defense) reinforced by the assertion of the experimenter that he will assume all consequences for any harm to the learner, thus helping the teachers deny not only their motivation but also its consequences. In this light we should consider whether much of what passes as the result of leaders' orders is actually leaders' granting permission to their followers to do what they want to do anyway but are too guilty and embarrassed to know it. Could it be the psychological function of leaders to provide plausible psychological deniability to their followers, as well as to shelter them from the consequences of their desires?

This interpretation, though, is not yet an explanation. Even if Hitler's executioners were willing, as Daniel Goldhagen puts it in the title of his 1996 book, *Hitler's Willing Executioners: Ordinary Germans and the Holocaust*, we need to think about what "willing" means. Why *would* people want to hurt others? The answer is not so easy as it might appear.

In the psychoanalytic tradition, sadism is generally associated with masochism, and both with sexuality; sadomasochism is the sexualization of relationships of power and domination. In recent years, however, some analysts have been applying the term "sadism" to the pleasure obtained from hurting others, regardless of whether sexual excitement occurs.[5] What distinguishes sadism from aggression is not the sexualization of domination and destruction but the sadist's intense identification with his victim.[6] *Sadism is the form that aggression takes when it is fleeing its doom*, a formulation that fits Freud's account of the origins of sadism in the *Todestrieb*, the drive toward death and destruction which can be turned within or without, toward oneself or others.[7]

It is this that Milgram captured, creating a world in which there are only two roles, or so it seems: victim or executioner. Drawing from a rigged lottery, subjects believed that they had a fifty-fifty chance of being the victim. (The third role, that of "experimenter," not devoid of sadism, was unavailable. "There but for the grace of odds go I. . . .") It is a world in which one is drawn into the role of executioner step by step, shock level by shock level, encouraged not so much by the orders of the experimenter but by the cries of the victim—as though the victim were whispering, "You could switch places with me in a minute. Unless you kill me." At least that is what the cries must sound like to the terrified executioner.

Sadism is the joy of avoiding victimhood, though that puts it too passively. Sadism is the joy of having taken control of the experience of victimhood by inflicting it upon another. Above all, sadism is about control. One prisoner, a murderer, put it this way: "I didn't care whether I killed the guy or not. I just wanted to be his God for a little while. . . . No, that's not enough. I wanted him to know it."

Every informant was told about the Milgram experiment in some detail and asked to discuss it (question 6). In addition, prisoners were asked to read a brief summary of the Milgram experiment titled "If Hitler Asked You to Electrocute a Stranger, Would You? Probably."[8] The first thing Mr. Acorn does is rework the title: "If the State Asked You to Electrocute a Stranger, Would You? Hell Yes." Mr. Acorn is covered with tattoos, some quite artistic, though not to my taste: a flaming death's head; a voluptuous woman with a skull between her legs; a swastika; and a rifle barrel encircled with the words "white power." He wears a confederate flag as a bandana. A biker, he wants to open a little tattoo shop when he gets out. One might argue that all this disqualifies him from understanding the Milgram experiment. Consider the possibility that it qualifies him. Mr. Acorn, like most prisoners, lives closer to the edge, including the hard edge of violence. About some things this characteristic makes him obtuse; about violence he is a savant: "Man, people love violence. Television and movie companies make millions on it. People love to watch violence, and they love to do violence. They just don't want to admit it. So, here this dude tells them to do it, and they must love it, man, a fuckin' fantasy come true: a chance to do their violence and pretend it's all in a good cause." The other prisoners nod. One calls Mr. Acorn "caveman." It's a term of affection; it means he speaks the primitive, brutal truth—not just about their own potential for violence but of others'. They sense that "half the citizens of the state would love to see us fry; hell, they'd be lining up for the job."

Most free informants interpreted the experiment as Milgram does— as a story about being placed in a terrible bind in which there is so much pressure to conform and obey that decent people do awful things. "People are naturally weak, but they are not naturally sadistic" is how one puts it, summarizing the view of many free informants but only a few inmates. Most inmates understood that the "teachers" did it because they wanted to, because violence is attractive, because they had a good excuse. "A scientist told them to do it," says Mr. Money. "But it's not why they did it. They did it because they wanted to."

Philip Zimbardo, who constructed a simulated prison in the basement of Stanford University and watched the "guards" run amok, reached a conclusion similar to that of most free informants: "Our results are also congruent with those of Milgram who most convincingly demonstrated the proposition that evil acts are not necessarily the deeds of evil men, but may be attributable to the operation of powerful social forces."[9]

Wait just a minute! Milgram did not demonstrate any such thing, he just concluded it. Only if we presume that evil is a situational attribute, not a quality of mind or heart, does this conclusion make sense. Only if we tacitly assume that normal men and women cannot be evil in the first place does it make sense not to attribute evil to those who created the situation that apparently forces them to do evil. What if this is just what these normal men and women want, to find themselves in a situation that absolves them of responsibility for their sadism, just as the teachers did in the Milgram experiment? Then, of course, finding that these men and women are just reacting to their environment would miss the point. It is what they want to pretend. "The inherently pathological characteristics of the . . . situation itself . . . were a sufficient condition to produce aberrant, anti-social behavior."[10]

The statement is nonsensical. Zimbardo cannot mean that these conditions were sufficient by themselves. If so, then there were no humans involved, just robots who responded to conditions but brought nothing to it, no tendencies, no potentialities, no love, no hate, no nothing. What Zimbardo seems to mean is that the conditions of the study, a drama in which the role of disciplinarian was offered to all, were sufficient to bring out the evil in normal men and women, their sadism. The assumption that normal men might be evil is the hidden variable, the most straightforward and obvious explanation of all, the one that cannot be uttered.

Only a fool would argue that these experiments prove that the imagination of man's heart is evil from his youth, as Genesis 8.21 puts it. What they prove is how difficult it is for social theorists to call humans evil, even—or especially—when they do evil things. Not because the theorist does not believe that "evil" is an appropriate social-scientific category: Milgram and Zimbardo both use the term, considering that it properly applies to acts of sadistic cruelty but deciding that it does not apply in their particular cases. In fact, both theorists have to work hard to avoid the obvious conclusion.

Prisoners know different. Not so sheltered from the world's violence or their own, they know something of its boundary-shattering power, and its allure. Mr. Acorn continues:

> Society likes violence. It just likes to be able to control it. Imagine that a guy built an electric chair in his basement, plugged it in, and then went out in the street and kidnapped people, dragging them into his basement, where he put them in his homemade electric chair and electrocuted them. You know what would happen? After he did this a few times (the state's not too swift, it takes them a while to catch on) they'd catch him, and throw him in jail. Then they'd put him in an electric chair and throw the switch, and his eyeballs would pop out of his head. And we'd call that justice.

The state's executioner follows public procedures to exact revenge; the man with the electric chair in his basement is a freelance predator. One subjects his sadism to the demands of the state; the other takes his sadism freelance. It is the difference between the subjects in the Milgram experiment and the criminal; it is the difference between civilization and chaos. But it is not the difference between sadism and obedience. Nor is it necessarily a difference in basic psychology.

Prisoners are like the rest of us, only more so. They are more adrift, morally, psychologically, personally. If you listen to their stories long enough, you will be struck by their lack of place in this world: they just don't fit anywhere. Marriage, family, school, work, military: only a minority of prisoners have made a go of any of these, let alone more than one. Prison is the only place many fit, which is why it is so attractive, the "concrete mama" they love to hate.

It was not my experience that the inmates in my group (not a random sample of prisoners) were more aggressive and sadistic than the free informants. But the sadism of some inmates is more visible, more likely to be freelance, less bound to institutional forms. Indeed, this is virtually the definition of criminal behavior—not its violence, for who is more violent than the state? Nation states kill millions. It is the freelance quality of criminal violence which makes that violence socially intolerable to a civilized society. It is not obvious that that quality makes the violence more evil. Its presence does thwart our consideration and confrontation of the organized evil of states and societies, as we tend to confuse organization, rationalization, and legitimation with goodness, at least when the state is our own. Norbert Elias made this argument in 1939 in *The Civilizing Process*, and it still stands.[11]

Ockham's Razor, Ockham's Fork

Let us apply Ockham's razor, itself a sadistic image, to the problem of sadism. If people hurt others, they do so because they want to, because it gives them pleasure. As Tom A. puts it, "How could there be all this war and killing, and people not want it to be this way? People say they don't want to do evil, but where's it come from? I had a professor who said people do what they want, or they wouldn't do it. The rest is excuses." And history.

Pleasure in evil may be complex, about the pleasure in avoiding one's fate, and the joy that stems from the illusion of inflicting that fate on others. It is complex, but it is simple—something Milgram and Zimbardo have forgotten. Augustine holds that evil is chaos and confusion, whatever keeps us from seeing clearly. Let us mitigate evil by not eliminating the simplest and clearest explanation of evil of all. People like to hurt one another, obtaining great pleasure and satisfaction from doing so.

Daniel Jonah Goldhagen has made just this argument in *Hitler's Willing Executioners: Ordinary Germans and the Holocaust*.[12] Germans killed Jews because they wanted to kill Jews. What else could explain the fact that Germans would violate orders against killing Jews, shooting babies in hospitals, continuing to beat and kill Jews during the death marches, long after the war was lost? Goldhagen is right, and Goldhagen is wrong. He is right to emphasize that people like to hurt and kill others. It is, I believe, the reason his book has been so well received by the educated public. Although often reluctant to know the allure of violence, the educated public is not so invested in structuralist explanations, as they are called, explanations that attribute the Holocaust to everything from the nature of bureaucratic irresponsibility to the abstractness of modern society;[13] that is, explanations that explain violence for every reason but one, that people like it.

Nevertheless, Goldhagen is wrong to assume that people simply like to hurt and kill others, that it is a pure pleasure, like the pleasure he imagines two concentration-camp guards having while lying together in bed. "Did one relate to another . . . the rush of power that engulfed her when the righteous adrenaline of Jew-beating caused her body to pulse with energy?" There is no pure pleasure, as Goldhagen seems to recognize in this little story, whose sadomasochistic aspect is apparent, but not developed. Recall the theory of sadism, that people like to hurt others because they identify with the victim. It may be that the pleasure in hurting others stems from relief at not being the victim, an argument developed in Chapter 5. It is important to be simple and straightforward about evil. But not too simple, and not too straightforward either. Perhaps Goldhagen is not as straightforward as he seems either. An author who writes sexual fantasies about the perpetrators knows more about the pleasures of cruelty than he is letting on.

"There are so many different types of evil. We ought to have half a dozen different words for it, like the Eskimos have a dozen different words for snow." Some informants made this suggestion, one I have not followed. From a strictly intellectual standpoint, it is no doubt a good idea. The evil of a corrupt political regime differs importantly from that of a corrupt individual, which differs yet again from that of an individual who murders in an insane rage. Colin Turnbull describes the Ik, African tribesmen who laugh as they starve their children.[14] If the Ik are evil, their evil is of still a different quality.

From a perspective that stays close to experience, intellectual distinctions are not as important as the feeling quality behind them. Most who made distinctions about evil were seeking to let someone off the hook. Not always themselves; frequently it was a parent or loved one, as in "Maybe what [I, they, we] did was bad, but it wasn't really evil. Or it wasn't the worst kind of evil. Real evil is _____ [fill in the blank]."

Among inmates the fork is the leading image of evil: the forked tongue that lies, the devil's pitchfork, the fork in the road that represents a choice between good and evil, the cloven hoof, the fork stolen from the cafeteria whose filed-down handle makes a knife. The image is their version of Ockham's razor. Only instead of making evil simpler, the image makes it so complicated that we almost can't know—or feel— it. That obfuscation is, of course, the point, transforming feeling and experience about evil into the less emotionally taxing experience of its categorization. For some, the point is to fragment feeling itself, the feelings of the whole self impossible to bear.

I too make distinctions among evils, as any thinker must. The distinction between evil as what we do and evil as what we suffer is central to my argument. Nevertheless, those who equate understanding with classification may be disappointed. In particular, I have avoided the distinction, so popular among informants, between evil deed and evil person, as in "I do not believe individuals are evil, but some acts are definitely evil." It is too easy, separating the person from the act in a way that suggests that evil just happens. Evil, or at least a particular type of evil, happens because people do it. Where else could it come from? These people need not be totally or unredeemably evil, but separating the act from the person can only make evil even more terrifying, as we no longer know where it is located. Location is the topic of the next chapter.

I must mention another distinction, though I do not accept it either: an impulsive, explosive act of evil versus an evil way of life. Most of the inmates are in prison for an explosive act of evil, the murder of a parent, child, brother, spouse, or loved one. There *is* something different about this evil act than the evil of a big-time drug dealer or a Mafia don who makes a career of murder, to say nothing of the corrupt businessman or politician who builds a career on lying, cheating, and stealing. It is, say the prisoners, the difference between an act and a way of life. It is not, however, a difference we should make too much of.

An explosive act of evil, such as murder, is not just the expression of rage, but of hatred. Hatred is chronic rage, the presence of rage in history, and over time.[15] Every inmate who murdered or raped in a fit of rage was expressing his hatred, his or her act the culmination of years of cultivated malevolence. Mr. Smith spoke of how he used to take to his bed as a child, consoling himself with thoughts of how he would revenge himself on his family for ganging up on him. It took twenty years, but he finally did, killing a family member in an eruption of this rage. Such a murder often brings relief to its perpetrator . . . for a little while.

Hatred is, as a type of fusion, the desire to destroy the object forever —not just in the sense of obliterating it once and for all, but of remaining locked in a relationship of destruction for eternity. If we understand hatred as chronic rage, a hateful attachment to malevolence, then even an explosive act of violence takes on a historical quality, not necessarily a life of evil, but a life of hatred. In this sense it is continuous with the life of hatred that never explodes into a single obliterating act.

Most of the inmates who have done explosive evil are decent and honorable human beings. Who could say this about someone who lives a life of corrosive evil? Their decency though, does not lessen their (or anybody else's) evil, though it may mitigate our judgment of it. Decent human beings do terrible, terrible things. It is one of the imbalances we must come to terms with if we are to know evil. This is one distinction worth insisting on.

THREE   *The Ground of Evil Is Dread*

Alexa K., about fifty, talks about a dream she had twenty years ago. Recently separated from her husband, she dreamed of a malevolent figure who would paralyze and destroy her if she did not awaken. Who was he? "You know who I mean," she answers in a husky voice. "The opposite one, the opposite of God." At the last minute Alexa woke up, and has been on her guard ever since.

Sally L. is about twenty-five years younger than Alexa. She too talks about a terrifying dream: "Three times I dreamed it. A powerful force attacked me, like a demon. It grabbed me around the neck, making weird mechanical sounds deep in its throat. Slowly it turned toward me, until I could see its face. It was the grim reaper, with a skull for a face. I knew I would die. And the pain. I was in bed, but it was no dream. I know it was no dream. It was like a headache, only my pain was outside my head, throbbing. . . . It was, you know, weird, like the pain was outside of me trying to get in."

Many talk about similar dreams. All are certain their dreams have to do with evil, and none can explain the connection. I ask no questions about dreams. In every case the informant originates the topic.

For Kara T. the dream has to do with a neighbor to whom she was attracted. He came to her, held her in his arms, and suddenly began to paw her, all the while making strange, inarticulate noises from somewhere deep in his throat. He had turned into a monster, Satan, with claws for hands. She dreamed the same dream every week for a month.

Understanding an informant's inner world so as to better understand her use of the term "evil" is not about causal knowledge, what causes what. Coming between sleep and wakefulness, sleep paralysis (said to affect 4 percent of the population) often results in terrifying dreams that have the quality of reality and a content frequently related to paralysis, such as being overcome by an alien force. Several informants reported being sexually molested as children, but the memories were distinct, not dreamlike.[1]

Causal explanations like these, even if the incidents are true (and how could one know in any particular case?) would miss the point. Understanding how people employ the concept of evil involves taking informants' experiences seriously wherever they come from. Experiences influence how we use concepts, and it is the connection between experience and concept which counts. Where the experience "really" comes from, if it could be known, is not important from this perspective.

Not all precategorical experiences, as they will be called, concerned dreams. Most concerned experiences that seemed more real than reality. They were not always bad. Mary H., almost sixty, talks like a whimsical teenager. A few years ago she visited the zoo, and while looking at the monkeys she twisted her neck sharply and felt a shock go to her brain. In the moment in which she lost consciousness she had a beatific vision: "It was like a bowl of cottage cheese bathed in a golden light. Everything in the world was there, everything. . . . Each curd was good or evil, but they were all mixed up so you couldn't separate them. And the whole, even though there was evil in it, was good. It was good. Ever since then I've been more relaxed. I know that no matter how much evil it contains, the universe is good."

Andrew S. lost his wife a few years ago. Now he drives an hour to attend another church because he cannot enter the sanctuary where her memorial service was held. "It's like part of her is still there. I really can't explain it." This in response to a question about how his religion helps him understand evil.

A down-to-earth man not given to flights of fancy, Andrew speaks about living in London during the blitz. It was not the exploding bombs that got to him, but the silence of the buzz bombs (V-1 rockets) when they ran out of fuel. "You knew they were going to fall, but for a moment it was just silence. Nothing. It was strange, beautiful. Then you heard the explosion." This in response to a question about having experienced evil. He could not explain the connection, but he could make it.

Nietzsche had a doom experience, apparently a hallucination, when he was twenty-five, studying in Leipzig: "What I am afraid of is not the terrifying figure behind the chair, but its voice. No, not the words, but the horrifyingly inarticulate sound of that creature. If only it spoke in the manner of human beings." Erich Heller argues that much of Nietzsche's writing (he wrote like mad, dozens of unpublished works for each of the many he published) is aimed at silencing the terrifying figure, drowning out its horrifying inarticulateness in a torrent of human, all-too-human words.[2] Perhaps. Chapter 8 argues that Nietzsche's philosophy should be viewed in a similar fashion, as a defense against ineffable doom. In other words, Nietzsche understood evil.

Precategorical Experiences

I shall call these experiences precategorical, a clumsy but useful term denoting experiences that are prior not just to morality but to the categories that make morality possible, including such basic distinctions as self and other. Expressed in images and words, the experiences are nevertheless preverbal. The precategorical is the realm of mimesis, a world of mirrors in which the outer world is experienced as deep inside, the inner world as though it were part of the external—like Sally's throbbing pain, located somewhere between the surface of her body and infinity—as though skin is a semipermeable membrane.

I shall explore precategorical experience from two different perspectives that are really one, a precategorical approach to precategorical experience. The first perspective is rooted in psychoanalysis, particularly in Ogden's concept of the autistic-contiguous position. The second perspective is phenomenological philosophy's account of prepredicative experience, experience so fundamental that it is the foundation of the possibility of other experience. In the end these perspectives are one, or at least not two.

Henry A. grew up in one of the world's trouble spots. One day, just as he was to enter a market, there was a tremendous explosion, and he was thrown to the ground by the blast from a homemade bomb. Still dazed, he got up, brushed himself off, and went inside, where he saw a dozen wounded people, several dead or dying. "It could have been me. If I'd finished brushing my teeth one minute earlier, it would have been me." One of the merchants was washing away the blood from around his stall, and when Henry looked down he found himself standing in a river of diluted blood flowing over his shoes. In the river he could see the image of his face. Only for a second it did not look like an image. It looked like it really was his disembodied face, covered in blood.

In the precategorical experience of evil the intensity of the experience dissolves normal distinctions between subject and object, inner and outer, so that for a moment Henry thought that he had been killed or wounded, that he had been inside, not outside. The experience is not simply that evil is bad and should be contained. Rather, what is uncontained is itself experienced as evil *because* it is uncontained, overwhelming, beyond limits. Not every uncontained experience is evil, of course, only those in which the experience seems boundless, likely to overwhelm the self in a tidal wave of emotion. Evil is that which threatens to obliterate the self, overcoming its boundaries. This is what informants were saying.

D. W. Winnicott refers to the transitional object, such as the baby's blanket, which does more than represent the security of the mother. It is mother, and at the same time it is not. It is both at once, and only a fool would try to say it is really one or the other. The whole point of the transitional object is that we suspend the laws of noncontradiction for a moment, letting something be A and not-A at the same time. Precategorical experience has the quality of a transitional object. It is a transitional realm, self and nonself at the same time. Potential space, Winnicott calls it, the fount of all creativity, where we play with evil.[3]

Thomas Ogden writes about the autistic-contiguous organization of experience, the most fundamental and primitive mode of being. It is called autistic-contiguous because the state it represents is not of two skins or surfaces touching, but one that is two, two surfaces whose contact creates one reality, shared skin. Imagine, he suggests, that sitting in your chair you feel neither the chair nor the pressure on your buttocks. Instead, there is neither chair nor buttocks but simply "impression," a feeling with no inside, no outside, and no locus. That is autistic-contiguous experience.[4] Its paradigm is the mother-infant relationship, the infant unaware of where his surface ends and mother's begins, aware only of a boundary that is not so much boundary as experience, an experience of the other that is at once an experience of itself, an "impression," a shape without a frame.

At its best, autistic-contiguous experience expresses a profound rhythmic contentment with the world, such as Mary's golden creamy All. Autistic-contiguous experience is not just the realm of dread; it is also a realm of meaning and immediacy beyond, or beneath, words. It is the realm of the reality of bodily experience so immediate and so real that the distinction between bodily and symbolic experience is transcended, or perhaps "undermined" would put it better. If we did not have autistic-contiguous experience to draw upon all the rest of our lives, there would be something hollow and missing in life, a world of symbols whose connection to felt meaning would be obscure.

Although autistic-contiguous experience is not only the realm of dread, it may become transformed into dread in an instant, the experience of oneness with the All becoming an experience of loss of self in the blink of an eye. Autistic-contiguous anxiety is experienced as a feeling of leaking or dissolving, disappearing or falling into shapeless unbounded space.

Ogden relates his work on the autistic-contiguous "position" to Wilfred Bion's work on the container and contained, Bion writing about "nameless dread" to refer to an experience of being stripped of containment, meaning, and form. We should better call it "formless dread," writes Ogden. Ogden is just right. Formless dread is the fear of formlessness, the loss of context, meaning, and containment, where boundaries fail and things that should be separate flow into each other. For over three thousand years evil has been understood as a form of pollution, dirt, matter out of place—the topic of Chapter 4. The autistic-contiguous position is the source of that experience.

In the autistic-contiguous position there is no symbolization. Bodily experiences, impressions of shapes, forms, and rhythms take the place of symbols. Symbols require frames, a form to contain the symbol and set it off from the experience it represents. Without this frame there can be no symbol, only experience without locus or boundary. Ogden tells the story of how he inadvertently destroyed this frame. After dinner one night it suddenly occurred to him how strange it was to call this thing a napkin, the conjunction of the terms "nap" and "kin."

> I repeated the two sounds over and over until I began to get the very frightening feeling that these sounds had no connection at all with this thing I was looking at. I could not get the sounds to naturally "mean" the thing they had meant only minutes before. The link was broken, and, to my horror, could not be mended simply by an act of will. I imagined that I could, if I chose to, destroy the power of any and all words to "mean" something if I thought about them one at a time in this way.[5]

Ogden is writing about dread, the world disconnected from itself, from oneself, from meaning itself.

Ogden is writing in the tradition of Melanie Klein, who developed the concept of "positions" of experience. Unlike stages of development, positions are never outgrown. Nor does it make sense to talk about a regression to a position. Positions, including the autistic-contiguous position, accompany us all the days of our lives. Problematic is not the persistence of early positions but what Ogden calls the collapse of positions, in which one position dominates all the others, finding no counterbalance in them.

Klein introduces two positions, which she calls the paranoid-schizoid and depressive positions.[6] In the paranoid-schizoid position, we fear our doom at the hands of malevolent external persecutors who seek to destroy us and all the goods we possess. In fact, says Klein, these persecutors are our own projections, our rage and envy come back to haunt us, individual psychology the psychologic of *lex talionis*, in which we fear everything we would have done to others. It is easy to see how evil might be done out of paranoid-schizoid anxiety. If one experiences the world as the source of perpetual attack, the best defense may be to attack first. Thomas Hobbes understood the psychologic. It is the basis of his account of the state of nature in *Leviathan*, in which preemptive attack is the best defense. Many inmates understand this logic too. It is why most let Eichmann off the hook: if everything is war all the time, there can be no innocent bystanders.

In the paranoid-schizoid position there is no history, because there is no space for the experiencing self, which in the paranoid-schizoid position knows itself only as an entity that is continually being acted upon by external forces. Hobbes knew this, the state of nature a place without civilization or culture, everyone devoting himself to survival. The claim of Agamemnon in the *Iliad* (19.86ff), that the gods made him seize Achilles' prize, expresses the psychologic of the paranoid-schizoid position perfectly. So does the assumption that a human being, a woman, may be a prize object.

Because there is no experiencing self to mediate symbol and reality, the paranoid-schizoid position is characterized by what Hanna Segal calls the symbolic equation, in which symbol and reality are one.[7] This is not the same thing as the complete absence of symbolization characteristic of the autistic-contiguous position. In the paranoid-schizoid position symbolization occurs, but in a way in which symbol and reality are likely to become confused, a concept I draw on frequently in Chapters 6 and 7 to explain evil.

The depressive position, according to Klein, emerges soon after the paranoid-schizoid position, sometime during the first year of life. (Many, like Ogden, find Klein's positions useful but ignore Klein's tendency to read them back into the earliest months of life.) In the depressive position we come to experience genuine remorse and regret for harm done to the good object. At first this remorse is selfish, as in "I have harmed, or wished to harm, the goodness upon which my life depends; how shall I survive?" Soon, however, the depressive position comes to include a genuine love and concern for the other and a desire to make reparation for the damage one has done to the other's goodness.

The depressive position is the realm of genuine symbolization, in which the self mediates between symbol and symbolized, knowing the difference between them. The self is the frame. In the depressive position we know others as whole persons, not part objects. We know this in the depressive position because we are able to tolerate ambivalence, to recognize that very little in the world is all good or all bad. Satan and absolute evil are not depressive constructs, but paranoid-schizoid ones.

Some see Klein's view of human nature as rather dark, but they are in many ways mistaken. Although infants first experience the paranoid-schizoid position, it is no more fundamental than the depressive position.

For Klein, to love and care for others is as natural as to wish to destroy them. In fact, it is the conflict between these two desires which is the source of mental conflict. Klein calls it the depressive position, in part because one despairs of ever being strong and good enough to repair the damage to goodness one has wished or caused.

The autistic-contiguous position, Ogden's construct, precedes the paranoid-schizoid and depressive positions, but not by much, and sequence is not really the point. The point is the way in which the three positions need one another, each acting to temper the other two. It is the force field among them that counts. Ogden puts it this way:

> Psychopathology can be thought of as forms of collapse of the richness of experience generated between these [three] poles. . . . Collapse toward the autistic-contiguous pole generates imprisonment in the machine-like tyranny of attempted sensory-based escape from the terror of formless dread. . . . Collapse into the paranoid-schizoid pole is characterized by imprisonment in a . . . world of thoughts and feelings . . . that simply happen, and cannot be thought about or interpreted. Collapse in the direction of the depressive pole involves a form of isolation of oneself from one's bodily sensations, and from the immediacy of one's lived experience, leaving one devoid of spontaneity and aliveness.[8]

Though Ogden uses the term "dialectical" to characterize the proper relationship among the three positions, it may be more helpful to conceptualize the relationship among the three positions in terms of a triangle whose form stems from the tension created by the three angles.

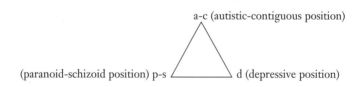

a-c (autistic-contiguous position)

(paranoid-schizoid position) p-s   d (depressive position)

The title of Ogden's book, *The Primitive Edge of Experience*, suggests that the autistic-contiguous position is the lower edge of the paranoid-schizoid position, what he calls the underbelly of the schizoid personality organization. Seen from this perspective, we should not expect to see autistic-contiguous phenomena by themselves, but rather mixed with paranoid-schizoid experiences, and even with depressive ones, insofar as autistic-contiguous experience may be symbolized. Ogden's book is a depressive frame for autistic-contiguous experience. This is the best humans can do.

Consider, in this regard, Ms. Warden, an inmate who is unable to read, but not because she is illiterate. "When I read," she says, "it's like the book is talking in my head. I don't know whose thoughts are whose anymore, like I'm losing my mind, like my thoughts are flowing onto the page. I'm not going to read anymore until I know exactly what *I* think." Hers is an autistic-contiguous anxiety, but she is not in the autistic-contiguous position. If she were, she could not use words to form the feeling. She is on the borderline somewhere, a borderline that touches on all three positions at once.

She is in the autistic-contiguous position, however, insofar as her dread is not of being attacked and devoured by persecutors but of losing herself, melting onto the page. She is in the paranoid-schizoid position insofar as she experiences the book as somehow penetrating her mind, and she is in the depressive position insofar as she can use words to frame the feeling. We could argue about which position is dominant. I would argue for the paranoid-schizoid position, but the argument is not important. Important is how the positions converge in reality for good and ill, the significance of the triangle.

The dread that leads to evil takes place along the left side of the triangle, the side that connects autistic-contiguous with paranoid-schizoid experience. In fact, one might argue that dread transforms an equilateral triangle into an acute one, the left side becoming shorter and shorter as these two positions collapse into one. Something like this is happening with Ms. Warden.

From this perspective, evil is a paranoid-schizoid attempt to evacuate the formless dread by giving it form via violent intrusion into another, the other's body giving presymbolic form to the dread that is evacuated there. Ogden refers to a patient who mimicked his every gesture, using Ogden's body to experiment with what it might feel like to be alive. Ogden was touched, as he should have been. It was a type of love, imitation the sincerest form of the autistic-contiguous position. But Ogden should also have been worried, and so should we all. Here too is the ground of evil, using others' bodies to give shape to our own formless dread. Putting our dread into the other by terrorizing and victimizing him, we give form to our dread. It is as though the other were the frame for the picture of our dread, a picture that must be framed before we can paint it, and destroyed immediately afterward, lest it remind us of our dread.

Destroying the other, we destroy our dread (or so the fantasy goes), separating from it after having given it protosymbolic form in the body of another. This process applies not just to physical violence but to the cutting remark, the hurtful gesture, and perhaps even the purposeful neglect of the humanity of others, as though some must lose their humanity for others to possess it.

From a strictly theoretical perspective, it may be useful to ask whether the evil act in question stems from a position closer to the paranoid-schizoid angle of the triangle than to the autistic-contiguous angle. Violence, whether physical or mental, that has a quality of evacuative attachment—in which one connects with the other in order forcibly to share an unbearable feeling so as to at once communicate and be rid of it—would come closer to the paranoid-schizoid position. "I made him love me and then left him so that I would know that at least one person in the world knew the hurt I feel every day of my life," says Tracy D. in response to question 8, about evil she had done.

Violence that seeks to create an edge, a boundary, as though to say you must suffer and die so that I can live, would come closer to the autistic-contiguous position, violence a defense against merger. "I knew that someone was going to die that night, but I just didn't know whether it was me or him," says Mr. Marcus.

In general, however, the dread that motivates evil operates through both positions at once, and it is not terribly important to sort them out. Important is the principle, the way in which paranoid-schizoid anxiety expresses and defends against autistic-contiguous dread. In subsequent chapters I argue that avoiding evil depends on the ability to symbolize dread. Symbolization is the realm of the depressive position. Avoiding the evil that stems from dread depends on the ability to bring all three positions into play—not in order to overcome our dread, if such a thing were even possible (and it is not), but in order to find a form to express it that does not involve using the body or mind of another in order to contain it. The transitional space that Winnicott writes of, the transitional space that is an alternative to inflicting our dread on others, is created when we use two sides of the triangle to frame the third.

Kleinians tend to idealize the depressive position. In fact, it is the autistic-contiguous position that is the realm of the most profound experiences of meaning and vitality, a realm religion seeks to tap and articulate in symbolic form. From this perspective, evil is an attempt to experience the vitality of the autistic-contiguous position without subjecting oneself to the dread, to experience vitality in and through the body of the evildoer's victim, as though the victim must contain the dread if the evildoer is to live. Not only is this attempt cheating, but it does not work.

Evil as cheating means that evil seeks to possess the vitality without experiencing dread. Evil pretends. It pretends that vitality need not have the same roots as dread, that one can know the joy of living without the dread of dying. Evil pretends that one can split the autistic-contiguous position, taking the vitality for oneself while leaving the dread for others or, rather, inserting it there. Excitement is not living, and living is always close to dread. As Ernest Becker puts it, "Full humanness means full fear and trembling, at least some of the waking day."[9]

One might argue, much as Socrates does (*Meno* 77b–78b, *Protagoras* 353d–58e), that the evildoer is evil out of ignorance, failing to understand that inflicting dread on others cannot bring him to life. If this is so, the ignorance will not be corrected by information, not even psychological theories about dread. It is a matter of teaching people how to symbolize their dread, so that they may contain it in more abstract and knowable forms. It is an education that begins with mother and baby and ends with our culture's finest achievements, such as art, religion, and music. In between is the art of everyday living with our dread, the most important space of all. The chapters that follow are about these spaces.

The Phenomenology of Precategorical Experience

Though illuminated by psychological insight, precategorical experience is a phenomenological concept, an account of experience. Even were the theory of the autistic-contiguous position mistaken, this mistake would affect not the validity of the experience but only the theory behind it. First of all, precategorical experience *is*. If my research-based approach to evil has not taught me anything else, it has taught me this—the priority of the experience.

Precategorical experience is a version of what Edmund Husserl called prepredicative experiences: experiences so fundamental that they are the foundation of the possibility of other experiences. Phenomenological reduction is a fancy name for a simple idea: imagine what one's original experience of the world must have been like, must be like, in order to live in it as humans do. In this original experience, Husserl argues, all thought has the quality of intentionality: it intends or aims at something. It is, however, a mistake to conclude that thought that intends an external object, such as a tree, is different from thought which intends an internal object, such as a feeling, like dread. In our first experience of the world, differentiations that later become distinctions between psychological and natural science do not exist: "Natural science is supposed to be based on outer, psychology on inner, experience. . . . What is actually experienced is the world as simply existing, prior to all philosophy and theory. . . . Why does the whole flowing life-world not figure at the very beginning of a psychology as something 'psychic'. . . . why is this experience not called psychological experience rather than 'outer experience,' supposedly by contrast to psychological experience?" [10]

Through the method of phenomenological reduction (actually, an act of imagination), Husserl grasps what Ogden grasps, what some informants grasp as well. The distinction between inner and outer, man and world, is not a fundamental but a secondary construction. At the most fundamental level of experience everything is subjective, flowing in and through us. What informants call evil is the reactivation of this experience in the realm of terror, what I call dread.

If precategorical experience makes no firm distinction between subject and object, then what of categorical experience? Ponder Kant's founding act of morality, the categorical imperative. "Act as if the maxim of your action were to become through your will a universal law of nature." [11] You might want to lie in order to get someone to loan you money. But what if your maxim "Lying is the best policy" became a universal law and everyone did it? The world would become hell and you would be its first citizen. Though Kant denied the identity of his maxim with the golden rule (Lev. 19.19), the idea is similar. Do unto others as you would have them do unto you.

Consider what is involved in the categorical imperative. You must know yourself as separate from other people, with your own interests and projects. If you do not, you would see no conflict between your interests and theirs; all would have the same desires. Not for the same thing, but literally the same desires. While separate and distinct from others, you must care about others. Not just about their behavior, but about their inner worlds, so that you can imagine them being like you, but not you. They too feel pain and joy at many of the same things you do, but not exactly the same things, and not exactly the same pain and joy either. The other is separate, different, yet similar, so that you are obligated to treat that person with as much respect as you treat yourself.

The academic might argue that Kant's categorical imperative cannot properly be contrasted with the phenomenon of precategorical thought. By "categorical" Kant means universally binding upon all; its opposite is not precategorical, but hypothetical, provisional. Kant is a moral philosopher, concerned not with the origins of experience but with how we must live if we are to regard ourselves as ethical beings. One might object that I am contrasting apples and oranges, even if one is called pre-apples.

Seen from the perspective of the history of ideas, such an objection is correct, or at least relevant. My argument is not, however, a play on the terms "precategorical" and "categorical." My argument is operational: what psychological operations, or distinctions, must one be able to make in order to act morally? All the distinctions that are assumed as given and obvious in Kant's categorical imperative. Precategorical thought is properly contrasted with Kant's categorical imperative if we recognize that the categorical imperative makes many assumptions about psychological development, assumptions not operative in precategorical thought. Morality depends on one's being able to make basic distinctions between self and other, distinctions so obvious they are often assumed to be given, available to all. In fact, they are made. Avoiding evil depends on how they are made.

The developmental achievement represented by the categorical imperative may be conceptualized in terms of the separation of self from object. The child loses the mania for omnipotent control and sees objects as existing "independently of the state of needs," as Heinz Hartmann puts it.[12] One cannot be moral if one values an object only when it serves the needs of the self. To do so gives us the "little girl who fell in the well" syndrome, in which our moral concern is for whoever meets our need for a good cry. Morality takes imagination, and moral imagination requires a concern for others whose existence and suffering is independent of our needs.

Sometimes the opposite is argued—that morality depends on the ability to identify with another so completely that the boundaries between self and world are suspended, as in precategorical thought. That is also not a good basis for morality, for identification can as readily lead to evil acts as to good ones. Susan Smith, much publicized for drowning her children, said that she was really trying to kill herself.[13] If we save others to save ourselves, then we may kill them to kill ourselves and torture them because we are tortured. "I just had to share my feelings," says one inmate who tortured his victim, sounding like a guest on the autistic-contiguous version of the Oprah Winfrey show. Above all, morality respects boundaries, finding a place for the other outside the boundaries that define me but inside the boundaries that define the human world we both share.

Under the influence of precategorical morality I may do awesome things, such as sacrifice my life for another. But such sacrifice is not necessarily moral. It may be an act of love, as when a parent sacrifices for the child with whom she so closely identifies that their fates are one, the child's good fortune the parent's own. But it is not a moral act; it is not immoral either. It is prior to both. Morality depends on the recognition of separateness, in which I choose to be bound by the same rules I would apply to others, because I recognize others as similar but nonidentical. This insight is what is captured in Kant's categorical imperative, and for this reason I contrast that imperative to precategorical thought, under which it is quite impossible. Kant's categorical imperative captures some invariant features of morality. Whether Kant's categorical imperative is the best and only way to conceive moral obligation is another issue.

Precategorical thought is neither pathological nor undesirable. All art depends on it, even as art is impossible without access to the frames and forms that define categorical thought. Undesirable is how the dread carried in precategorical thought may isolate it in the mind, so that it becomes impervious to categorical reflection—that is, morality. Creating a two-way traffic flow between dread and morality may lessen evil, but only if we can find the symbols to embody our dread. In the absence of symbolization, evil gets lodged in the body, acted out rather than expressed in more abstract, less destructive forms.

"I just wanted someone to know how terrible I really felt," says one who murdered an innocent man. "I just wanted someone to feel me for a little while." Reflect on the double meaning for a moment. It is the psychologic of the autistic-contiguous position, in which feeling someone else (in this case with a knife) and being felt by them are one, like the impression without a locus made by the chair-buttocks which Ogden writes of. Here is an explanation of much otherwise-incomprehensible violence, the victimizer feeling as though he were the victim. In the autistic-contiguous position he is.

Mr. Deacon wishes he could wire his mother to a feeling machine and turn on the switch, "so she could feel what I felt for just a little while." It sounds as though he wants to electrocute her, and that may not be far from the truth. She used to beat and torture him with an electrical cord. (Ogden characterizes the autistic-contiguous position in terms of being trapped inside a machine with no way out.)

"No!" cries out Ms. Paine to Mr. Deacon. "We should never do anything like that. The evildoer is sick, and needs help." Ms. Paine killed her child. Mr. Deacon knows this, and because he is a decent man he relents. "Well, even if there was such a machine, I couldn't hook anybody up to it." Evil is a nonfeeling machine, the way we inflict our feelings on others, so that we need not experience them ourselves.

"Evil is a·feeling of doom, the feeling we get when we depart from God's law," is how Mr. Caine puts it, capturing the psychologic perfectly backward. "Perfectly," because this is just how his mind works, confusing the experience of doom with evil, when it is actually evil that is the defense against doom, as though we could inflict doom on others and so rid ourselves of it, as though doom were a concrete thing that could be moved from place to place, preferably with a gun, not with the symbolic abstraction of a feeling.

Most free informants have strong precategorical experiences of evil, in which normal distinctions between self and world, inner and outer, part and whole, are suspended. Few inmates do. Many can hardly understand the experience. "That's just insane!" says Ms. Ball when I recounted the story of Henry, who saw his face covered with blood. Few free informants are so quick to dismiss the experience. The difference points the way to our understanding evil.

The Dread of Being Human

All precategorical experience is not dreadful. But all precategorical experience traffics with dread, the experience of dread giving our epiphanies the quality of awe, such as Mary H.'s vision of the creamy All bathed in a golden light. Evil is awesome in the way that it exceeds the normal, going to every excess and beyond, including beyond what humans can stand. This is the meaning of the English term "evil," related to the German *ueber*, "over" or "beyond." Not every "beyond" experience is dreadful, but there are sound reasons to insist that the experience of awe is powered by dread.

A good Middle English word, "dread" frequently translates the German *Angst*. Both connote not only awe-filled terror but anticipation. "An apprehension of the future, a presentiment of a something which is nothing," is how Kierkegaard puts it in *The Concept of Dread (Angst)*.[14] Dread is primordial, the terror of human limits, of living and dying in a single human body. Above all we dread being human. For Alfred North Whitehead, the two sources of evil are that "things fade" and that "alternatives exclude"[15]—another way of saying that evil is what reveals to us the limits of being human.

We dread what it is to be human—not just because we shall soon die but because the limits revealed to us by our choices make it so hard to find meaning in anything. In *The Symbolism of Evil*, Ricoeur writes of ethical dread, terror at the inability to love or care, despair at the incapacity to invest the transitory world with value.[16] The love of money is the root of all evil, according to 1 Timothy 6.10. But that is not quite right. The root of all evil is the inability to love or value anything, and the dread this inability to invest in the world evokes.

Epiphanies like Mary's, good and evil bathed together in a golden glow, are a defense against terror, awe momentarily split off from dread. If we understand dread as the awe at being merely human, and all too human, it does not seem immoderate to argue that all epiphany has the quality of dread.

Charles Baudelaire's title *Les Fleurs du Mal* suggests that he is writing about flowers that sprout from evil. (*Mal* may denote sickness, not just evil; but standing alone as it does, it can only mean evil.) However, his topics are, for the most part, not about evil at all, but about ugliness, old age, decay, and death. His images of a decadent old lecher devouring the battered tit of a doddering whore and of maggots packed close to the skull[17] are ugly, base, and disgusting. And they are part of life. Dissolution, corruption, and decay are the themes of most of the poems, and they have nothing to do with evil, except in the biblical sense of misfortunes that plague us all. This, though, may be what evil is really about, the fantasy that the misfortunes of old age and death can be inflicted on others to save ourselves.

Dread is abstract. Pain, abandonment, and helplessness are not. Empirical correlates of dread, to use a clumsy term for a moment, they are how we experience dread in our everyday lives. In *Women and Evil*, Nel Noddings goes further, arguing that male writers such as Paul Tillich have taken refuge in abstraction, writing about the great existential terrors: death, guilt, and meaninglessness. She brings these terrors down to earth and makes them real.[18] It is an interesting point, though it is hard to see why we must choose between dread and its correlates. Pain, helplessness, and abandonment elicit dread and frequently stand for it. There seems no good reason to make this trio of terrors more fundamental, or less.

We experience dread as physical pain that will not stop, so that one's body becomes the enemy. It is why so many want the option of physician-assisted suicide, so that we need not feel utterly helpless in the face of the body as torturer. In pain the body betrays the self, overwhelming the self with its suffering, as though the body were speaking to the self in the only language they share. Only it is not speaking, it is wailing.

We experience dread as abandonment. Noddings writes of "the absolute terror on the face of the child lost in a supermarket."[19] It is the face that all who want to face evil ought to look at. Not Eichmann, not Hitler, but the face of a terrified child. Not because a terrified child is necessarily the victim of evil, but because it is the child's terror that we seek to escape by facing evil, looking out instead of in.

For many of us, two of the three correlates of dread, pain and helplessness, will arrive as illness, intensifying the fear of abandonment no matter what our friends and loved ones tell us. In puzzling over why Jerzy Kosinski and Bruno Bettelheim, both Holocaust survivors, killed themselves when they were in poor health, a friend suggested that perhaps they could not tolerate being helpless a third time. Childhood and old age are all most people can bear. Primo Levi killed himself for a different reason. He was, he says, afraid that people were already beginning to forget. That too is abandonment.

Evil inflicts pain, abandonment, and helplessness on others, so that the evildoer will not have to experience them himself. It is that simple, and that complicated. It is why torture is the paradigm of evil, master of all three terrors at once. All evil has the quality of torture, inflicting dread on another so as to escape it oneself. Hence, all evil has the quality of sadism, defined in Chapter 2 as the joy of having taken control of an experience of victimhood by inflicting it on another.

Terril T. Gagnier and Richard Robertiello write of "sado-masochism as a defense against merging," but that is only half the story. Arnold Rothstein comes closer to the mark when he writes of "sadomasochism . . . as a pathological compromise formation." It is a compromise between merging and separation.[20] Sadomasochism is fusion, seeking to merge with the other in order to get the other to contain one's dread, a fusion that is the essence of what I call the psychopathic moment. Suddenly the other is cut off to suffer alone, scapegoat to the sadist's doom. Sometimes, in the case of a few of the prisoners, this cutoff is literal.

In Dante's *Inferno*, not just the images of torture but the rhythm of the poetry embody the experience of dread, communicating with the body as well as with the mind. The *Inferno* is an encyclopedia of terror, a catalog of dread transformed into art, so that we might bear it.

From each hole's mouth,
a sinner stuck
but only half;
just the feet
and legs showed,
and only to the calf.
The soles of their feet
were on fire,
and their joints convulsed

with so much power,
they'd have snapped rope,
or baling wire.
As flame will flow
on oil-soaked things,
lightly on the surface, so
it slithered here,
back and forth,
from heel to toe.

(Canto 19;
C. K. Williams, trans.)

This for selling indulgences, high up in the fourth circle of hell.

Dante is not writing just about the tortures of hell. He is writing about despair, the torture of life. His poetry understands what his theodicy must reject, the sheer dread at the caprice and arbitrariness of life and death, to say nothing of the hereafter. All made worse by the reigning Augustinian theodicy of predestination, God's choosing who shall be saved long before they are born. What must it be like to live in a world in which God hated Jacob's brother even before he was born? Did he hate me too? And you? Is that why we suffer so much? The *Inferno* makes sense of this experience—not philosophical sense, not even theological sense, but experiential sense, finding a creative form to express and contain the torture of despair and self-doubt. It is the only alternative to inflicting dread on others.

Noddings's interpretation of dread brings us back to the surface of the earth. But only to the surface. Dread is also about the ambiguity of surfaces, the feeling of doom which arises when surfaces no longer contain, what Ogden calls autistic-contiguous anxiety. In putting words to dread, we must not forget that dread is about the ineffable, experiences that involve not loss of others, not even loss of hope, but loss of self. This view does not make Noddings wrong. On the contrary, it suggests why the empirical correlates of dread are so powerful, evoking an experience that is prior to the empirical, the precategorical experience of evil. (A note on terms: one's doom is one's death; dread is abstract doom —pain, abandonment, and loss, as well as their existential correlates, meaninglessness and nothingness. Dread is fear of a living death. Which term is employed, "dread" or "doom," depends on the context.)

The psychopath is frequently considered the epitome of evil, so cold and remote he remains untouchable while treating others as objects of contempt, manipulation, and destruction. Many free informants, and some inmates, talked about evil in terms that are readily translated into the experience of psychopathy, such as "coldness," "inhuman unresponsiveness," "snake-like," and "using others as food." It is interesting to reflect on psychopathy from this perspective, seeking not to demonize the psychopath but to see what we all share with him. To do so opens another door on evil. Like all doors on this subject, behind it is a mirror. Evil is a psychopathic moment in which we all share.

There are several theories of psychopathy. In 1948, Harrison Gough, working in the tradition of George Herbert Mead, characterized psychopaths as suffering from a deficient role-playing ability. Almost two decades later, Hans Eysenck defined the psychopath as a genetically predisposed deficient learner. Robert Hare, who developed the psychopathy checklist (PCL-R) referred to in Chapter 2, understands psychopathy as a failure of inhibition, the psychopath never learning what it takes to avoid punishment. There are other theories, such as H. Cleckley's in *The Mask of Sanity*, but none is analytic. One might argue that none is truly psychological, if by "psychological" we mean concerned with environmental and developmental sources of dynamic emotional states.[21]

Current research follows two paths. The checklist approach, as it might be called, aims at better identifying inmates and others likely to be unresponsive to treatment or punishment. The neurological approach aims at discovering biological correlates, such as the discovery that many deemed psychopathic "exhibit excessive amount of slow-wave activity" on the EEG, as Hare puts it. There is probably something to all these approaches, as Dennis Doren argues in *Understanding and Treating the Psychopath*, but they have the disadvantage of heightening the difference between the psychopath and the rest of us.[22] One advantage of a psychoanalytic perspective on psychopathy is that it captures the continuity between the psychopath and us all, much as Freud captured the continuity between neurotics and normals. An analytic approach to psychopathy allows us to see the roots of everyday evil in everyday psychopathy.

The analytic approach I draw on is that of J. Reid Meloy in *The*

Psychopathic Mind. Meloy explains psychopathy in terms of developmental failure at an early age—a failure involving the "stranger selfobject," a term he borrows from James Grotstein. Grotstein believes that the stranger selfobject is a built-in, image-based expectation that the stranger is to be feared as a dangerous predator. This expectation is the basis of the stranger anxiety that seems to affect all infants.[23] For most infants most of the time, parents act to quell stranger anxiety, allowing the infant to find a place for his fear. What happens when a parent, particularly the mother, herself becomes the stranger selfobject, because of failed empathy, intrusiveness, abandonment, and lack of attunement on a massive scale?

Rather than internalize the stranger selfobject as a scary part of himself, the future psychopath identifies with the stranger selfobject, becoming the stranger selfobject to himself. Psychopathy is a pure (that is, unmediated by the depressive position) paranoid-schizoid defense against profound autistic-contiguous anxiety. The stranger selfobject is identified with so completely because the terror of dissolution is so strong, as though only perfect identification can protect against total annihilation. As far as I know, there have been no attempts to explain psychopathy in terms of Ogden's autistic-contiguous position. It is, however, a fruitful perspective, helping to explain why the psychopath is so devoted to his victim, without whom he would become "something which is nothing." Paranoid-schizoids need enemies. Psychopaths need victims to quite literally (since this is the realm of the presymbolic) hold their dread.

One inmate deemed psychopathic said his previous study of mortuary science gave him a greater respect for life. The "full refrigerator" down at the morgue, packed with all those young bodies, gave him pause. Not enough, apparently. He resumed his criminal career, murdering several competing drug dealers before being returned to jail. Once a corpse he was embalming moved its arm and struck him, a muscular reaction to the embalming fluid. Did it scare him? "I don't get scared. If it had been a monster, I'd have killed it. If there's any monster around, then it's me. I'll out-monster the monster." His reasoning is perfectly psychopathic: if there's any monster around here, it's going to be me.

Neurotics, and most borderlines, internalize their fearful objects, making them a part of the self, the self containing within it aspects that are hostile, bad, and alien to it. W. R. D. Fairbairn refers to these alien aspects as the antilibidinal ego or "internal saboteur."[24] It is these parts, and their relationship, that I listened for in my interviews. Such listening does not work with the psychopath, or rather what one hears is a vastly simplified psychic drama, the psychopath identifying so completely with the stranger selfobject that he becomes it, finding his only human relationships in persecuting others, as though he were his world relating to him in the only way he knows—as predator.

"It is my hypothesis," says Meloy, "that the psychopathic process is fundamentally a virtual failure of internalization."[25] Identifying so completely and concretely with one internal object, the predatory stranger, the psychopath has no room for others. His relationships with others are not really object relationships at all, at least not human ones. Except as means, tools found strewn about the world, others do not truly exist. His is a great defense at a great price, the loss of an inner world, what it is to be truly human.

The psychopath defends against his autistic-contiguous anxiety, the dread of losing himself, by means of total identification with the persecutor, becoming evil to share its power. One might argue that the process is akin to what Anna Freud calls identification with the aggressor, the terror whose only solution is to become the terrorist. But that would not be quite right. Identification with the aggressor has the quality of fusion with a feared and admired object. It is, says Anna Freud, the way in which the oedipal conflict is resolved, the little boy identifying with the father who threatens to castrate him for his presumption.[26] In this regard, identification with the aggressor has the quality of an oceanic relationship, a merger that stops the leaks in the self by binding with another.

Identification with the persecutor is more primitive, not a merger with the threatening All, but becoming the part-object that threatens to obliterate the self. Like the shark, the predator can never stop moving, never stop preying on others, lest he be destroyed. When you are a shark, not even oceanic merger offers a respite, not even for a moment.

Absent an internal world, the psychopath finds his only relationships in predation. But strange relationships these are, the other as food for the psychopath's ego, with no hint of attachment. This accounts, says Meloy, for the common experience of the psychopath as cold, reptilian: "The reptilian, predatory eyes are, in a sense, the antithesis of the affectionate mirroring of the infant in the eyes of the mother. The nascent self is reflected as an object of prey, rather than an object of love. . . . The interaction is socially defined by parameters of power rather than attachment."[27]

Recall how many informants define the evildoer in terms of the cold, creepy feeling he engenders. Because such feelings often mislead does not mean that the psychopath does not exist. Feelings mislead because there is a little psychopath in each of us: sometimes we find him in others when we cannot know him in ourselves; sometimes we fail to see him in others for the same reason.

Unreachability—the fear that there is nothing one could say or do that would move the other to recognition of our subjectivity—is a key dimension of dread, the dimension reflected in the experience of evil as cold and inhumane. Referring to the Milgram experiment, one informant says, "If it had been me locked in that little room, I'd have thought of something to say, something to make him stop."

What if you couldn't? What if there was absolutely nothing you could say or do? Not a word, not a cry, not a whisper? Then what? Greta R. goes pale, and for the longest time says nothing before responding in a small voice: "Then I guess I would just die." Sadism is catching, and I'd caught it. I hope the lesson was worth the pain.

Precategorical dread evokes the helplessness of infancy, in which the responsiveness of the other is the condition of life itself. It is not just mothers who bond. Babies bond with their mothers, quickly learning (evidently the knowledge is built in) how to evoke her life-saving responsiveness. Gross failures of maternal responsiveness are so terrifying they lead the nascent psychopath to identify with the unresponsiveness itself, a failed merger that is the only merger around, the union with the stranger predator.

It is not only the psychopath who experienced failed responsiveness. We all did, and do. Like the psychopath we identify total unresponsiveness with evil. Unlike the psychopath, we do not become it, at least not totally. The responsiveness we have experienced keeps the unresponsive self at bay.

"I stood over them and watched them die," says Mr. Leotine. "I shared their last moments, their pain, their sorrow. For once my family was close." Mr. Leotine is talking as if his parents died in a car wreck, as if he had rushed to the hospital to share their beautiful deaths, as if he hadn't shot and killed them. His eyes close for a moment. I think he is experiencing bliss, an oceanic merger with the idea of his parents separated from their awful reality.

He wanted to be close to his parents and free of them at the same time. Only he could not do the abstraction, the distinction between his real parents and their mental representation, internalizing their image while leaving their bodies behind. Or rather, the intensity of his hatred bound him to them so that the only way he could have their image was to destroy their bodies. He killed them to have them all to himself.

One psychopath, put it this way: "What I needed to have was a particular experience with a person, and to possess them in the way I wanted to: I had to evict them from their human bodies."[28] The psychopath kills to possess the body without the bother of the other's subjectivity, soul, or will. Mr. Leotine killed in order to possess the souls of his soul-murdering parents without the bother of their bodies: the terrible, and terribly complex, reality of their hatred, their power, and their love, totally under his control for the first time in his life.

Since he killed his parents, Mr. Leotine dreams about them almost nightly. He likes it that way. "While they were still alive, I never dreamed about them. I was too angry. It's better this way. Now I can have them in my dreams." Mr. Leotine seeks an idealized spiritual attachment to his parents. For this reason alone (there are others) he is not psychopathic. Still, it would not do to draw the distinction between psychopath and lost soul, like Mr. Leotine, too sharply. Although only the lost soul wants the connection as well as the power, both the psychopath and the lost soul identify with the power of their persecutors.

We all do. The psychopathic moment is a virtually universal moment in all lives. When we are faced with intolerable, uncontainable dread, the natural tendency is to identify with the persecutor, becoming the agent of doom, as the only way of controlling it. Evil is the attempt to inflict one's doom on others, becoming doom, rather than living subject to it. In this sense evil is bad faith, the lie that one could escape one's fate by inflicting it on others.

To explain dread in terms of a psychopathic moment is not to imply that it can be cured as a mental illness is cured. If evil is a mental illness then it is a universal one, the illness of being human, an illness that at best can only be ameliorated. The value of seeing the experience of dread in terms of the psychopathic moment stems from the way in which it exposes the complex identifications involved. We do not feel terror and *then* identify with the aggressor, or at least that is not the whole story. The terror stems *from* the identification with the aggressor, his aggression suddenly our own, directed against those we care about and depend on, including ourselves and our values.

For most of us this happens only occasionally. Or we identify with the aggressor indirectly, participating in social systems that inflict the terror of helplessness downward, on select populations such as the poor or prisoners. But we do it. Unlike the psychopath, most of us feel guilty, at least sometimes. Neither guilt nor empathy will change this tendency to inflict terror on others, however. Individuals and societies are quite capable of hardening themselves against their guilt, blaming the victim, and all the rest. The only thing that will change this tendency is the ability of individuals, and societies, to traffic with their dread, to give dread creative form so as to be able to live with it. This is the theme of the remaining chapters.

FOUR   *Suffering Evil, Doing Evil*

In *The Symbolism of Evil,* Paul Ricoeur writes about the precategorical experience of evil, though he does not call it that. He writes of the paleosymbolic prehistory of evil in which the leading experiences are impurity, defilement, dread, and loss of wholeness, resulting in alienation and nothingness, what he calls loss of root and bond, an anchoredness in the world. What unites these primordial experiences is the loss of boundaries, the way in which inside and outside are no longer distinct, and the dread this loss incurs. It is what Matt C. means when he says, "I felt evil." It is what Ogden means when he refers to the "formless dread" of the autistic-contiguous position. Dirt, says William James, is matter out of place, as good a definition of impurity and defilement as any.

Like Andrew S., Spury F. fought in World War II, a PFC with a rendezvous with history, among the first troops to liberate Dachau. It is an experience that will stay with him to his grave, but it is not what he thinks about when he thinks about evil. He thinks about the seventeen months he spent at the front and about how hard he worked to keep himself pure. Sexual purity was a big part of this struggle, not having sex with whores, not leaving his seed on foreign soil. Not talking dirty was important too. Equally important was fighting fair. "I had this German officer in my sights. He'd just gotten up, and was out in front of a farmhouse doing his sit-ups. I didn't shoot him. How could I shoot someone while he was taking care of a part of his body?" Later, when the German sat down behind his machine gun, Spury shot and killed him. He felt bad. "I searched his papers; he was fifty-two. The war was almost over, and he wouldn't be going home. But he was looking down the barrel of his machine gun. I had a clean shot, and it was a clean kill. I didn't debase myself."

Spury tells horrible stories about the front, losing half his platoon, best friends blown to pieces. After a while everyone just kept to himself; it hurt too much to get close. Spury thought he was going to die, knew his fate was in God's hands, but this fate no longer concerned him much. What concerned him was keeping pure, so that if he lived he could go home again, be close with his family, especially his mother.

"I overheard her talking once. I was in the basement working in my shop, but the floors were cracked and I could hear right through them. Mom was in the living room with Dad, talking about some local girl who got herself pregnant. Mom said she knew it wasn't any of her boys. Dad asked how, and Mom said because she knew her boys wouldn't do anything like that. . . . I wish I hadn't heard her say it though. It's been a weight on me."

Whether Spury died in the war was in God's hands. Whether he could go back home again if he lived was in his own. Could he could keep himself pure and uncontaminated in a morally corrupt environment? If he could, he might return home the same person who had left his small mining community two years earlier. Upon arriving home he threw his uniform and gun down an abandoned mine shaft. He has not held a gun or worn a uniform since.

War threatens more than death; it threatens loss of wholeness. Loss of physical wholeness, and loss of moral wholeness too, being contaminated by the things one is exposed to, becoming someone who cannot go home again, lest one contaminate and destroy everything one values. Home is wholeness, the root and bond that Ricoeur writes of, an anchoredness in the world, alienation from it tantamount to dread.

Ricoeur writes as if this experience is historical, part of the prehistory of the species, a superstition located long ago and far away. What if what Ricoeur has described is not historical evolution at all, but different aspects of the experience of evil in everyday life? As Joanna Overing puts it, "Ricoeur has not presented us with . . . an evolutionary typology of evil, but he has rather distinguished for us various ways in which evil can be experienced, symbolized and judged—many of which can be incorporated within one and the same system of ethics."[1] One might argue that Ricoeur has confused historical with personal development, but that would not be quite right. Although the capacity to experience precategorical evil, what Ricoeur calls the experience of a basic fault in being, precedes the capacity to judge evil categorically, developmental primacy is only that.

Natural and Moral Evil

The distinction between precategorical and categorical evil has an affinity with the more familiar distinction between natural and moral evil. The Old Testament makes no distinction, blaming God for both. Evil, *ra*ᶜ, is anything bad, displeasing, or harmful to man (Isa. 45.7; Jer. 4.6; Amos 3.6; Mic. 2.3; Eccles. 1.13; Job 2.10). Evil is not yet a philosophical problem, theodicy not yet an issue. Evil just is. "The ethical order of *doing* ill is not distinguished from the cosmo-biological order of *faring* ill," says Ricoeur.[2] *Pace* Ricoeur, let us at least consider the possibility that this lack of distinction represents a hard-won insight, not a developmental lag.

For well over a century, the Lisbon earthquake of 1755 was the paradigm of evil. Tens of thousands perished, Voltaire wrote *Candide*, and God's justice, theodicy, was questioned as never before. Now the Nazi Holocaust is the paradigm of evil, the Lisbon earthquake a geological event. Is this really intellectual and moral progress? Yes and no.

Consider Hannah Arendt's thesis of the banality of evil. With that term Arendt invokes the "sheer thoughtlessness" of Adolf Eichmann, who "never realized what he was doing," not because he was stupid but because he lacked the imagination and will to acknowledge his actions.[3] This is what she means by "banal," a term she contrasts with "diabolical," "demonic," and "evil instincts," which she would apparently attribute to such characters as Iago and Macbeth.[4] Evidently Arendt believes in the existence of evil, at least in the abstract; she just does not find it where we might expect her to, in such characters as Eichmann.

Has not Arendt transformed human evil into something closer to natural evil, an event causing horrendous suffering in the absence of an equally horrendous intent? Which is not to say she is wrong. There *is* frequently something out of balance about evil, cause and effect hardly corresponding with each other.

Arendt's thesis of the banality of evil preserves the key insight of the Old Testament, that evil is not readily located. Evil is not spatial but situational, as much about how we experience suffering as what causes it, as much about a world that cares nothing for humans as it is about humans who care nothing for one another. It is a property of the human heart (Gen. 6.5–6; Jer. 17.9; Ezek. 6.9; Eccles. 9.3), but that is only one of its many residences. Above all, evil is. Everywhere. Evil is prior to the wide-awake and rational distinction between subject and object, between action and reaction. Which neither means nor implies that we should not hold its perpetrators responsible. Lack of agency does not necessarily mean lack of responsibility. It does, however, suggest that we rethink the meaning of this much-vaunted term.

Responsibility and Regret

It is part of the folklore of prisons that prisoners never take responsibility for the crime that sent them to jail. Quite the opposite is true of most inmates. Not only do they take responsibility for their crime, they take responsibility for everything that ever happened to them, including maternal abandonment. "My mom left me when I was a kid," said Mr. Beaty, "but I had a choice of how to feel, how to react." Sure.

The emphasis on responsibility is in part an artifact of the prison's therapeutic aims, which stress individual responsibility above all else. Certainly it is an ethic that finds great resonance in American life. Only the prisoner who acknowledges responsibility for his fate is deemed reformed. Prisoners know this and act accordingly. Only it is not a posture. Most believe that taking total responsibility is better than total powerlessness.

Of all the inmates who struggled with whether the Holocaust was evil, only Mr. Smith said, "Sure it was evil. Even if most Germans didn't do anything bad. It's evil if you just don't care about others." It was a simple statement, but few informants, inmate or free, uttered its like. The tone was new. He was not talking only about responsibility. He was talking about regret, about how sad and tough it is to live in a world where people just don't care.

Mr. Alter comes closer to the norm. "I knew right from wrong," he said. "That wasn't my problem. My problem was that I couldn't administer myself in stressful situations. But I'm learning, I'm learning that if I don't control myself, someone will control me." Responsibility without regret, it might be called, the ethos of the remediated prisoner.[5]

Better an ounce of tears than a pound of responsibility. The mass media chatters on about Americans' failure to accept responsibility, but it misses what is really lacking, a sense of regret, of sadness for the way things are and for what one must do to survive. Our culture does not encourage citizens to linger in the depressive position, as Klein calls it. Probably the majority of free citizens substitute self-administration for self-knowledge. Certainly many of the prisoners will manage to stay out of trouble if they can learn self-administration. It is just that with many prisoners the stakes are so much higher, the administrative self set on top of a volcano.

Ms. Paine describes how she was walking down the stairs with a group of inmates. Suddenly she was afraid that one might push her down the stairs. "Then I thought about it a minute, and decided that maybe I wanted to push someone down the stairs." The group congratulates her on her insight. But we might also consider that it is not unlikely that someone did want to push her down the stairs. It has happened in prison. The world is a scary place, the evil in it real. Some people really do want bad things for Ms. Paine, for you, and for me. Perhaps she is taking the evil into herself in order to control it, as though she said to herself, "God, the world is an evil and scary place. Maybe if I make myself the center of evil, put all the responsibility for evil in me, I can master it."

Mr. Marcus defines evil in terms of a *Star Wars* movie he saw as a child. Darth Vader is evil, Luke Skywalker good, life a contest between them. The mythologist Joseph Campbell points out that after Skywalker slays Darth Vader, he sees his own face behind Vader's mask. The hero is the villain, his evil alienated in another and fought there as though it belonged to someone else. That is the mythological message, and it is true.

But it is not the whole truth. The whole truth is that there is evil all around us. The face behind the mask is not just yours. It is your wife's, your husband's, your mother's, your father's, your child's, your teacher's, your lover's, your friend's. It is the stranger against whom the psychopath (and all of us in our psychopathic moments) defends by becoming the stranger to himself. It is sad and troubling to find evil in oneself. It is different, but equally sad and troubling, to find it in others.

It is important to know the difference, lest our dread overflow the world. As Ms. Paine passes photographs of her two children around the group, Mr. Smith begins his "women are the evillest creatures there is" mantra, a theme he has been belaboring for weeks. I ignore him, admiring Ms. Paine's attractive children, about to ask about the third when I remember. She was seventeen years old, living alone with three children to care for. One dark morning she lifted her two-year-old up and threw him to the floor. He cracked his head on the stove, went into a coma, and died the next day.

Mr. Smith pretends it is Ms. Paine's mother, who visits her frequently, to whom he is attracted, but in reality he is attracted to every woman in the prison. It is this that leads him to call women evil, as though to say his need is so great it must unman him. This is not supposition. He says it. "Women are the evillest creatures because they make men need them. They make us lose our manhood, make us do anything to keep them. Man, when I think of the changes I've put myself through for a woman. Ninety percent of the men in prison are here because of a woman."

Why do you call women evil, I ask? Why not say that it is your need that's evil? I think you make evil into a type of weakness. Mr. Smith thinks for a moment. "No, evil couldn't be weakness, that doesn't make sense. Evil is strength and power, the most powerful thing there is."

In fact, evil is both. Evil is the dread of a need so bottomless it threatens the self, the self that knows it would do anything to fulfill itself, including lose itself to the object of its desire. Evil is also the defense against this experience, as though we could master our desire by terrorizing its object. It is a distinction mirrored in the more familiar distinction between evil as what we suffer, and evil as the suffering we inflict on others—as though we could avoid natural evil by inflicting moral evil. This, at least, seems to be the unconscious fantasy, whose motto might be "Do anything but simply suffer." Sometimes, avoiding doing evil is about simply suffering.

Evil Is a Discourse on Malevolence and Suffering

Recall Patricia D., who defined evil as the feeling she was losing herself to her boyfriend, an autistic-contiguous anxiety so primitive as to be almost beyond words and symbols. Which is why she says, "Evil's just a word, you know. Just a tiny four-letter word."

In a way, Patricia is right. Not that evil is just a word but that it is an experience so powerful that it threatens to render words insignificant. We must try not to let it. Evil is a way of talking about profound and puzzling experiences of existence, particularly those precategorical experiences of dread, badness, malevolence, and loss whose locus is unclear. In a word, evil is a discourse, a conversation about the ultimate causes and meaning of human dread. In the Western tradition, this experience has come to be subsumed under the categories of sin and redemption. Yet, even in the West, that is not the whole story, as the concept of *ra*ᶜ in the Hebrew Bible reveals.

To call evil a discourse is to miss the point entirely, or so it might be argued. Evil is a real presence or it is nothing. Carroll Dale Short, a reporter, tells the story of being alone in a jail cell with a kidnapper. The title of the piece, "A True Thing," is from a line in Cormac McCarthy's novel *All the Pretty Horses:* "Evil is a true thing; it goes about on its own legs." Short recalls:

> At one point I became unaccountably apprehensive; the hairs on my neck stood up. I felt I was in the presence of an immense intelligence, which for the moment had rendered itself almost entirely visceral. . . . I had distinctly felt a third presence in the cell. Somebody, or something, that was clearly not [the kidnapper], and not me, but was equally as real—and was clearly, my instinct told me, evil. . . . I am increasingly convinced that evil is an actual force existing independently of human constructs and periodically making itself known through human behavior. I realize, even as I think it, that this is a dangerous way to think.

With the term "presence," Short means what Andrew Delbanco means in *The Death of Satan*, whom he cites. "Evil as a distributed entity with an ontological essence of its own . . . what some philosophers call 'presence.' "[6]

In my language, Short had an experience of precategorical dread and came to call it evil in order to give it a locus, a contained presence. He would presumably disagree. Though uncomfortable with the term (Short understands how much evil has been done in the name of fighting evil), he believes that to render evil anything less than a presence, a virtual entity, is to trivialize it.

I do not object—if "objection" is even the relevant category—as long as the experience of evil as presence is itself a topic of discourse, an experience that is worthy of puzzlement and subject to explanation, that is, to symbolic expression. If not, if presence just becomes tantamount to saying I felt it and that's that, then we are not very far from the psychopath who said about his unwillingness to argue or explain (that is, his unwillingness to use words) "whatever comes to my mind, I know it got to be right because I'm thinking it."[7] The comparison is not invidious: it captures the autistic dimension of precategorical dread, an experience etched so deeply in the body that its feelings are beyond (or perhaps beneath) words. That too is presence, the presence of dread. It is a view whose greatest danger is that it ignores (or rather, defends against) that dimension of evil we might call absence—that is, loss.

The term "evil" usefully encompasses both the Hebrew *ra^c* and the New Testament *kakía*. Like *ra^c*, *kakía* means "what is bad," such as pain, sickness, suffering, misfortune, and loss. Some Gnostic Christians, such as Valentinus, stressed the origin of *kakía* in the "anguish and terror" of being human, as the *Gospel of Truth* puts it. It was only the orthodox Christians who insisted that *kakía* was a moral category, a condition of the heart which leads to trespass against others.[8] Evil is all three at once: suffering and loss, "anguish and terror" at being human (what I have called dread), and a moral category. The suffering, anguish, and terror of being human may enrich our understanding of morality; they may also obscure it. Dread is not the whole of evil, but it is the most important part, in good measure because it may obscure the rest, evil as a moral category.

Sam T.'s father died suddenly when Sam was sixteen, and the experience defines evil for him. Evil is loss, the terrible emptiness it leaves, the lost opportunities it inflicts, and the bitterness that remains. For Sam, evil is what is taken from us. "Evil, it's not something we do, it's something that happens to us. I'm going to be bitter about it for the rest of my life." He will not accept his loss, but he accepts his powerlessness. It sounds easy, but it is not. Nietzsche could not do it. The Greeks call it *tuche*, which is sometimes translated as "luck" but is better rendered as all that happens to a man beyond his control. *Moira*, the fabric of a man's life woven by the three Fates, daughters of the night who spin the destiny of the world, is a cognate term. *Moira* is sometimes translated as "evil," suggesting the experience of human powerlessness which is at the root of our encounter with evil.[9]

Greek tragedy is the morality of powerlessness. At first the feeling is intolerable, the humiliation galling, the paralysis terrifying, the temptation to lash out irresistible. Most protagonists never get any further. Agamemnon sacrifices his daughter so that he can be a hero. He does not want to, but the thought of being called a "fleet deserter" is worse. Clytemnestra destroys Agamemnon so that she might be as powerful as the man who causes her to suffer such a loss. Medea destroys her children out of rage and humiliation. Of all the things she cannot stand, the worst is to be thought weak, powerless.

> Let no one think me a weak one, feeble-spirited,
> A stay-at-home, but rather just the opposite,
> One who can hurt my enemies and help my friends;
> For the lives of such persons are most remembered.
> (*Medea*, lines 807–10; Rex Warner, trans.)

Ajax destroys himself so that his father will not see his weakness (lines 473–75). All are weak before the gods, Techmessa reminds him, but it is no use. It is the weakness of his own mind, that it could not resist the madness brought by Athena, which is unbearable.[10]

Some protagonists learn acceptance. At the conclusion of *Oedipus the King*, Oedipus blinds himself in shame, but in *Oedipus at Colonus*, written and set years later, he embraces his fate, not just his death but his star-crossed life, mark of his specialness to the gods. Even Prometheus, the Titan whose rebellion against the gods results in an infinity of torture and rage, is finally reconciled with their power, if we can trust the surviving fragments of the trilogy. More of a theme in the pious Aeschylus and the reverent Sophocles, reconciliation with *tuche* is less central to the atheist Euripides, who writes not of man's folly but of his venality. Nevertheless it is not absent in his work, as the arrogant Admetus learns that he must die his own death. His wife Alcestis cannot do it for him, even if she wishes.

Morality in Greek tragedy depends on the acceptance of *tuche*, of our ultimate powerlessness before fate. *Arete* is what the Greeks called morality, the excellent performance of a human life, the goal being to become as richly and fully human as can be. Which means, above all, accepting and living within human limits. If humans do not accept their powerlessness before fate, we will be forever lashing out, generally at fellow sufferers. We will do evil. If we do accept, then we may learn pity. Why pity? Because to accept humanity's vulnerability and powerlessness means to stop fighting one's fellow sufferers, joining with them in human solidarity against a world that cares not at all about human suffering unless perhaps to inflict it.

Kant defines radical evil not in terms of the enormity of the deed but of the human inclination to corrupt morality so that it becomes a servant of self-love. Let us put the same idea a little differently. Evil inflicts one's fate, doom, on others. Radical evil justifies this exercise of power by calling it morality. Sometimes it does so explicitly, as with Nazis and other racial, ethnic, and sexual supremacists. More frequently the corruption is implicit, as when a high-sounding ideology of liberty and equality is used to justify short, painful, hopeless (that is, dreadful) lives for some so that others might have long, full, and happy ones. It happens every day all over the world. One might argue that morality should aim higher than living with evil. Perhaps, but since morality frequently falls lower, failing as it does to take the power of evil seriously, this is a good place to start.

The Incorrectness of Satan

Elaine Pagels opens her biblical study, *The Origin of Satan*, with an account of the death of her husband of twenty years in a hiking accident. Her son died shortly after her husband. Loss caused her, she says, to appreciate what it was to live "in the presence of an invisible being— living, that is, with a vivid sense of someone who had died. I began to reflect on the ways that various religious traditions give shape to the invisible world."[11] Her book about evil is, evidently, an attempt to come to terms with her own sorrow and loss, but its theory does the opposite, finding a place not for these emotions but only for the paranoid ones, the ones that locate our pain in the malevolence of others.

Pagels grasps how pain leads us to locate the source of our discomfort in others. She quite fails to appreciate that evil may also be a meaningful way of talking about more differentiated experiences, those recognized as stemming from within, even as their source is external. Suffering and loss are other dimensions of evil, but still evil, like the terrible loss Sam refers to, evil as what we suffer. It is, apparently, where Pagels wants to go, but she cannot get there from where she begins and ends, evil as hatred of the other.

Pagels writes of the biblical concept of evil, particularly in the New Testament, as an essentially sociological phenomenon, the demonization of the other. We make others evil in order to secure the loyalty of our own group, whose fragmentation threatens us with anxiety and loss. Not surprisingly, most of her examples concern the demonization of Jews by Christian zealots.

At its worst, *The Origin of Satan* transforms evil into a problem of political correctness, the solution being the tolerance of difference. Her last sentence reads like an encounter between postmodernism and Christ: "Concluding this book, I hope that this research may illuminate for others, as it has for me, the struggle within Christian tradition between the profoundly human view that 'otherness' is evil and the words of Jesus that reconciliation is divine."[12] One might be inclined to let Pagels off the hook by arguing that the one-dimensionality of her account of evil stems from her source, the New Testament itself—except that the overwhelming number of references to the devil and evil in the New Testament have nothing to do with stigmatizing the other but with personal morality, particularly with the threat to righteousness posed by desire.[13]

From a Kleinian perspective, the experience of otherness is not, by itself, the root of all evil. Otherness is tolerable unless it is experienced as monopolizing the good. Envy, she says, is the root of all evil, the desire to destroy what is good because one cannot have or be it. Carefully distinguishing envy from jealousy and greed, Klein argues that envy wants not merely to have all the goodness in the world for oneself but to destroy the good because one cannot be it. The very existence of goodness outside the self generates a destructive narcissistic rage that would destroy goodness because it is good. There are sound reasons, says Klein, to call envy the deadliest sin of all. She quotes Chaucer: "It is certain that envy is the worst sin that is; for all other sins are sins only against one virtue, whereas envy is against all virtue and against all goodness" ("Parson's Tale").[14]

If there were an adequate psychological definition of evil, this would be it. Evil is the special quality of badness called envy, the desire to destroy the innocence and goodness for its own sake, because the very existence of innocence and goodness outside the self is an intolerable insult to the grandiose but empty self. Augustine's definition of evil as the privation of good (*Confessions* VII.xii.18) is frequently seen as failing to capture the maliciousness to which the human heart is prey—but it does not fail, however, if we see privation as an active process, the willful depletion of good. Then it would be tantamount to envy.

While Augustine's definition of evil at least alludes to its malicious destructiveness, Kant's does not, and it is here that his concept of radical evil is not radical enough. For Kant, radical evil is a defect (*malum defectus*) not of reason but of will, the tendency to make morality servant of desire, so that we can do what we want with a good conscience. In fact, evil is more: not just a negation of the good but a destruction of the good because it is good (*malum privationis*), tantamount to what Klein calls envy.[15] Evil is not just the devaluation of otherness because otherness is scary and bad. Evil is the destruction of the other because the other is *good*, an even harsher truth that both Kant and Pagels fail to recognize.

Most people most of the time deal with the conflict between their hateful and loving impulses by locating good and evil in watertight compartments that never touch. Heaven and Hell, God and Satan, Good and Evil, the saved and the damned: these and so many other Manichaean distinctions have their origins in paranoid-schizoid anxiety: that one's hatred and aggression will spill over to damage and destroy the good. This splitting is the defense of choice in the paranoid-schizoid position, separating good and evil so that one does not corrupt the other, and ourselves.

It will do no good to implore people not to demonize others. People demonize the other not out of ignorance or intolerance but to protect their own threatened goodness. Demonization of the other is a defense against doom. That the doom is self-inflicted, the aura of one's own aggression, makes this defense more poignant but no less destructive.

Throughout history the paranoid-schizoid position has ruled, our doom attributed to a mélange of persecutors whose historical variety is endlessly monotonous. It is not, however, the only possible world view. In the depressive position we still fear our doom, ultimately our death and its symbolic equivalents, such as abandonment and helplessness. Instead of attributing our doom to others, we come to accept its necessity. Not love it. Klein's depressive position is not Nietzsche's *amor fati:* "My formula for greatness in a human being is *amor fati:* that one wants nothing to be other than it is, not in the future, not in the past, not in all eternity. Not merely to endure that which happens of necessity . . . but to *love* it." [16] *Amor fati* is bad faith. To love all that happens pretends that if I love it enough then it is almost as if I chose it, as if I have power over it. *Amor fati* pretends a control it does not possess.

The depressive position does not love the sorrow and the pity but reluctantly accepts it. Reluctant acceptance—the path that passes through sorrow, mourning, tears, and grief. In the depressive position we mourn not just our own doom, and that of those we love, but a world that is filled with malevolence, suffering, and loss, a world of almost incalculable sorrow.

Xerxes, watching his army cross the Hellespont to invade Greece, pities the shortness of man's life, that so many will soon die. "No, King," responds Artabanus, his uncle, "weep rather for this, that brief as life is there never yet was or will be a man who does not wish more than once to die rather than to live" (Herodotus, *Histories* 7.46). No, Artabanus, weep for both. In the end they are one, every terror and heartache a little death, a piece of dread.

Evil presents itself in the paranoid-schizoid position as malevolent Satan, the bringer of doom. If, however, we can come to accept our doom we may transform evil. Malevolence and envy, our own as well as others, become no less real or destructive, but they can be grieved. Evil becomes an occasion for sorrow and pity, something to be suffered instead of inflicted. Jesus Christ had a few words to say about this too. It is, however, a long road from here to there, and our culture does not help very much. One should include *The Origin of Satan* as part of this culture, a document of an age and academic subculture that see intolerance as the root of all evil. Why the culture is so unhelpful is addressed in each of the remaining chapters.

FIVE *Identifying with Eichmann*

Was Adolf Eichmann evil? He didn't kill anyone, but he orchestrated the murder of millions. Does this not make him evil? (In question 11, Eichmann is the "good German." Originally I referred to Eichmann by name, but not a single informant, young or old, knew who he was.) Most said no. Inmates and free citizens alike assume he would have been killed if he had not gone along. But, as Hannah Arendt points out, such punishment was unlikely: "In the Nuremberg documents not a single case could be traced in which an S.S. member had suffered the death penalty because of a refusal to take part in an execution. . . . To be sure, in individual cases, one had to be prepared for a certain disciplinary punishment. A danger to one's life, however, was not involved."[1] The truth of informants' assumptions is not at issue, though it is interesting to consider why many not only assume that Eichmann would have been killed if he failed to obey but talk as if this assumption were written into the question. "Look, he was just a cog in the machine. If he didn't do it, someone else would have. Besides, he would have been killed if he didn't, and you can't ask someone to die for others."

Although most inmates and most free informants hold Eichmann not to be evil, their reasoning is different, at least on the surface. The difference is a key to understanding evil. All free informants who find Eichmann not evil use the "just a cog in the war machine" argument: he didn't have any choice, he was just doing his job, if he didn't do it someone else would have, and he would have gotten himself killed for no reason at all. Very few inmates use this argument. Instead, inmates see the world in Hobbesian terms, a perpetual war of all against all in which there are no innocents, only victims and executioners. As Mr. Acorn puts it, "It's total war, man, and in total war there's no bystanders. Everyone is a soldier."

Even babies?

"Yeah, they just don't know it yet."

"All's fair in love and war," says Mr. Leotine. In prison for murdering his parents, he might as well have said "Love is war, war is war, everything is war, so anything is fair all the time."

Prison is the Leviathan that Hobbes wrote of, the all-powerful father whose omnipotence provides the security under which freedom is meaningful. Prison is also a mother, "concrete mama," cold and hard, but at least she's always there, always waiting to take you back. In a word, prison is form and frame. Just as the reality of the ghetto mirrors in exaggerated form the reality of middle-class life (threatened families, teenagers raised by peer groups and mass media, the cultivation of violence and toughness as the currency of every relationship), so the reality of prison reflects the values of the free world. The prisoners who can make no distinction between the mass murder of innocent civilians and the clash of armies, dividing the entire world into victims and executioners, are expressing in slightly exaggerated (and not always exaggerated) form a world view common among a majority of informants.

Connect the "only a cog in the war machine" argument with the assumption of almost all free informants who found Eichmann not evil: that he would have been killed if he had not followed orders. Is this not really a bureaucratized and rationalized version of the war of all against all? It's still total war, kill or be killed. Only now the chaos is contained within the bureaucracy, so that instead of a war of all against all it is a war of some against others. If the some don't carry out their orders, they will be killed and replaced by others who will. It is the serial version of the war of all against all.

Most prisoners are closer to their dread than others are; it is less contained, less well managed. This proximity makes them dangerous, more in need of prison walls. It does not make them and their reasoning fundamentally different. On the contrary, they know something about the horror of victimization, the sense of living in a world in which one is either victim or executioner, which free informants feel but can't know. Or, rather, cannot know in such bitter and unmediated form.

In such a world, power and caprice are the only variables. It is no wonder that many prisoners have trouble obeying the rules, rules that seem to have no justification but power. Rules make more sense to free informants. If rules are still nature-like (beyond reason and critique: they just are), it is nevertheless a more predictable nature, the nature of general principles as well as of earthquakes.

Yet, what we think about rules makes little difference as far as the judgment of evil is concerned. Evil will not be overcome by rules, not even the categorical imperative. Rules may limit the arbitrary and capricious, much as prison walls do, and so allow us to know our dread. By themselves they will not prevent us from inflicting that dread on others, though they may rationalize its infliction as freedom and justice.

Were the informants, free and inmate alike, who assume that in Nazi Germany it was invariably kill or be killed responding merely from ignorance? Or are they projecting something of their own terror, as well as their understanding of how in the last analysis all societies rest on their willingness to use violence against their citizens? It is impossible to know for sure, but it is striking that most informants do not merely *assume* that Eichmann, or the German officer, would be killed if he did not kill others. They posit it.

"Assume" means to fail to question one's presuppositions, the background knowledge one brings to every new situation. Most informants did no such thing. Most actively read the assumption into the question itself, though it is not there. "I thought you said they would be killed if they did not follow orders. That was the point of the question. It wouldn't have any point otherwise, would it now?" Some put it this way, John B. in just these words. Employed in such an aggressive fashion, the "assumption" that Eichmann or the German officer would be killed for failing to kill is actually a defense, though of course one can still argue about what it is defending against, dread or guilt—for example, the guilt of the living.

The "Iron Cage": Power and Victimhood

If the "war of all against all" and "cog in the machine" arguments are truly continuous, one would expect to find informants having difficulty finding a way out: a third path between that of victim and executioner, domination and submission, evildoer and victim of evil. One would expect that informants would experience this world as having no outside, no exit. Many do, with consequences for how they view evil.

This critique of modern society has been made many times. The analysis of Herbert Marcuse and the Frankfurt School of Critical Theory finds this totalizing tendency not just in totalitarian regimes but also in liberal democratic ones. It is not, however, a critique limited to the left. Its original and most famous proponent is Max Weber, who wrote of the modern world as an "iron cage" of icy polar darkness and night, every aspect of life the subject of administration.[2]

For prisoners the iron cage is no metaphor, though it is striking how many feel that they are more free in prison than without. For free informants the iron cage is more metaphorical, more multidimensional too, but no less real, the world providing few choices between doing evil and suffering it.

Grace E. turned down a commission to be a fighter pilot in the Air Force because she knew she could not drop bombs on people. Now she is in an aerospace engineering program, learning how to design better bombs. "I hate it, but where do I draw the line? How do I draw it? Where does the responsibility stop? How far do I have to go to get away from evil?" She thinks Eichmann was evil because he knew what he was doing.

Terry P. sat in the hall reading her Bible before her interview. Her lesson was Psalm 52, which is about not lying. She thinks that Eichmann was evil. "We all have a choice, including the choice to die for what we believe." But she is bothered by the question, obsessing over it, stating several times, "There but for the grace of God go I." She is not identifying with his victims. She is identifying with Eichmann. She hopes, but is far from certain, that she would have had the wit and courage to refuse. Because she knows what it is like to be morally lost, adrift. She had been there before converting to Christianity several years ago.

Andrew S. fought in Europe during World War II. "I was the youngest second lieutenant in the army, just like Bush in the Navy." He is certain that Eichmann was not guilty. "He was just a cog in the war machine, just like the rest of us." The German officer who shot Jews was guilty, but Andrew quickly changes the question around: "Now, if they'd been partisans, blowing up the railroad or something, then he would have been within his rights."

Spury F., who liberated Dachau, also holds Eichmann to be without evil. It is not that Spury does not know or feel the consequences of Eichmann's acts. The image of a line of corpses at Dachau as far as he could see still haunts his memories. Were the men who did this evil? He does not answer directly. Instead he refers to the camp guards at Dachau who exploited female inmates sexually. "The ones who did the things with women, with the female inmates. They were evil."

Ricoeur's distinction between fear of defilement and the morality of sin seems to work here, Spury is so concerned with his own purity, and sexual purity generally, that he does not see mass murder as evil. It is wrong—he knows that—but it is not evil in the same way that threats to his purity are, except that after seeing Dachau he felt better about killing the German machine gunner. "For the first time I knew why I was fighting."

All but Andrew identify with Eichmann, not the victims. (It is not clear who Spury identifies with, perhaps his mother.) It is a key point, and a subtle one. Five Jewish informants, all under the age of thirty-five, identify with Eichmann. This identification does not mean that they do not think he is evil, though three do not, and one is not sure. It means that Eichmann's victims and their suffering do not enter the picture, except as abstractions. They see the issue strictly from Eichmann's viewpoint, from his eyes. His problem becomes theirs. "You grow up in Nazi Germany, you hear all this stuff for years, you come to believe it. It all depends on how you were raised. People will believe anything if you brainwash them long enough."

One might argue that my question is posed from Eichmann's perspective, so of course informants identify with him. But question 11 simply asks whether the Eichmann-type individual (the "good German" who does not necessarily hate Jews, knows about the "Final Solution," and above all likes to carry out his assigned duties) is evil. It is the informants' choice to see the question from behind his eyes, a choice so simple and natural it took me a while to see how strange that choice truly was.

Rachel B. remembers back to grade school, when her teacher had the class draw family trees. She couldn't. All her relatives had been killed in the Holocaust. Her family did not talk about them, so it was as if they had never existed.

What evil have you done?

"Once I wished my baby sister had never been born." For Rachel that is the consummate evil, not to harm another, not to kill her, but to wish another had never been born. Informants identify with Eichmann not because they want to, but because identifying with the meaningless deaths of his victims is too terrible to contemplate. In such a disordered world power is the only currency. Victimhood can have no meaning when there is no one to witness, remember, or understand. We live in a world of executioners and "dead meat," as one puts it. Not all the time, but when push comes to shove. Except for Andrew, the World War II vet, who identifies with a regime that once, at least, combined power with righteousness, even if this did not always keep it, or him, from doing evil.

A number of theorists of the Holocaust, particularly the structuralists, as they are called, stress the modern, bureaucratic nature of the destructive process. The Holocaust, at least for most participants, was not about hate. It was about obedience, distancing, task segmentation, and the like.[3] They are as mistaken as Milgram was, failing to appreciate the intrusion of doom and dread into modernity. They fail to understand, in other words, how scared people really are. Though it is not clear that Daniel Goldhagen understands this fear any better, *Hitler's Willing Executioners* better grasps the sadism that unites the executioner with his victim, if only for a moment.

The bars of the iron cage are made of power and victimhood—the perception that these are the only choices. These were, it will be recalled, the only choices that many subjects in the Milgram experiment perceived, shock or be shocked. The iron cage is made more confining still by the failure of cultural memory, which makes of meaningful victimhood an oxymoron. How can being a victim—living and dying for a belief or value rather than power—be meaningful in a world in which being a victim is tantamount to having never existed? Primo Levi said that he would take his life when it no longer served to remind people of the Holocaust, when people no longer wished to remember. Robbed forever of the joy of living, his life had meaning only as witness, and only as long as others were willing to be witnessed to.

The problem is not the failure of memory per se. It is the failure of the culture to preserve those categories of experience which make victimhood meaningful, so that the meaning might be available to make the memory meaningful. It is how MacIntyre should be interpreted in *After Virtue*. What the culture has lost is not just a narrative unity that makes sense of values. It has lost the narrative resources to make sense of the experience of victimhood, above all the dread of what it is to be truly human. It has, in other words, lost the sense of tragedy. We are all victims, victims of life and death. It is against the victimhood of being merely human that evil is dedicated.

Against this conclusion, the contemporary culture of victimhood might be cited as counterevidence, groups vying with one another for honors as victim of the month. This though is a somewhat different phenomenon, a matter of identity politics, part of the struggle for a bigger piece of the pie in a world in which the claim to merit based on excellence has become suspect. The experience of individual victimhood is different, and less tolerable. "Don't call me a crime victim!" said one informant pointedly. "I'm a survivor; that's what we call ourselves these days."

Reason Cannot Overcome Dread

The Frankfurt School of Critical Theory, whose intellectual founders were Max Horkheimer, Theodor Adorno, and Herbert Marcuse, understood that power cannot overcome dread. They also understood the persistence of the illusion that it can. They called this illusion the dialectic of Enlightenment, referring to how progress in enlightenment culminates in the resurrection of myth. Capable of transforming the external world, reason is finally powerless before the dread that motivates this transformation: dread of limits, of mortality, of meaninglessness, of vulnerability and loss. It is the dread that Creon would overcome with political power in *Antigone*, subjecting the doom of death to politics. It is the same dread that science and technology and industry would overcome with their mastery of the material world.

Lead author of *The Authoritarian Personality*, which seems to explain the Holocaust in terms of the prevalence of authoritarian types in the Nazi regime, Adorno took a vastly more complex position. In *Dialectic of Enlightenment*, written with Horkheimer and published in 1947, Adorno argues that people turned their reason to the domination of nature because of the terrors unconquered nature held for them. Not just science but philosophy expressed this ethic of domination. Reason as rage at a world too sparse to be dominated is how Adorno puts it elsewhere. Marginal groups such as Jews, blacks, and prison inmates are identified with unconquered nature, in the vain hope that with their containment or destruction the terror of nature itself can be overcome.[4]

Dialectic of Enlightenment is not the last word. It does, however, grasp the way in which the irrational stealthily intrudes upon the rational, leading to what C. Wright Mills calls crackpot realism, the deployment of rational methods and argument in the service of delusion.

If you go to the Holocaust Museum in Washington, D.C., you may find that it is not the photographs, or even the piles of shoes and hair, that overcome you. For better or worse, many seem to have become immune to the pathos of such images. Overwhelming is the perverse rationality of it all, the elaborate categories of beings to be destroyed, the Institutes for Racial Hygiene, the Offices of Purification of the Reich, the Departments of Special Procedures. The Holocaust was science, industry, and bureaucracy driven by images of doom, impurity, and dread, the stuff of precategorical evil. The Holocaust was the instrusion of precategorical dread into modernity, where it is not supposed to be. Modernity has no categories for it, just primitive superstition, so that it is all the more vulnerable.[5]

Though Andrew is not walled off from his own precategorical experiences, such as the awesome silence of the buzz bombs over London, he steadfastly refuses to let these experiences influence his moral judgment. Evil he defines as the irresponsible lack of self-restraint, a refusal to face life's seriousness. He ran a department store in a poor section of the city, and he and I both know he is talking about blacks. But he will not say it.

Andrew guides his life by his father's motto, "the fittin' thing to do."

It means fitting in with the values and needs of one's group no matter what, but not because these values are objectively right in every case. Andrew is surprisingly relativistic about the German and Japanese aggressors, recognizing that from their perspective they may have been acting morally. This view, though, does not confuse him; it only reaffirms his belief that loyalty and morality are one, about commitment to one's group no matter what. Nor does his relativism assuage his fury at the "historical revisionists" who want to paint the atomic bombing of Japan as wrong: "You want to know what's evil, that's evil. Historical revisionism is evil. The bomb saved my keester. I'd already been wounded in Europe. I'd have been a dead man if they sent me to Japan."

The utter conventionality of Andrew's morality means there was nothing he would not do for his group: nothing right, nothing wrong, nothing. Andrew is in touch with precategorical experience, though it would be more accurate to say that the precategorical is in touch with him, as when he feels his late wife's presence in the church so strongly he cannot return there. But it does not translate into reflectiveness about anything, including morality. He is surprisingly relativistic, but in ways that only enhance his loyalty to the one thing he can believe in, "the fittin' thing to do."

Andrew is the dialectic of Enlightenment living out its final days in Retirement World, with his images of precategorical dread, like the silent buzz bombs, defended against by perfect loyalty, and rage at the "historical revisionists" who would wish his death on the beaches of Japan. Or so it seems to him. In a postmodern world myth no longer masquerades as reason. For better and worse, it is all fiction these days.

By and large, younger informants are more cynical than Andrew. Less vulnerable to the evils that stem from unreflective, conventional attachment to one's group, they are more vulnerable to the belief that morality is not about what you do in this iron cage of a world, but about who you are. For all his faults, Andrew believes that individuals can act together to overcome aggressors like Hitler. For many younger informants, real freedom is what takes place deep inside. Inmates share this belief; they just have better reasons for it.

Among those who let Eichmann off the hook, Tom A. is speaking for a majority when he says, "You'd really have to know what he was thinking, wouldn't you? I mean down deep. And how could you, how could anyone? So you just can't judge. I mean people in glass houses shouldn't throw stones." In Tom's world there is no place to hide, except perhaps deep down inside, where all that is important in judging good and evil resides. The outside, "it's just what I do, not who I am."

Tom's is not a great morality. There is an objective quality to evil which it ignores, abandoning the world to the powerful and the damned. But this morality is real, and must be dealt with. It is interesting to learn about how people understand evil, for it is interesting to learn about the world. It is, however, more than interesting. It is morally important, so that we might have a dialog about evil, a dialectic that connects surface belief with core experiences, precategorical dread with categorical morality.

SIX   *Splatter Movies*
       or Shiva?
       A Culture of Vampires

Ralph C. is an emergency medical technician. He has long greasy black
hair, wears leather, and is overweight. He wants to please. A little button
with a skull and cross-bones is pinned to his vest. "Kill Everybody," it
reads.

What's it mean?

"Don't discriminate," Ralph replies. Some of his best friends are black.
Ralph says he used to wear another button: "Going to Hell Would Be
Redundant."

What does that mean?

"I'm already there."

Ralph has been having bad dreams lately, and worse awakenings.
He came upon a corpse recently, victim of a stabbing. He still can't get
over the expression on the dead man's face. The look was not of
terror, or even surprise. Though he does not have the words, Ralph
is talking about the chagrin of dying. "God, what's come over me? Is
that it, is it all over? Forever? What a fuss we make over such a silly
thing." Though he does not put it quite this way, this is what Ralph
seems to think the dead man would have said to him if the dead could
speak.

Ralph is terrified that someone will die while he is trying to save his
life. "Sometimes we have to give the kiss of life, artificial respiration. We
use a plastic airway, it's not really kissing, but if anyone dies on me I

84

know I'll die. It's the only thing I couldn't take." Ralph fears that even his breath of life is deadly to others.

Recently Ralph has taken to sleeping with a Swiss Army knife under his pillow. "I don't know why. It just makes me feel better, you know?"

Aren't you becoming overwhelmed?

"No, I'm actually very desensitized. On my day off I go to splatter movies. You know what they are? Lots of blood and gore, body parts all over the screen. I need it so I can chill out. You know what I mean?"

Maya is Indian, a Hindu, born in the United States. Her parents are strict, and only in the last couple of years at the university has she felt free. Highly acculturated, she talks as though she watches a lot of MTV, music videos. A psychology major, Maya loves to figure people out.

To herself she remains a mystery, surprised at how competitive and jealous she has become, stealing a friend's boyfriend just to see if she could, things like that. Mostly she is surprised that her evil (if that is what it is) thrills her. "You read about ——— [a student charged with rape], didn't you? He asked me out a couple of months ago. It could have been me, he could have raped me. I keep thinking about it. Just the fact that he could do it, that he wasn't who I thought he was. Or maybe he was. . . . The whole thing zoned me out for a week."

Only when she talks about her religion does Maya come fully alive. She practically glows. "I pray to Shiva. And Kali, the black mother, all scary, with wild eyes, lots of hands, always sticking her tongue out. She's the dark side, goddess of revenge. When Indiana Jones rips out the heart of some guy, he prays to Kali. But it's Shiva who's my patron saint. They're the same, you know."

How do they help you understand evil?

"Maybe there's no evil. I bought an Indian picture a few years ago. It's on the wall in my dorm room. I take it everywhere. Freaks my parents out. It's Shiva, stepping on a demon while dancing his dance of ecstasy. Only Shiva's dance is so extreme, the sound of his bells so loud, the world is shaken to its foundations and destroyed. But out of destruction a new world is born. I think the world's like that, good and evil all mixed up, so that out of destruction comes something new, something better. Maybe evil is destruction, maybe it's creation." Suddenly Maya has become articulate, as though she's been thinking about this for a long time.

Have you ever been to India?

"I went there a couple of times with my parents, and it was wonderful. It was like being cocooned, like living with a safety net, Mom's and Dad's families always around, always caring for me, all this beauty everywhere."

Culture Is a Frame, not a Mirror

Maya has found the cultural resources to give containing form to her precategorical dread. Ralph has not, he can only reenact it in the desperate hope that he might somehow desensitize himself. What he really needs is to sensitize himself. He cannot because he does not have the resources. Not just personal, but cultural, a repertoire of stories to give narrative form to his doom, so that he need not be so terribly alone with his demons.

Maya has found these resources, but they hardly resemble the resources MacIntyre writes of in *After Virtue*, a coherent tradition. Maya has constructed a meaningful narrative out of an incoherent tradition, bits and pieces that MacIntyre decries. For Maya it is evidently enough, this mix of Hindu mythology, American experience, and MTV.

I ask her what she thinks the cliché "evil spelled backward is live" means? It is my favorite question (number 14), evoking more wonder and consternation than any other. Maya cannot even begin to answer it. She cannot think, cannot imagine that it means anything, asks to come back to it. We do a couple of times, and finally she says, "I'll call you if I think of anything. Can we go on now? I have to go soon." She never calls.

She cannot get it because it is only the meaning of her life. Somehow evil makes her feel alive, at least in small doses, like stealing someone's boyfriend or identifying with a god who destroys the world. Blind to the meaning of the cliché, she constructs her beliefs around it: that evil is part of life, inseparable from the good, maybe even the creator of good.

Perhaps most who do possess a tradition are blind to its deep connection to their inner lives. Perhaps this blindness is necessary, lest we discover how fully we have made the connection, lest it lose its objective power. T. S. Eliot said we do not inherit a tradition. We obtain it at great labor. Most of which, it should be added, remains invisible to us.

Most younger informants come closer to Ralph than to Maya. The cultural resources available to them either are experienced as irrelevant, such as religion, or do little more than revivify their terror, mimicking their fears in a narrative that lacks the form and meaning to contain them.

Culture is about the meaning of life. Or rather, it is about the meaning of life in the face of death, the doom that confronts us all. It is that simple, and that complicated. Culture is of no value when it mirrors the experiences that terrify us. When it does, culture is talking the language of the autistic-contiguous position, imitation without understanding or integration. The evening news is not culture, though it is the number-one source of the free informants' examples of evil. Nor are most movies culture.

A meaningful culture stands at a distance, connecting with our experiences but not becoming them. Maya, so Americanized, went to India (at least the India in her mind) to find the distance, and did so. Not, however, for the reasons that MacIntyre describes, not because the narrative was coherent and shared, part of a grand tradition, but because it was not. Its incoherence gave her room to create, room to stand at a distance from what she had made, so that it could become more than herself. So that it could become her meaningful world.

People have always worked with tradition this way. Whether made or found, those who use it make it their own, adapting and adopting it in a million idiosyncratic ways, most of which they hardly know. It is this process that makes us individuals, not cultural dopes—the freedom to make our own traditions out of the material available. But we do need material. Are there cultural resources available for young people to construct their own narratives? Movies and TV do not seem to lend themselves to such active constructions, being experienced more passively, a parade of icons across the screen, like the shadows on the walls of Plato's cave.

A Culture of Vampires

Younger informants frequently refer to a cultural icon of some importance to them, vampires. The local bookstore divides its fiction into three categories, "Classics," "Contemporary," and "Anne Rice," author of popular novels featuring vampires. For every informant who refers to the devil, three refer to vampires. Vampires are the leading cultural icon of evil, at least for younger informants. What does that mean, the devil replaced by the undead? (Fifteen of 24 free informants under 26 years refer to vampires, 11 at length. Five of 18 free informants between 26 and 50 years do, 2 at length. No informant over the age of 51 refers to vampires.)

Inmates seem utterly uninterested in vampires. "Only kids and weirdos believe that stuff. It's for babies."

What if it's not about believing, but telling a good story?

The distinction seems to make no sense. If it isn't true, it isn't real. So important among younger informants, vampires have no resonance among inmates young or old. Perhaps we can learn something about evil here.

One older informant cannot even utter the name "Satan," whispering reverently about "you know, the One who's opposite of God." No one whispers about vampires, none talk reverently about them, though several are in awe: "Oh man, that's what I want to be. I'd give anything to be a vampire," says Ralph C., who likes vampire epics almost as much as splatter movies. "I could go anywhere, do anything. No one could stop me."

Tom A. tries to figure out how something so evil and scary can be so exciting. "They're so sexy," he says. "I didn't even think about it until an English professor said so. But they are. It's all about sex."

Pregenital sex, that is. Vampires do not have intercourse with their victims; they suck them dry. It is a relationship of pure power with a strange twist. It is the living who possess the life force, the vampire destroying life to preserve its unlife. The vampire is a parasite, like a little baby, totally dependent on its mother's milk for survival. At the same time, the vampire symbolizes perfect freedom, able to live forever, if that is what life really is. "I feel sorry for vampires," says George W. without a trace of irony. "They've got to live too."

The vampire is the perfect baby, perfect, in the sense of being so dependent it knows nothing of the limits of its power, the way its unlife depends on others' real lives. It is the way life ought to be—but only for babies. Psychoanalysts use the term "primary narcissism" to describe this state, a state of dependence so unconscious and complete that the other's power is an extension of one's own. "I'm so powerful and perfect I need no one but you without whom I wouldn't exist" is what the narcissist's unconscious would say if it could. The unconscious thinks like this, pure paradox.

Primary narcissism is also a state of terror—that one's weakness will be discovered, one's vulnerability exposed, one's powerlessness apparent for all to see. Shame is the narcissist's terror, the narcissist constantly working to prevent exposure, like the vampire who cannot bear the light, seeking absolute freedom in a dependence on the lives of others so extreme it can be realized only in the dark. Though Christopher Lasch does not write about vampires in *The Culture of Narcissism*, he does write of cultural narcissists in just these terms, so terrified of their own primitive lust for fusion and destruction that they turn the world into a mirror image of this terror, transforming a truly scary world into an unbearably horrifying one.[1]

The vampire is the undead, living and dying on the border between life and death, a messenger of death to the world of the living. What is its message? That there is no hope. The world is the way it appears to be to the perpetually hungry narcissist, people feeding off one another unto death, life a contest to see who can eat whom. Vampires represent the transformation of a world of victims and victimizers into a world of the living and the dead. Only in this world the dead have won.

Consider what it means that the vampire has replaced the devil for many free-world informants, becoming the leading image of evil. Evil is no longer a force in the world, no longer about temptation of the soul. Instead, evil is lodged in the body, and has become weakness.

Faust sells his immortal soul to the devil, but anybody can become a vampire—all it takes is one little bite. How readily informants segue from mythical to metaphoric vampires. As Patricia D. puts it, "Louis [the vampire in Anne Rice's *Interview with the Vampire*] is a saint compared to my former boyfriend. Talk about a blood feast, he'd have taken every drop of me if I'd let him."

In talking about vampires, my young informants are talking not just about former boyfriends but about themselves, about anybody, everybody who depends on others—on government, society, friends, lovers, spouses—but who cannot admit it. Admitting real dependence becomes tantamount to dread, paralysis and powerlessness in a world in which only perfect freedom can overcome the shame of being merely human. It is, I have suggested, why most informants identify with Eichmann. To identify with his victims represents unbearable dread.

Vampires are messengers from the realm of precategorical experience, carriers of doom who are nonetheless external, a little campy, distant enough to tell stories about. Only sometimes the stories lose their fictional quality, and the doom bursts forth.

Rachel B. is talking about portrayals of evil in the media. "Like vampires. They look just like anybody else, like the neighbors, only one day they possess and destroy you, turn you into the walking dead." Suddenly she blanches. "My God, it's like the good Germans who turn away when the SS comes to take you to Auschwitz. I never thought of it that way before." She looks as if she is going to rush from the room. Instead she cries.

"Revenants," the generic term for the undead, are subjects of myths and legends all over the world. To my informants, however, vampires are clearly fictional, not folkloric. Although one scholar reports that 27 percent of her North American respondents answered "yes" to the question "Do you believe it is possible that vampires exist as real entities?"[2] this response is not evidence of their integration into the culture. Instead it is evidence of how shallowly rooted modern rationality truly is, the point of Horkheimer and Adorno's *Dialectic of Enlightenment*.

All vampires cross the boundary between life and death, but only fictional vampires plot to take over the world by creating an army of the undead. Folkloric vampires are generally a morose and gloomy lot. Consider the modal revenant, a plump peasant with mottled red face and one eye, dressed in a dirty smock, stealing from the cemetery to revenge himself on the living, then returning to the isolation of slow decomposition in a shallow grave. Scary but hardly admirable, and his victims avoid him like the plague he so often represents. None desires to follow in his footsteps, a wish tantamount to wanting to become a disease-carrying rodent.[3]

The fictional vampires of informants are symbols of social isolation, not cultural integration. The folkloric vampire represents how difficult it is to come to terms with the otherness of death, how difficult it is to mourn. In mourning we must separate the memory and spirit of the dead one from the physical body, so that we can bury the body and hold onto the image.[4] Folkloric vampires speak to us about how difficult this is. Fictional vampires are also about mourning. Only instead of linking us with our concern about how difficult it is to mourn *others*, they link us to the difficulty of mourning our own mortality, our own limits, our own doom.

Read closely, fictional vampires may help us do this, however. Louis, fictional vampire of Rice's *Interview with the Vampire*, would give anything to be human again.[5] Many informants regret only that they cannot have it all, that they cannot be as powerful as a vampire without giving up being human, without giving up life itself. "If I didn't have to be dead first, I'd become a vampire in a minute." So says George W. in a wonderful and pathetic burst of honesty.

Varieties of Vampires: Satan, Hardmen, Faust

The vampiric impulse, that strange combination of idealized power and shameful humiliation, is not unique to revenants. Consider Milton's Satan, for whom serving a power mightier than himself is such a terrible narcissistic wound that he chooses hell. Satan is an impressive creature, creator of his own identity, deeply reflective (he has five soliloquies), in some ways more like Macbeth than an epic hero, becoming more inward as he goes along. But he cannot transform this inwardness into creation. All he can create is himself. His inwardness is too narcissistic, unable to combine with matter to make something new.

God creates from matter, inserting his active creation into the givenness of matter, bringing it to life. Satan does not, seeking to create entirely out of himself, unwilling to be dependent on anything, not God, not even matter. With great energy Satan and his legions make hell, training for battle, singing, and apparently building a richly adorned civilization, Pandemonium. But pandemonium it remains, all chaos and dynamic energy but hollow at the core. Action is not necessarily creative. Creativity requires bringing something new into the world not just rearranging the pieces.

Paradise Lost is a very erotic poem; Adam and Eve brim with sexuality. Procreative sexual intercourse is Milton's vision of creativity, vitality combining with matter to produce something new. Satan is nonsexual, lusting and envious of Eve, but eventually his need and desire become hatred of her beauty. Instead of procreating with another, Satan procreates Sin and Death out of himself, children of incest and his own imagination. Sterile in his creativity, Satan would inflict his dread on the world, a narcissistic terror of helplessness and dependence so extreme he is unable to combine himself with anyone or anything to make something new.

In *Seductions of Crime*, Jack Katz analyzes the appeal of criminal violence. The goal of much violence, he argues, is transcendence, the power of not having one's subjectivity affected by anyone or anything.

> In his everyday doings, the hardman transcends the difference between how he and others experience everyday situations by insisting that his subjectivity remains firm as he moves into and out of others' worlds. In street language, the challenge arises when others try to take him through "too many changes." . . . The project is to move, without being visibly impressed, emotionally affected, or spiritually swayed between "here" (wherever you are "at" at the moment) and "there" (all situations defined by others.) . . . For the badass, transcendence is essentially a *presence;* the badass strives to be so intimidating that he becomes virtually any situation he is in.[6]

The hardman's goal is autarky, not to be touched by anything. Stasis —not being moved by anyone or anything—*is* transcendence, of a world that is always trying to put one through changes.

The world of the hardman is an almost-pure expression of the autistic-contiguous position, in which a touch is tantamount to an invasion, a disruption of the fragile equilibrium of stasis (homeostasis) which must lead to destruction. It is as though the hardman is so soft he will melt into any situation he finds himself in unless he resists being touched at all. Instead, he touches, or rather penetrates, seeking to *become* the situation that threatens to become him, as though these were the only choices. In reality they are but a single choice, like the autistic-contiguous "impression" made by the chair on your buttocks, located everywhere and nowhere, no distinction between self and world. There is no relationship involved, not even with the chair, because there is no other, and really no self, just the impression of the situation.

Satan is the hardman. The transcendence at stake is not just that of good and evil but of a world that does not bow down, that puts one through changes. In this the vampire shares the world of hardman and Satan, the vampire not so much a parasite as a leaky jar that can be filled up for no more than a moment before the life blood begins to seep away.

Goethe's Faust is another vampire, sick to death of pouring over sterile, meaningless academic tomes, lecturing about dusty old books to callow students. He uses symbols just fine, but they have lost any connection to the vitality and meaningfulness represented by the autistic-contiguous position. He is depressed in both senses of the term: isolated in the depressive position, unable to make contact with the world of feeling, so depressed he is about to take poison and end it all, so that his striving soul might find respite from its dread.

Faust's conviction of meaninglessness, that there is not enough meaning inside to fill the empty world outside, is akin to what Ricoeur calls ethical dread: the inability to love and invest anything in the world. Empty striving is the most common way of keeping dread at bay. Prozac is a close second. "Evil spelled backward is live" is the third, Faust choosing Satan in the hope that the magic he represents, the magic that denies the boundaries of this world, might bring his own inner world back to life.

"All Nature's workings, to my inner sense made clear," is all Faust wants (line 441). That and an enchanted cloak to soar above the world, to know everything without effort, to have anything without striving. The answer to dread is magic, effortless knowledge of the All, effortless possession of anything, including Helen.

Mephistopheles promises Faust that he will finally have enough. He can have it all for all for eternity as long as he never asks to stop, never wishes to hold a moment in his hand (line 1700).[7] In other words, as long as he never wishes to just be.

> Procure a girl whose roving eye
> invites the next man even as I lie
> in her embrace. . . .
> Show me that fruit that rots before it's plucked
> And trees that change their foliage every day!
> (lines 1683–88)

The moment Faust wishes to savor mortal life, his soul will belong to the devil forever.

The worst bargainer around, Faust would pay with his soul for what he dreads above all, a life of meaningless striving. Why? Because it is the only defense he knows, the only alternative to despair and suicide. Once despair meant the conviction of damnation, and the hopelessness that went with it. Faust trades despair for despair, his for the devil's.

God likes the devil. They get along. "Among the spirits who negate / The Ironic scold offends me least of all," says He (line 339). Without the devil, man would sink into laziness and stupefaction. He needs the devil to keep him busy. Together they make a good team, like the light that needs the darkness to make it shine. "Evil spelled backward is live." That is the theme of Faust. It is the devil that makes us do it, anything worth doing, that is.

Striving is the way of the world, a principle of nature, neither good nor bad, but likely to cause harm, since it is incompatible with care. Without striving we would not be human, Goethe seems to say. Morality is not the principle of life in this amoral world, striving is. Goethe's readers appreciated this. Faust was widely admired, especially in Germany, "Faustian striving" still more compliment than criticism. Even a "Faustian bargain" may be admirable.

It is ironic, Faustian striving being ultimately barren. Faust brings nothing new into being. He does not really want to know, he wants to have and experience. The devil, though, wants to destroy. The Lord of the Flies is pure negation, activity without creation.

> I am the spirit of perpetual negation;
> And rightly so, for all things that exist
> Deserve to perish, and would not be missed—
> Much better it would be if nothing were
> Brought into being. Thus, what you men call
> Destruction, sin, evil in short, is all
> My sphere, the element I most prefer.
>
> (lines 1338–44)

If he could, Mephistopheles would transform all into Nothingness (line 1365).

Faust gets confused, calling the devil the enemy of striving. Quick to agree when Faust gets it right, Mephistopheles says only that they will talk about it later (line 1379–87). The devil is not the enemy of striving; he is its cause. What Faust would say if he were more acute is that striving that stems from dread is always at risk of emptiness, a destructive, grasping enterprise that does not know the difference between destruction and creation. Faust does not know. He knows he has not been creative, but he does not know what creativity is anymore, if he ever did, preferring magic, control, and ceaseless new experience. But only forever. Eventually Faust too chooses life, love, and the mortality that goes with it.

Vampires, the hardman, Milton's Satan, Goethe's Faust: in each case the principle is the same, the quest for power to overcome dread ends in lifelessness and failed creativity. Precategorical dread does not originate in society. It comes from within. But a dark and empty cultural space, like the basement of which so many informants were terrified, can make life so much more difficult to bear—so difficult that the only alternative to dread may seem to be its infliction on others. This too is vampiric, transforming others into the undead because it hurts too much to be among the living while feeling dead inside. The vampire does not need to murder. The infliction of abandonment, helplessness, and pain is more than enough. This happens all the time.

The difference between the vampire and Satan is analogous to the difference between violence and more subtle ways of victimizing others. Vampires suck the life out of you when you least expect it, and there is nothing you can do. Satan requires your cooperation, your will. He needs your soul, not just your body, and he wants that you want to give it. It is the difference between Rice's *Interview with the Vampire* and C. S. Lewis's *The Screwtape Letters*. It is the difference between infantile and adult icons of dread.

"Stomping for Knowledge," Appropriating the Victim

Prisoners do not talk about vampires, but they talk about the vampiric impulse. One calls it "stomping for knowledge."

"I read about this Nazi soldier," says Mr. Leotine. "He didn't just kill his enemies, he spent hours lovingly stomping them to death."

Why?

"He wanted to get to know his victim. He wanted a close personal relationship. He wanted to know the other man's secret."

What was the secret?

Mr. Leotine doesn't know. Another inmate chimes in. "You know why Jeffrey Dahmer ate all those guys? Because he wanted to know them better, so he could have them inside him. I'm not saying it's good. I think it's crazy. But that's what he said."

Do you think it's true?

"Only for faggots," says another. He wasn't being cruel, just literal, concrete.

What if the secret is simply that we are all, each one of us, so terribly alone in the world? So alone that sometimes the only way we can make contact is through our hate and rage at being so alone?

Another inmate compares the vampiric impulse to deer hunting. "To be a good deer hunter you have to put yourself in the place of the deer, be like the deer, think like the deer . . . become the deer. When Indians killed a deer they thanked the deer for giving up its life blood, its substance."

Isn't there a ritual about drinking the deer's blood?

"It's just a couple of drops, and only after the first kill."

"Banking" is what the inmates call a group assault, several inmates jumping on a guy and beating him bloody. Why call it banking? They weren't sure; one thought it must be some kind of investment. Perhaps it is, an investment in another. The only way you can count on anyone is to pile on him until the blood flows. That you can count on. It was not accidental that this discussion took place as we were renegotiating whether to continue the group for another six months. Could they bank on the group, on one another, on me? Is there any way to bank on someone that does not involve physical coercion? "If you don't continue the group, then we'll just have to hold you hostage," one says jokingly. He is banking on me.

Is this the root of all evil? The desire to eat rather than to see, to have rather than to be, to possess rather than to relate? Because we are so scared that if we let go we shall have nothing. Because we fear that we are so evil and destructive we deserve nothing. Evil is an intense relationship that wants all the other person has to offer, without the fearsome bother of having the other person around. So you try to take what they have and kill them, or throw them away, use them up. Suck them dry, and throw the empty husk away.

The impulse to possess the other totally is the human impulse: the desire to have and take rather than see and relate. We will not be rid of it, and moral injunctions that fail to recognize the dread behind the impulse will always be ineffective. Desperately needed are stories about the impulse, so that we might use narrative to discover and know it, giving evil a form that we and others can live with. Satan stories like the Faust legend are better than vampire stories, because Satan believes in the human soul: a soul in conflict, a soul willing to do anything to have power over its own dread, decay, and doom. Vampire stories are pregenital accounts of merger, of the narcissistic baby dependent on the lives of others for its substance.

It is not a good sign that younger informants and inmates sound more alike than different, at least as far as vampires are concerned. The culture that could provide better and richer narrative forms by which to contain their dread is failing both, and failing us all.

At the same time, we should not neglect the differences. Fantasies about vampires, about becoming a vampire, are still fantasies, vampire stories better than no stories at all. Of all the differences between free informants and inmates this is the most striking: free informants are more imaginative about evil. Consider the possibility that being able to imagine evil is the only real alternative to doing it. If you can imagine evil, you can imagine the consequences of doing it, including the terrible loss it inflicts on others and oneself. You may even be able to imagine how terrible you will feel later.

Imagination does not always work that way. For psychopaths and some others, violent fantasy is a rehearsal for action, a stimulus, not an alternative. Is pornography that degrades women an incitement to sexual violence? For most men no; it is an alternative. For a few it seems to be an impetus.[8] Violent fantasy is similar. Even for those for whom fantasy is an act of preparation, however, there is often something monochromatic about the fantasy, as though the act were necessary in order to give life to the details of the fantasy image. Deficient in fantasy, the act of violence (particularly, but not exclusively sexual violence) becomes a means to a richer fantasy life. Perhaps this is why some inmates seem so in love with their crime, it's reality not so important as its value as a resource for fantasy. If only they could fantasize better in the first place! Why they, and so many others, do not is addressed in the next chapter. It is probably the most important thing to be learned about evil.

SEVEN # "Evil Spelled Backward Is Live"

Evil is attractive—more attractive in theory than in practice, more attractive as literature than as reality. "Imaginary evil is romantic and varied," writes Simone Weil: "real evil is gloomy, monotonous, barren and boring." C. S. Lewis describes hell as a vast, gray city in the British Midlands. M. Scott Peck compares it to an endless room of slot machines, exciting but monotonous, always promising more than it delivers.[1]

Where does it come from, this romantic, creative vision of evil, Faust as culture hero? Why is it so persistent, so attractive, and ultimately so misleading? Does Satan really get all the best lines in *Paradise Lost*, as William Blake claims? Should he?

Evil is an attempt to recapture the vitality of autistic-contiguous experience. Trapped in a world of dusty tomes and empty lectures, Goethe's Faust has lost the meaning of life, his world of symbols unconnected to sources of vitality lodged in the rich immediacy of experience. Autistic-contiguous experience helps, says Ogden, to "make bearable the awareness of the separateness" of existence, providing "a healing sensory experience."[2] If autistic-contiguous experience is a source of dread, it is also a source of deepest satisfaction, the meaning of life.

From this perspective, one might think of evil as an attempt to get the satisfaction without the dread, making contact with ultimate reality inside the body and spirit of another, by various forms of physical and spiritual violation. Only the psychopath does so literally, like the psychopath referred to in Chapter 3 who "had to evict [his victims] from their human bodies." But all evil has the quality of psychopathy, becoming the monster so as not to be the victim, becoming dread so as not to live it. The cost, I have suggested, is life itself, a disconnection from autistic-contiguous satisfaction because the evildoer has become the autistic-contiguous dread he so fears.

What does the cliché "evil spelled backward is live" mean? If I had but one question (number 14) to ask about evil, this would be it. The answer is not as important as the struggle to get it. To get it one has to own up to the idea, like a gestalt image that leaps out from the background only when one realizes one has seen its like before. Without some experience with the attractiveness of the idea (more precisely, without a willingness to acknowledge it to oneself), the sense of the cliché is incomprehensible. As Toni D. puts it, "I don't want to tell you what it means, because then I'll know, and you'll know I know."

Of course, the cliché has several senses. It may also mean that we cannot live without suffering evil. A full understanding of evil requires an understanding of both senses, particularly the way in which the excitement of inflicting evil serves to anesthetize the pain and terror of suffering it.

Evil is an attempt to feel alive, even when we are just playing at being bad. "There's only one thing worse than not feeling," says Mr. Acorn. "Not knowing you don't feel anything." In order to feel, Mr. Acorn drove his Harley at 130, "a bitch on the back, weaving in and out of traffic, it doesn't get any better than that." He covers his body with tattoos, stimulating his skin, marking him off from the world, containing his dread in the skin envelope that he knows is real because it hurts, because he feels the pricks. Somehow it works. His evil, if that is what it is, is all display, penny ante stuff.

Among many psychiatric patients, cutting and scarifying the body is a common practice, a response to stress and psychic pain. Many hide away razor blades and other sharp objects, so that one will always be available should the stress get too much. Cutting the skin defines the self at its body boundary, creating a real physical pain to define and contain the ineffable psychic pain, as well as the ineffable "formless dread" of leaking away. The experience of dread is not just an uncontained experience; it is an experience of being uncontained, without limits or boundaries to the chaos and fear.

Prisoners deal with razor blades a little differently, secreting razor blades to cut another. It is as good a distinction between madness and criminality as any: the mad one cuts himself, the criminal another. Most inmates do not play with razors. Those who do prefer double-edged blades, usually obtained from a visiting wife or girlfriend who smuggles the unwrapped blade in her mouth and transfers it to the inmate with a passionate kiss, a practice that gives new meaning to the term "secreting razor blades."

Were the prisoner and his visitor to wrap the blade, they would miss the thrill of living and loving on the razor's edge. Evil is a version of cutting. In evil we cut another rather than ourselves. We may do it literally or figuratively, as in a cutting remark, but the goal is the same: to implant our dread within another, and so define its boundaries, its limits, containing the uncontainable in the form of another so we might live.

Whether we cut another rather than ourselves makes a moral difference, but it makes almost no difference at all so far as the psychologic is concerned, the psychologic of dread which makes no real distinction between self and world. That is why morality is so readily corrupted by precategorical thought, which knows no boundaries. We do evil so as to feel the boundaries for a little while, even false ones. In evil we scratch the surface of the other in order to mark the separation. At the same time we do the opposite, acting as if there are no boundaries, no limits, my access to your body limited not even by the envelope of your skin, which I slice open before you even feel the pain. This dualism, evil creating the limits it would destroy, is the psychologic of narcissistic omnipotence, your boundaries nothing more than an expression of my will.

Evil and Creativity Both Play with Limits

Evil is attractive for the same reason that vampires are fascinating: both transgress boundaries, violate taboos. Still, this explanation is not so much an answer as another question: why is such transgression attractive? Because limits are as terrifying as their absence, because they tell us that we are human, subject to constraint, isolation, contingency, morality, and death. Everything we are, everything we become, precludes our being and becoming a thousand other things. We can have different jobs, roles, lovers, spouses, and friends, but each of us can live only one life and must leave a thousand others (actually, an infinity) unlived.

Limits are at least as terrifying as no limits: the experience of vertigo, of the world fallen away, the feeling that everything is possible, so that nothing is given, reliable, substantial, real. We live our lives between claustrophobia and agoraphobia, between the terror of limits and the terror of limitless being. This is the secret of dread. The knife that cuts in order to limit also cuts through limits, or so it sometimes seems.

We play with limits, a version of repetition compulsion, to quell the terror of their presence and their absence. We play to sustain the illusion of mastery, or at least acceptance, as though we had a choice. Mardi Gras is about this illusion, so is Carnival. Both turn the world upside down. The latrine cleaner becomes king for a day, and adultery is smiled upon by the gods for one night.

Evil partakes of this play with limits, or at least its highly institutionalized and ritualized manifestations do, like Carnival or ritual sacrifice. Like books about vampires or Satan. Like Dionysos, symbol of the transgression of boundaries, the transformation of limits, the joining of opposites, and the separation of unities.

The evil obliteration of limits is not always so dramatic, at least not on the surface. It may also be bureaucratized. In *Memory, History, and the Extermination of the Jews of Europe*, Saul Friedlander writes of the *Rausch*, the intoxicating thrill that seems to have seized Eichmann and other bureaucrats as the number of dead piled up, as the ideal of a *Juden-Frei* Europe came closer. Friedlander attributes the *Rausch* to the "mystical Fuehrer-Bond," the thrill of perfect obedience, perfect belonging.[3] Violating a taboo may be experienced as equally thrilling, a transgression of the most sacred boundaries—especially when the taboo runs deep, not just against the murder of individuals, but against the extermination of a people. If down deep the desk murderers were thrilled, then we shall have to rethink the meaning of the "banality of evil."

Creativity also plays with limits, subverting limits, obliterating limits, restoring limits, and subverting them all over again. *Creativity is evil that submits to the requirements of abstract form.* Instead of expressing our doom in and through the bodies and minds of others, we express it in abstract media, in words not deeds, in images not actions. An implication is that Kleinians such as Hanna Segal are mistaken to hold that art is an expression of the depressive position, an act of symbolic reparation.[4] This is only half the story.

Art is the submission of paranoid-schizoid destructive impulses to the requirements of abstract form, forms that are expressions of both the autistic-contiguous and depressive positions. Shape, texture, and rhythm are the artistic forms of the autistic-contiguous position. Art is an act of paranoid-schizoid destruction that submits to reality: the reality of morality, the reality of consequences, the reality of love, and above all the reality of otherness. In other words, art submits to the morality of Kant's categorical imperative, the morality of separateness and care, even as it plays with precategorical experience.[5]

Art is not just, or even primarily, an act of reparation, as Segal would have it. Segal, like many Kleinians, sees art as an attempt to restore what the paranoid-schizoid impulse would destroy, but she would not admit this struggle into the work of art itself. Art comes afterward. My argument is that this struggle *is* the work of art. Behind every work of art, including the art of creative living, lies the narrowest of victories over evil. As Nietzsche puts it, "Good actions are sublimated evil ones; evil actions are coarsened, brutalized good ones."[6] (The next chapter argues that Nietzsche's art does not succeed in grasping evil.)

Evil and creativity come so terribly close that it is important to grasp the crucial difference. Torture is a good place to start, particularly because torture is frequently couched in the language of drama, a work of art. The torture chamber is called the "production room" in the Philippines, the "cinema room" in South Vietnam, and the "blue lit stage" in Chile.[7]

In fact, torture is the reverse of drama. In drama, a transformed larger world is acted out on small stage. In torture, the world is reduced to the body of the victim, the difference between creativity and evil in a nutshell. In a creative work, the body is projected into an artifact, where it can be transformed, enhanced, played with, even used ruthlessly because it is not really the human body, but a body of work. In creation we animate the world, bringing the dead material world to life with the spirit of mind.

Torture is reverse animism. It reduces the world to the human body.

Rather than non-body symbolizing body, body comes to symbolize a world reduced to its bare essentials, pain and power. "Symbolize" is a misleading term, however, suggesting a degree of abstraction not present. It is not that the body comes to symbolize the world; the body becomes the world, it is the world.

We are now in a position to understand what Arendt means by the banality of evil, perhaps even better than Arendt herself, who seemed so puzzled by the stir she created. "Banal" is an aesthetic category, referring to a lack of creativity, originality, or inspiration. It properly applies not to people but to the uncreative quality of evil itself, the way evil substitutes body for symbol, turning in on itself, as Milton's Satan does, attempting to create out of himself alone. Evil is uncreative because it abandons the quest to translate dread into abstract form and instead evacuates dread into the bodies and minds of others. Evil is the failure of creativity, and banality is its slogan.

Spury F. talks of evil as a "performance." He is referring to a relative, a priest who has been accused of molesting young boys. The priest "performs" evil because he pretends to serve God while actually serving another, his own desire, maybe the devil himself. Evil is an act. Goodness is transparent will. Spury sounds like Augustine. In fact, the performance is more complicated, even for Spury, who long ago changed his name to mean "deceitful." "It's a challenge. Everyday I have to overcome my name, show people my name isn't me, that I'm not what my name says."

Spury owns commercial property. Our interview took place in the first-floor storefront of a vacant office. Sitting behind a huge plate-glass window, talking about evil as hundreds of pedestrians walked by, we were as transparent as could be. Except that the cavernous room was dark; it was easier for us to see out than for passers-by to see in, as if we were wearing sunglasses.

Spury says, "I know what 'evil spelled backward is live' means, and I won't play." But he does, challenging the "performance" of evil with his own transparency, a transparency that in the end is not so clear as all that. How could it be? If creativity is the alternative to evil, then the difference between good and evil cannot be the difference between transparent will and performance. Instead it will have something to do with the quality of the performance itself, how well it traffics with the precategorical. Spury traffics better than he knows.

Complexity and Confusion

The trouble with complex performances is that they readily segue into confusing performances. Most people deal with evil by becoming confused. It is the most popular defense around. One might respond, following Klein, that it is really splitting that is the most popular defense, dividing the complex world into watertight compartments. Klein treats confusion as a type of serial splitting, dividing and subdividing the world into so many discrete units of experience that nothing makes sense after a while. In this regard, confusion is a paranoid-schizoid defense.[8] It is for this reason that I have not sought to draw very many distinctions between types of evil, or between evildoer and evil deed, as discussed in Chapter 1.

The problem, or perhaps it is just the complex reality, is that confusion is not just a defense where evil is concerned. Confusion is part of the experience of evil itself, reflecting its origin in the experience of dread as an uncontained force, within and without and at the same time. It is no accident that confusion, chaos, mist, fog, and the knot are leading images of evil, most handed down to us by Augustine (*Confessions* II.x.18, III.xi.19, VI.iii.4, VII.iii.4–5).

Mr. Leotine studied religion to figure out who was evil: he or his parents. With all the evil about, with all the fear and loathing he felt, someone had to be. He took courses, wrote papers on evil, thought about it for years. But he could never decide. His parents had done evil things to him, that was clear. But he wasn't pure either; his thoughts were filled with terrible things. In desperation he bought a gun and some pills. "I didn't know who was evil anymore, or even where it was coming from. But if I killed everybody, the evil would die with us. I had that much figured out." With the gun he killed his parents. The ninety-six Sominex he took afterward just put him to sleep for the night.

"Kill Everybody," the motto on Ralph H.'s pin, is a version of a motto he attributes to the U.S. Army Rangers. "Kill 'em All, Let God Sort 'em Out." To leave the sorting out to God abandons any attempt at clarification, finding solace in ignorance and confusion—as in the relief we feel when we finally throw up our hands and exclaim, "God knows!" Mr. Leotine and Ralph mistook the experience of dread, the confusing experience of evil as uncontained, everywhere and nowhere, with its solution.

The fact that confusion seems to have been their choice, or at least not an unwelcome experience, raises the question of whether confusion is itself a type of autistic-contiguous satisfaction, becoming part of the chaos that is the All. We like to be confused, at least sometimes, so that we do not have to be distinct, including distinctly separate and responsible.

On the morning of May 28, 1995, Sinedu Tadesse, a junior at Harvard, stabbed her roommate, Trang Ho, forty-five times while Trang lay sleeping in her bed in their Harvard dormitory. By the time police arrived, Sinedu had hanged herself in the bathroom. In a campus memorial service shortly after their deaths, the university chaplain eulogized them this way: "For all that was good in these girls, Lord bless them; for the forces of evil beyond their control which overcame them, Lord forgive them."[9]

The Rev. Peter Gomes was not entirely mistaken in conflating the killer and the victim. Something about evil seems to envelop victim and executioner alike, as though they were lost in the same fog. This has been my argument throughout, and it will be developed further. Nevertheless, it is important not to indulge this experience or to use it as an excuse for confusion, that is, as an excuse not to judge evil. If evil overcame Sinedu, it overcame her in a different way from how it overcame Trang, and we should insist on this distinction, the distinction between inflicting and suffering evil. It is not the distinction, but the failure to make it, that fosters confusion.

Jean-Paul Sartre says that we never choose evil, that we must first call evil good.[10] Socrates makes a similar argument: no one ever does evil knowingly; people do evil only because they confuse wrong with right (*Meno* 77a–78b). Assume for a moment that these views are correct. Then the confusion, the fog that Augustine equates with evil, becomes even more problematic, an invitation to evil in the name of good. Evil is complex and confusing enough without our indulging it.

How can it be denied that good sometimes comes from evil, evil from good; that destruction often precedes creation; that it is not always easy to tell good from evil; that we know evil, in part at least, only in contrast to good? Above all the world is, and in the world as it is good and evil are almost always found together, even—or especially—in a single person.

Whether these insights constitute a defense or revelation, or both (perhaps all insight has the quality of a defense against further revelation) depends on how these insights are held, a judgment frequently more subjective than logical. About such a difficult and complex issue as evil, an excess of clarity is at least as dangerous as confusion. It is good to respect confusion, or at least lack of clarity. But it is not good to worship confusion or to halt our questioning prematurely.

In *A Grief Observed*, written about his crisis of faith after the death of his wife, C. S. Lewis says, "God has in fact—our worst fears are true—all the characteristics we regard as bad: unreasonableness, vanity, vindictiveness, injustice, cruelty." Lewis seems content to deal with the issue as Ralph does, embracing the confusion, finding relief in human ignorance. "Peace, child; you don't understand" is what God seems to say to him. For Lewis it is enough.

Confusion and lack of clarity are virtues only after we have struggled like hell with a problem, finally deciding either that it is beyond our ken or that confusion and lack of clarity are aspects of reality itself. Accepting confusion and lack of clarity is a valid conclusion, but only after we have tried everything else. Lewis eagerly embraces confusion out of his desire to abandon himself to divine paternalism.[11]

Creativity and Consolation

There are sources of consolation other than the divine. Adrian Leverkuehn, in Thomas Mann's *Doctor Faustus*, has written an oratorio, "The Lamentation of Doctor Faustus," as counterpart to Ludwig Beethoven's *Ninth Symphony*, an "Ode to Sorrow." It is, according to Serenus Zeitblom, the narrator, "the most horrendous human and divine lamentation that has ever been intoned on earth, starting from the individual self, but then spreading out further and further until it engulfs as it were the entire cosmos." The *Lamentation* is cold as crystal, but it is not the coldness of the devil, whose appearance is always preceded by a chill. It is the coldness that knows the only consolation in the universe stems from the ability to give voice to suffering. Zeitblom continues: "Here toward the end the uttermost accents of mourning are reached, the final despair achieves a voice, [denying] any other consolation than what lies in voicing it, in simply giving sorrow words . . . that out of the sheerly irremediable hope might germinate. It would be but a hope beyond hopelessness. . . . Then nothing more: silence, and night." [12]

It is no accident that Mann sounds like his friend and fellow exile Theodor Adorno, who writes that "advanced music has no choice but to insist on remaining 'hard,' without any concessions to those humane values whose tempting offers, wherever they are still to be found, it sees through as the mask of inhumanity." [13] Perhaps we misunderstand what humanity really is, equating it with warmth and tenderness, Disney humanity. Perhaps it is much simpler, a willingness to contain one's dread and terror, not inflicting it on others, transforming it into art, including the art of living. Everything else is detail.

What does Leverkuehn lament? The losses of his life, especially Echo, his beautiful little nephew who dies such a bad death. Above all, Leverkuehn laments life's relentless losses: "Thus it is." "Alas, it is not to be." Zeitblom exclaims, "How the words stand, almost like a musical direction, above the choral and orchestral movements." [14] Recall Whitehead's sources of evil: "Things fade," "alternatives exclude." Evil is what reveals to us the limits of being human. In creativity, "a voice is given the creature for its woe." That is the only alternative to evildoing.

Doctor Faustus is filled with fuzzy boundaries, unclear transitions. Leverkuehn's father takes special delight in blurring borders, transgressing boundaries, collecting different species of plants and animals that look like one another, growing crystals that look like plants. Water is the leading trope, seeping from one entity to another, holding its form only when tightly contained. It seems like blood. Such confusions and transgressions are the paradigm of creativity, the creative analog of evil. But creative transgression is not evil. Nor is Leverkuehn Christ, no matter how often Mann evokes his Ecce-homo countenance. These are simple points perhaps, but the world is confused and confusing enough about evil that when we can be clear we should be.

Doctor Faustus is as much about music as words; it is about rhythm, raising the question of whether rhythms of ice-cold lucidity and crystal clarity can still be soothing. The answer is yes, for rhythm is the "language" of the autistic-contiguous position. Though perhaps "soothing" is not the right word. The "consolation" that Ogden writes of might be a better term, except that to listen to Leverkuehn's oratorio is to be stroked ever so gently with an icicle. It's soothing, but you know it's cold.

There are few rhythmic consolations in the industrialized modern world other than music. Consider the rhythms and forms of the premodern world: the rhythm of nature, of the stars and planets, of the seasons, of the sun rising and setting. Then there is the silence, the silence that envelops and contains in its emptiness, like the silence of the Moroccan desert at night that Paul Bowles writes of in *The Sheltering Sky*, an autistic-contiguous satisfaction that lives just next door to dread. Think about night, its darkness barely broken by artificial illumination, and then only for an hour or two. Consider the Great Chain of Being that bound everyone to his station, and his station to the cosmos, a life lived in a single place, the same place one's ancestors lived and died in for generations.

Rhythm, place, space, darkness, silence, death: these are the themes of the autistic-contiguous position, experiences that dissolve dualities. Not into oneness, but into impressions, shapes, rhythms, feelings, and a sense of location which is all the stronger for having no locus. When it is not dreadful, autistic-contiguous experience is about a space without a place, everywhere and nowhere, like the oceanic experience that Freud writes of, being at home in the universe.

Contrast preindustrial experience with that of the modern industrial world, of a life lived at a vast distance from the rhythms of nature, filled with light and noise and cars, movement and sound bites. Modern industrial society has its satisfactions, but autistic-contiguous satisfaction is not one. More and more we live in a world devoid of connection to rhythm and place. We do not even die at home, where once people died in the bed they were born in, or could hope to. Icons, images, and symbols are omnipresent, but we are ever more removed from the autistic-contiguous floor of experience. If this loss generates a longing for immediacy and reality which is virtually ineffable, we might expect the temptations of evil to become greater, as individuals seek a shortcut to authentic experience. If so, then education about evil will become more important still, putting into words the ineffable longing. The more a culture is removed from the autistic-contiguous satisfactions of a life lived close to the rhythms of nature, the more important it is that the culture provide rich depressive forms within which to frame and form the longing. Even if our depressive forms were as good as those of the ancient Greeks (and who would argue that?), they might not be enough.

Containing Evil

The problem of evil is to know our dread, so that we may contain it in ourselves rather than inflict it on others. This has been my argument, and it is too simple, at least as it stands. Although the result of playing with evil is an increased ability to contain it, that containment is achieved not by holding it in but by projecting it: into cultural symbols rather than onto the bodies of victims. Inmates are not, for the most part, torturers. But many think like the torturer insofar as the body of the victim becomes the world, icon of all reality.

Tattoos mark the borderline between torture and creativity, bound to the body but pointing to the world. Of all the "languages" of the autistic-contiguous position, the tattoo is among the more complex.

Why do you do that to yourself? I asked an inmate with more tattoo than skin. "Because I want to possess a permanent piece of art," Mr. Torey responds. An immortal work of art that perishes with the body would seem to be a contradiction. Not so for the tattooed artist, eternity reduced to the life of a single inscribed body. The flaming death's head is the most popular image, but some are more elaborate, brave works of art frequently on flabby bodies, the torso not integrated into the work of art but occasionally poking through it, a nipple emerging from a fiery sun, pentimento of the corpus delicti.

It is the inability to know and contain their dread that most sharply distinguishes inmates and free citizens. This distinction is reflected in the divergent answers of these two groups to the question "Is it evil to think evil?" (number 9). Most free informants said no. Most inmates said yes. It is also reflected in the fact that most free citizens talked of precategorical experiences and few inmates did.

Though the evildoer inflicts his dread on others, it would be wrong simply to state that inmates who have done evil put more of their evil into the world than others do. Rather, they put it into the world in a way that is insufficiently abstract, so that symbol and the reality are virtually one. This is why, I believe, inmates are far more likely to equate thinking evil with doing it.

Mr. Deacon says that he read somewhere that Hell is ten thousand times hotter than the sun. "I just don't think I can believe that. Have you ever walked down the street on a hot summer day? Even then the road is melting, and the sun is far away. The tar sticks to your feet. How could hell be ten thousand times hotter? It would melt all the rocks and earth and everything? It just doesn't make sense."

Many inmates are trapped in their bodies. We all are, of course, but they more than most have difficulty using language to capture and reflect their feelings. Mr. Deacon was tortured by his mother. She made him collect switches from a tree in the backyard. Braided together, they made a whip covered with knots. After soaking the whip in oil, she beat him in such a way that the whip wrapped around his body, removing his skin as she pulled it loose. Twenty years later the scars still show. Is it any wonder that Mr. Deacon has trouble with abstraction, getting stuck in the physical world? Is it any wonder he broke into the house of a woman who, he believes, threatened his life, and then stabbed her to death?

On hearing this story, Mr. Leotine compares torture to a work of art. "It's sick, but it's artful, a type of perverted art, like that picture over there." The picture is of cute little rabbits frolicking in a meadow, a paint-by-numbers picture. (Inmates had begun to bring art with them, leaving it around the room.) Mr. Leotine is more insightful than he knows (or perhaps just more insightful than I know), torture about as artistic as a paint-by-numbers picture, so bound to the contours of the body it can never be free. "Oh, man, that's just one of those paint-by-numbers jobs," says Mr. Prior. "Lots of the guys have that one. He didn't even do the one of the Last Supper. Now that's art!"

Mr. Deacon has some idea of what happened to him, and this awareness helps him. God knows what happened to Mr. Albright, a member of the group for only a short while, the only psychopath to have been a member.[15] Mr. Albright twists and turns in his seat, sometimes preening, sometimes covering his face with his undershirt or putting his hands in his baggy pants. I ask him if something is bothering him, if there is anything he wants to say. "Evil is the darkness cast by the shadow of goodness," he answers, a response whose connection to the thread of the conversation is, to say the least, obscure. Whatever he is feeling in his body is not making it into words.

Melanie Klein's most famous patient was a little boy named Dick, who could barely speak or play, so inhibited was his use of symbolism. One day while looking at some pencil shavings from the sharpener he'd been playing with, Dick said of them, "Poor Mrs. Klein."[16] For Dick, the wood shavings did not represent Mrs. Klein, they were Mrs. Klein after he had put her through the grinder. Yet, even this image was progress: at least he was able, however concretely, to use one thing to represent another, a pencil and its shavings for her body.

Inmates are not so regressed, but they need much the same thing as Dick did. So do we all: a cultural reservoir of symbols, images, icons, and narratives into which we can pour our dread, allowing it to be formed and reformed by the image before we reintroject it into ourselves in more contained, less terrifying form. Actually, I put it too passively. We experience the forming and reforming as Maya experiences Shiva, a symbol that acts on her understanding. In fact, the forming and re-forming is an active, unconscious process, in which the cultural symbol is used as the child uses a transitional object, investing it with the power of self and other, creating meaning out of things.

Consider, for example, a fairytale told to a child who is afraid of abandonment. The tale concerns a motherless child who is cared for by wild animals. The fairytale does not say that everything turns out okay, that mothers always return. Instead, it gives narrative form to an inchoate dread, so the child might be able to know, locate, and contain it, ultimately in a narrative form that will be at least slightly different for each who hears it. Bruno Bettelheim made a similar argument in *The Uses of Enchantment* many years ago, and it is still convincing—not just for fairytales but for all narrative forms. They exist so that we may know our dread.[17]

In response one might argue that what counts for the child is not the tale but the teller, the experience of hearing a scary story while sitting in a mother's or father's lap, the terror contained by physical love, not by abstract narrative. Mr. Beaty said it straight out: "Most of us didn't get enough lap time. And we're still angry about it." Trouble is, adults seldom get much lap time, especially in prison.

If we think about culture as Winnicott does, as a transitional object existing somewhere in the realm between self and world, not clearly in one or the other, then the distinction between physical containment (a parent's lap) and cultural containment (narrative form) is not so clear. Inmates and others who have experienced barely enough lap time may be able to use narratives and other cultural forms as though they were a parent's lap, a source of comfort and containment. Form is synesthesia, the experience of one thing in the realm of another. Symbols connect body with the world. If we are lucky, symbols can connect us to other bodies we long for.

Some inmates, and not just inmates, cannot make the symbolic connection. Instead they use their own bodies as containers, embedding their dread in the flesh. Seeking to be shriven of their dread, they inflict it on the bodies of others. For them, the prison must remain the ultimate container, a narrative of concrete and razor wire.

Here we see the limits of depressive form, narrative form. Important as it is, it cannot completely substitute for the "sensory floor," as Ogden calls it, of the autistic-contiguous position. For a person with no experience of being contained in a presymbolic mode, what Mr. Beaty calls "lap time," the richest symbolism in the world will remain unusable. In its place there is only Pa Tuxent and the concrete mama, terms inmates use to refer to the prison. It is why some inmates flourish in prison and fall apart in the uncontaining world.

One might ask why anyone would *want* to use symbols in place of bodies. In some respects, at least, bodies are much more satisfying, the symbol a poor substitute for the real thing, at least when the body is beloved. One answer is that we can have the symbol when we cannot have the body. The ability to symbolize is the ability to control, but only in the realm of imagination. Symbolization requires that we abandon fantasies of narcissistic omnipotence, acknowledging something of our terrible dependence on others.

Another reason we turn to symbols is to protect the body of the beloved. Janine Chasseguet-Smirgel, following Melanie Klein, puts it this way: "Symbol formation derives from the need of the child to protect his object, or parts of the object, from the effects of his attacks."[18] Prisoners are, in my experience, not deficient in love, but they are frequently deficient in finding symbolic substitutes for their rage, in large measure because they cannot give up the object in reality so that they might have it again in the realm of fantasy.

Culture and Containment

To state that the Freudian concept of sublimation remains undeveloped is to say nothing new. It is undeveloped not because the concept is unimportant to Freud and his epigoni, but because Freud was never able to distinguish sublimation from repression in terms of his energetic model.[19] Ricoeur puts it well when he states that the concept of sublimation is both "fundamental and episodic" in Freud's thought. Joel Whitebook argues that sublimation is a "frontier concept."[20]

Whereas a drive stands on the frontier between psyche and soma, sublimation stands on the frontier between psyche and culture. An implication is that successful sublimation depends not just on psyche but on culture. Or as Ricoeur puts it, the very disproportion between the psychological transformations of desire, which are limited, and the vast variety of forms which sublimation can assume, implies that the process cannot be adequately accounted for by "the economics of desire."[21] The success of sublimation will depend on the interaction of psychological potential with cultural resources.

I am making a similar argument about cultural forms, an argument that does not depend on the vagaries of Freud's concept of sublimation. Whether or not people are able to come to terms with their dread, finding cultural forms in which to embody, express, and contain it, depends not only on individual psychological development but on the resources of the culture.

Roy Schafer writes of "storylines," master personal narratives as they might be called, by which people organize their experience, using themes such as imprisonment, rebirth, and odyssey.[22] It is not my argument that our culture is deficient in storylines. Storylines are so basic and abstract that any going society will have a sufficient repertoire. It is my suggestion that our culture lacks sufficiently rich and complex roles (similar to what Schafer calls "self-representations") within storylines. Alasdair MacIntyre makes a similar argument in *After Virtue*. Indeed, it is his theme, and his bête noir.

Roles are the form in which individuals enter and participate in storylines. In the absence of sufficiently rich and differentiated roles, individuals lack the capacity to express their dread in narratives. To be sure, rich roles are not enough. Many inmates could not take advantage of even the richest roles. It is one reason they are prisoners, one of the most structured roles around. For many of us, however, the availability of complex and developed roles will make a difference in how we give form to our dread, and so limit our evil.

An example would be the role of "meaningful victim," whose victimhood does not rob his life of meaning, but on the contrary may enrich it. It is a role we all play, the human role par excellence. Whether we can invest ourselves in it, rather than devote our lives to trying to get someone else to play it, depends in good measure on whether we can see our life, and death, as standing for something meaningful. It also depends on whether one has confidence that the world will not soon forget. Conversely, many informants, and most inmates, see victimhood as merely shaming. As one inmate puts it, "If I don't do evil, then evil will do me. If I weren't evil, I'd be shit." Free informants frequently make similar, albeit more modulated comments, such as "I know it's not supposed to be this way, but all the world really cares about is a winner. If you lose, you're history." Consider what history means here: not remembrance, but obliteration. Taken to its logical conclusion, such a storyline offers only two roles, victim and executioner.

The Risky Business of Playing Evil

Mr. Marcus and his girlfriend found a way to play at the roles of victim and executioner. Because it was play, their "role-playing fantasy," as he calls it, represents a genuine symbolic achievement, the sublimation of dread. Nevertheless, their play lacked sufficient symbolic distance from the act.

From a used-clothing store they concocted fine costumes: slave, innocent virgin, sorcerer, and sorceress. He would climb into her window, cut her clothes off with his blade, and rape her at knife point. She would bind and whip him. Then they would switch costumes. "It just kept going and going. It was evil, man, like there weren't any limits. I didn't know where it would stop."

When did it stop?

"When I got arrested."

Mr. Marcus is mistaken. Nothing about this game was evil. On the contrary, it expresses several virtues—an ability to trust, a deep desire to know another from the inside out (to live inside another's clothes), a desire to satisfy the deep, almost unspeakable, needs of another. But Mr. Marcus was right to be worried. It was risky business.

It was risky because their play with evil was insufficiently abstract. To be sure, their play had the quality of a transitional activity: clothes, roles, props—a world of symbols. But the symbols were too condensed, too physically and dramaturgically embodied, insufficiently abstract. The form was too close to the act. Instead of recapitulating the act in another medium, such as thoughts, words, or pictures, the role-playing drama, as he called it, *was* the act, stopped just short of its completion. He was not playing with evil, or even imitating it. Mr. Marcus was tempting evil, acting as though he could walk right up to the line, daring himself to step over.

It is why Mr. Marcus says that "thinking evil is the same as doing it." Ethically and morally he is mistaken. But he is right to be worried. When the thought is so concrete, its symbols having the quality of Dick's pencil shavings, the thing-in-itself, then it will be experienced as more than thought: as action in another medium.

Exactly why Mr. Marcus became so captivated by role playing is unclear. I believe that he was seeking to restore a sense of vitality and meaning to his life. All he really got was a thrill. Evil cannot restore vitality because it will not submit to the reality that is the natural ground of vitality: the reality that is death and vulnerability as well as life and vitality. You cannot have one without the other. Mine is not a metaphysical claim about some ultimate reality, but a practical one, the reality to which I refer the reality of everyday life . . . and death.

Mr. Marcus was not arrested for rape or assault on his girlfriend. He was arrested for beating a policeman on the head with a hammer. He believes that he was evil to play rape games, and he knows that evil was present when he beat the policeman, who he believed was about to shoot him. But where exactly the evil was located on the night that sent him to prison for sixty years he is not quite sure.

EIGHT *Evil Is No-thing*

Evil is nothing, no-thing. I do not mean in the sense of Augustine, for whom evil is nothing but the absence of good, an interpretation that seems to deny human malevolence—unless it interprets privation as envy. To see evil as privation and loss captures an experience of evil which gets too little attention these days, an experience on the cusp of categorical and precategorical: utter and devastating loss, like the loss of his father that Sam T. experienced, a loss that threatens to empty the world of goodness and life, a loss we never get over.

In his *Confessions* (VI.xvi.26), Augustine says that while longing for his mistress he fell to discussing "the nature of good and evil" with his friends. Evidently it helped. Intimate conversation is the shared creation of a narrative form in which to experience, contain, and re-form his loss.

Evil is nothing because it is no-thing. It is not an entity, not an experience, not a feeling, though it may be all these and more. It is not a definition, even if we desperately want to make it one. We define evil because it scares us, because we do not know where it starts, or stops, so we try to confine it with a definition. We define to confine, to keep evil from becoming a precategorical blur. We define evil so that it is something, rather than no-thing. It is precisely the no-thing quality of evil that is so disturbing. Definitions are the easiest thing in the world. What is tough is to be true to our experience, and to our doubts.

The need for a definition is itself a reflection of precategorical dread, an attempt to give shape and boundaries to an experience that we fear possesses neither. Perhaps this is the most terrifying aspect of evil, its unbounded quality, neither inside nor outside, but both, passing through us, possessing us in ways we hardly know but deeply fear.

Recall how Kierkegaard defines dread as the "presentiment of a something which is nothing." It is what we fear most, nothing, no-thing, total loss. Not just of those who mean the most to us, but the loss of ourselves, the ethical dread that Ricoeur writes of, the loss of the ability and spirit to invest the world with meaning. The loss of the ability to love, to care, to be. Total meaninglessness, total loss . . . nothing. Heart of darkness and the core of evil: that we have lost the pulse of the world, so that to care about anything must be in vain.

It is still not enough, you might reply. Evil cannot be nothing. Better that evil be a demon one hundred feet tall and breathing fire than nothing. How could humans be so scared of nothing? Because the nothing that we fear is really something, the emptiness of our lives, the threat not merely that we shall die but that our lives and deaths will be meaningless, pointless, that we shall be unable to invest our selves in the world. To love evil is to love nothing, says Augustine (*Confessions* II.viii.16). Though one might call this *depravatio* (privation), it is far worse. To love nothing is not to love anything, an ethical and moral catastrophe, the essence of dread.

What if we define evil as a discourse?[1] What if we define it as a discourse about human suffering, malevolence, loss, and the meaning of human life—and death—in the face of all this? This time you might reply that the definition is too much, that the study of evil becomes tantamount to the study of philosophy and religion. How could it be otherwise? The question "What is evil?" represents a particular take on these subjects; it stresses some experiences and problems more than others. But it concerns them all.

You might also reply that to define evil as discourse makes it too philosophical in another sense, about words rather than feelings. There is some truth to this objection, though the real objection would be not to the concept of evil as discourse but of evil as philosophy, the philosophy that Nietzsche defines as the desires of the heart filtered and made abstract by reason. Discourse is more akin to what Augustine was talking about, feeling one's feelings in the company of others so as to construct a shared narrative able to contain and explain them.

Assume that evil stems from the pleasure we obtain in inflicting our doom on others, that it is a species of sadism—a species, because its origin is not in pleasure in hurting per se but pleasure in containing and controlling one's dread in others. It is genuine pleasure, pleasure in the illusion of controlling one's fate or escaping it. Evil is an intense object relationship. It seeks a hot, intense connection of power and control to manage the cold, isolated dread within.

In this way, evil is not just something to be inflicted on others. It is a relationship, a friend. Inmates read excerpts from Milton's *Paradise Lost*, concluding with Satan's first soliloquy. "So farewell Hope, and with Hope farewell Fear, Farewell Remorse: all Good to me is lost; Evil be thou my Good . . ." What did they think these lines mean? They mean, said Mr. Prior, that evil was the only friend Satan had left. Better to sell one's soul to the devil than to have no bidders at all.

When an Explanation Isn't Enough

This book has sought to explain evil. Evil is the attempt to inflict our dread on others. Evil is the presentiment of something which is nothing. Evil is a hot relationship to warm a cold heart. Evil is a discourse on suffering and loss. Above all (or perhaps I should say beneath all), evil is a refusal to submit to the conditions of being human: that the vitality of life is fed by the autistic-contiguous experience that lives just next door to dread—not just the dread of pain, helplessness, and abandonment, as though that were not enough. Autistic-contiguous anxiety is about the way these experiences evoke the fear of losing oneself, falling through the net of the world.

Freud approvingly quotes the dramatist Christian Grabbe, who consoles his dying hero with the reassurance that "we cannot fall out of this world. We are in it once and for all." Such consolation, continues Freud, invokes "a feeling of an indissoluble bond, of being one with the external world as a whole."[2] Ogden makes a similar claim about the autistic-contiguous position. The difference is that Ogden knows how close consolation stands to dread. Under the pressure of pain, hopelessness, and abandonment the indissoluble bond returns as its dark twin, a bond with the All that threatens the integrity of the self, the self melting into the All, the essence of dread. It is against this experience that evil is dedicated, seeking to master dread by mastering the selves of others.

What happens when a cause is no explanation? Even should you accept these explanations, you may find they provide no satisfaction, no relief. In "Survival in Auschwitz," Primo Levi writes of a guard who said "There is no why here." This remark captures the atmosphere of the death camps perfectly, Kafka plus mass murder. Louis Micheels, a psychoanalyst, disagrees. We should not adopt an S.S. decree in a death camp as our own: "There *should* be a why."[3] Perhaps. Or perhaps the trick is to figure out *what* we really want to know, why we want to know it, and if this "why" can ever be satisfied. Maybe *why* isn't really what we want.

What if the most important question about evil is not why people do it? What if the most important question is why the world is as it is in the first place, so that evil exists in it, so that there are people who take pleasure in destruction, people like you and me? Not only does this "why" frequently have nothing to do with cause, but causal knowledge only makes "why?" more difficult to answer. "Cause and effect"—the very term implies some balance in the world. What if there's not?

Henry A. is a member of MENSA, an association of people with high IQs. About evil he is virtually tongue-tied, halting in mid-sentence for what seems like minutes. Finally he says something that seems to ease the flow of words. "Evil is random in effect, and evil intent is quite unrelated to actual harm." He smiles. For a moment he's got it, if a world out of balance is something we ever truly get.

Henry is the young man who was almost blown up in a foreign market, glimpsing his image in a river of blood. Before this he had become friends with a young radical who was involved in other bombings. His friend was abducted on a visit to his mountain village, and Henry never heard from him again.

> My friend, he was a great man. You know the saying "One man's terrorist is another's freedom fighter." Well, Tarik was a freedom fighter. His brother was tortured and killed, half his family had been killed by [the authorities]. I'm sure Tarik is dead too. See, Tarik might

have killed me, it might have been his bomb. Not really, he'd already been abducted, but do you see the point? Good guys can kill you, blow off your legs. While a really malicious bastard might just give you a nasty look. It all depends on the circumstances, on luck. I think the Greeks defined evil as chaos, that's what my dad says. [Henry's father is a professor.]

Randomness kills.

Are such deaths really random? Aren't historical events a cause, the history of oppression of Tarik's people?

"History is for intellectuals," Henry replies. "What does history matter when you're eighteen years old and almost get blown up by some guy who doesn't even give you a thought? And if he did he wouldn't care. You're a bonus, or you're in the way. Either way you're dead meat."

What if Tarik had known you'd be in that market that morning?

"He'd have waited. But see, I'd be basically the same guy even if I didn't know Tarik. So would he. The only difference is that I'd be dead now. And now he's dead. . . ."

Henry plans to become a history professor.

Nietzsche: Claiming Evil as One's Own

A few informants hold a vulgar Nietzschean view of evil: doing evil, at least as society defines it, is essential to a full and meaningful existence. For Matt C., "evil is the rush, the satisfaction that hurting someone brings. I feel alive when I test the boundaries, and violating the physical boundary of someone is the ultimate test." Recall the *Rausch* that Friedlander writes of, the thrill the Nazi desk murderers felt as they neared their taboo goal. For Patricia D., "everyone wants to experience everything. Doing evil is something only the strong and brave can do, so it's special, the forbidden fruit that tastes so good because only a few can taste it."

Many informants, including prisoners, are reluctant, regretful Nietzscheans, agreeing that "evil spelled backward is live." Unlike Matt and Patricia, however, they do not like it very much. Instead of feeling a thrill, they find in the saying a source of enormous regret: that life is the way it is, demanding appropriation, self-assertion, and competition for scarce goods. "I commit evil everyday," says Judith K. "I don't even want to. But how can I live and not hurt others? I'd still be seeing [an old boyfriend] if I wasn't willing to hurt him. I hurt him bad. But if I didn't I'd be so miserable I'd kill myself."

How do you deal with the knowledge that you hurt someone you cared about?

"I pray for forgiveness."

Mark D. expresses a similar idea. "Life's a web. If I pursue my goals, even things I have a right to, like good grades, someone else is not going to make the Dean's List. Maybe they need it more than I do. I hate it, but what can I do?"

What do you do?

"Feel sad sometimes. That the world is such a jungle. And try to be responsible. Not to take more than I deserve."

Many expressed similar feelings. If you don't hurt others, or at least participate in a system that does, you can't survive, you can't even move. "It's not a question of freedom," says Judith. "It's a question of survival, literal survival." One might argue that informants confuse hurting others with evil, that it is not the same, just as aggression is not the same as sadism. Perhaps, but this is one of those confusions we should not be too quick to clarify, lest we miss the deeper point.

Although Judith's stress on survival gives her statement a paranoid-schizoid quality, Judith, like Mark, is speaking from a depressive position, expressing the deepest regret that the world is as it is. That regret is my most encouraging finding. Most informants are reluctant Nietzscheans much of the time. They just have trouble staying there, in what Klein calls the depressive position. Their terror of vulnerability and weakness is too great. (This conclusion about "most" [more than thirty free informants, more than ten inmates] informants stems not from their answers to a particular question, but from my overall impression.)

"Whatever is done from love always occurs beyond good and evil," says Nietzsche.[4] What if we say, in our darker moments, that our lives are also beyond good and evil? That not only is there no plan, no God, and no goal but that there is no "ought" that we can read back onto history, as in "it ought not to have been that way, at least we can know that, even if we can't change it." What if, in other words, the suffering that we call evil just hurts? Because it is.

One answer, Nietzsche's answer, is to love our suffering, so that we can make it our own, control it by becoming it. *Amor fati*, he calls it: love your fate, not just in this life but forever more, so that you wish that were your life to recur eternally nothing would be different. It is Nietzsche's most important teaching, called sometimes the doctrine of affirmation, sometimes that of the superman, and often just life. "Make your suffering great, make it shine, give yourself over to it, so that you might become the power of your suffering" is what Nietzsche might have said were he an informant. What Joseph M. said comes close: "I'm hard on myself, harder than anyone else ever could be. It's the way I make myself strong. One day you will hear my name again."

Theodor Adorno calls Nietzsche's *amor fati* "ignominious adaptation" to one's prison, and he is just right. Reality must be accepted and endured, but why must it be loved? "To redeem the past and to transform every 'It was' into an 'I wanted it thus!'—that alone would be redemption," says Nietzsche. Nietzsche has turned traitor against himself, willing his redemption by denying his desire. "I have harbored no desire. . . . I do not want in the slightest that anything should become other than it is." That too is a lie, one that holds the needy self hostage to its own desire.[5]

The Stockholm Syndrome, as it is called, happens when hostages fall in love with the terrorists who seize them. It is named after a hostage-taking in Stockholm. When it was all over, some hostages and would-be bank robbers emerged, after several days together in the bank vault, engaged to each other. So Nietzsche must love the fate that causes him to suffer so terribly, that he might become his fate and by an act of will alone choose what happens to him by choosing what has already happened. He claims stoic power, identification with fate, as though by becoming his fate he might gain power over it. But no one really does. One is actually "willing" that over which one has no power. It is really bad faith, pretending to power one doesn't possess in order not to feel so weak and hopeless.

How about this simple argument? With all the pain and suffering in the world, there are good reasons not to inflict more than already exists, more than is necessary. Nietzsche would disagree. For the strong, suffering is the anvil on which greatness is formed. "Man is the cruelest animal. Whatever is most evil is his best power and the hardest stone for the highest creator."[6] To reduce pain, to make life as free of pain as possible, is the path that terminates in the last man, whose world is as empty as it is easy. Or so Nietzsche argues.

As though one had a choice as to whether to live a pain-free or painful life, as though the strong suffer because they have chosen the path of pain. As though there are two types of suffering: the "self-chosen torture" of Christians and other last men, as Nietzsche calls them, who deny their own natures; and the higher and finer suffering of a few nobles who embrace their suffering with their natures, not against it. What if these distinctions are a fantasy? What if it is more than fantasy, what if it is bad faith, one more attempt to pretend to control what we all must suffer?

Life is appropriation, self-assertion, and competition for scarce resources. It is suffering and terror. This condition is something to be respected, occasionally embraced, more often regretted, certainly not toyed with. The appropriate attitude is that of native peoples who are said to pray to the soul of the animal they are about to kill—respectful awe at what we must do to survive. The trouble with Nietzsche, as Adorno recognizes, is that he takes these regrettable facts and turns them into ideals, so that he might gain some mastery over his own suffering. It is but a small step from willing one's own suffering to inflicting it on others.

Nietzsche appears to submit, affirming the world in all its sorrow and joy. In fact, he only pretends to submit, seeking in affirmation a type of backhanded mastery. This stance does not make Nietzsche evil. It makes him creative, his desire for mastery sublimated into symbolic form. It does, however, indicate that Nietzsche does not understand evil, writing as though one could experience the fullness of life represented by the autistic-contiguous position while mastering the dread by embracing it.

The psychoanalyst Otto Rank said that the neurotic "refuses the loan (life) in order to escape the payment of the debt (death)."[7] For Nietzsche we would have to change this to read "the superior man embraces his suffering in the hope that he could become its master." The strategy of the superior man is not the same as Rank's "neurotic," but it is not the opposite either. The *uebermensch* and the last man share here something important. Both try to cheat doom.

Nietzsche sent his friend, Paul Rée, to propose Nietzsche's marriage to Lou Salomé, only to discover that Rée and Salomé were lovers. Suffering terribly, Nietzsche wrote one of his closest friends that he is lost if he cannot "discover the alchemical trick of turning this—muck into gold. Here I have the most beautiful chance to prove that for me 'all experiences are useful, all days holy and all people divine'!!"[8] Nietzsche cannot suffer "mere" loss, gut-wrenching, heart-rending loss, the loss that makes our bones ache. He must make his suffering great.

There is a curious photo, taken evidently at Nietzsche's insistence not long before his proposal to Salomé, which shows Nietzsche and Rée pulling a little cart. In the cart Salomé brandishes a whip, but does not look very enthusiastic about it.[9] Recall what Nietzsche has the old woman say to Zarathustra. "Are you going to a woman? Do not forget your whip?" The cruelty and suffering that Nietzsche would choose for himself is so labile that he would inflict it on another in a minute, identifications so complex that who is really whipping whom becomes almost impossible to sort out.

This, at least, is the theory of sadomasochism, discussed in Chapters 2 and 3. People overcome their suffering by becoming it, like riding the tiger. Or rather, becoming the wild beast. I may suffer, says the sadist, but I shall not suffer passively, or alone. One way or another there will be others to share it with me. I'll make sure of that! Above all, sadomasochism is about fusion, and confusion: identification with the victim's suffering so profound that the victim must be destroyed in order to protect the sadist's separate existence.

Wonder at the intimacy of the sadistic relationship, a contact across boundaries which can only be called autistic-contiguous, like a vampire sucking blood. "Sad-ism" an esteemed colleague calls it, the sadness of one's separate fate dealt with by sticking (it) to another: sad i stic to you. Identification with the victim puts it too weakly; becoming the victim is more like it.

But only for a moment. To stick to the other who now contains one's doom is hardly a solution. Shared doom is still doom. A violent separation is necessary, sadism a scratch across the autistic-contiguous surface to separate the parties, damaging the other so as to know who really has the power, who really contains the doom, and who's in charge. The other's suffering is evidence of that, the position of victimizer the only position in which one's separateness can be known.

Sadism is a blemish on the mirror, distinguishing the image from the reflecting surface. The tattoo serves a similar purpose, defining the body in pain. In the sadistic act, the sadist seals his dread in the body of the victim, the victim become coffin, the victim's suffering the sadist's testament to his will to survive his pain. Why sadism is properly called sadomasochism is apparent; identification with the victim is central to the act, without which it would be pointless.[10]

In *On the Genealogy of Morals*, Nietzsche writes of the pleasure of being allowed to vent one's power freely on "one who is powerless, the voluptuous pleasure of doing evil for the pleasure of doing it, the enjoyment of violation."[11] Nietzsche is writing not just about whipping but about cutting the flesh from a debtor, piece by piece, ounce by ounce.

Nietzsche isn't just saying cruelty is part of life, a desire that must be felt before it can truly be mastered—or rather, lived with. He idealizes cruelty as the primordial pleasure of the truly strong. "How naively, how innocently their thirst for cruelty manifested itself."[12] Unlike the weak, who are cruel and sadistic out of resentment, the strong man slaps his slave, whips his debtor, and is done with it. Why? So that resentment doesn't build up in him, so that he can get it out—a nice, neat hydraulic exchange. "I'm angry; I hurt you in my strength that is abundant with life. I do this purifying deed so that the anger does not build up in me, like wine souring to vinegar. Then I go on to bigger and better things." Nietzsche does not say it just this way, but it is what he means.

In "Carnivals of Atrocity: Foucault, Nietzsche, Cruelty," James Miller concludes that both Foucault and Nietzsche "seem to be saying: Better externalized than internalized cruelty. It is healthier, more 'active,' rather than weak and 'reactive.' "[13] This is precisely my point. Sadism ("externalized cruelty") is an active attempt to control suffering in others rather than experience it in oneself. As Matt says, "When I hurt I just have to do something, you know, get it out, turn the tables. I can't just sit there." It is for this same reason that most informants forgive—to restore their potency, their power. It is human, all too human, but it is hardly the act of a noble man. It is the act of one who cannot contain and manage his terror of passivity in the face of the suffering that comes to us all. "I forgive to get back on top" is how Patricia puts it.

Miller continues that Nietzsche and Foucault would also hold that "better internalized cruelty than no cruelty at all." Internalized cruelty expresses "the continuing chaos of instinctive violence—the kind of chaos needed to give birth to 'a dancing star.' "[14] The statement is not all wrong, but it raises more questions than it answers, as Miller appreciates. First, the hydraulic model is too simple, an almost pure expression of sadomasochism: any pain that I do not inflict on others I must impose on myself.

Second, the issue is not whether cruelty is external or internal, but the *form* of the cruelty, its shape and structure—in particular, its degree of artistic and creative sublimation. Is a work about great cruelty, such as "The Flaying of the Satyr Marsyas by Apollo," a Hellenistic sculpture much copied in the Renaissance, externalized or internalized cruelty? In appreciating it, in experiencing a *frisson* of sadistic pleasure, have we externalized or internalized our cruelty? Miller suggests that these are instances of externalization, but is this so clear?[15] Is this hydraulic distinction really adequate? Would not a distinction such as sublimated versus nonsublimated cruelty come closer to the mark? The distinction between internal and external cruelty is itself so bound to sadomasochistic thinking that it is not very useful, reproducing the problem it is trying to solve: the deep identity between sadism and masochism. Certainly it does not account for the cycles of projection and introjection which define the way we use culture to contain evil.

You take Nietzsche too literally, a devotee might reply. His celebration of cruelty, like that of Foucault, is irony, dramatizing the fact that repressing cruelty and anger doesn't make it disappear. It just gets driven underground, expressing itself in more perverse and subtle ways. Nietzsche's apparent idealization of cruelty is actually melodramatic criticism of the subtle savagery of resentment, and Christian morality generally.

Correct as far as it goes, this defense fails to grasp the sadistic consequences of masochistic defenses against suffering. Imposing one's pain on another so as to control it there is the flip side of embracing one's suffering, making it grand and glorious so as to master it. "Flip side," because one flips over to become the other so readily, the reason analysts call it sadomasochism. Nietzsche's superior man is not so different from the suffering martyr after all. In the face of suffering both are unable to just be. Both must transform it into something great.

It is not accidental but central to the logic of sadomasochism that the idealization of one's own suffering becomes the idealization of inflicting suffering on others. Who is whipping whom in that curious photograph anyway? It is no accident because the logic is the same, to control suffering at any cost. Only the locus changes, from self to other and back again. To change the locus becomes—indeed is—evidence of control. If I can't make my suffering yours for a little while, how could I know I really control it? Here is the logic of sadomasochism in a nutshell. Seen from this perspective, the problem of sadomasochism is not peripheral to Nietzsche's work, the implication of a few melodramatic statements. Rather, it is central.

Nietzsche intensifies suffering to make it meaningful, an intensification so sadomasochistically infused that it cannot be contained, spilling over into the idealization of cruelty which fails to recognize the denial of separation this involves. Janine Chasseguet-Smirgel gets it right when she says that the telos of sadomasochism isn't pleasure or pain but the destruction of reality: the reality of difference, of individuality, of fate.[16] What reality would Nietzsche destroy?

In *The Gay Science*, Nietzsche asks, "How can we make things beautiful, attractive and desirable for us when they are not?" He has asked the question before, how to turn muck into gold. The answer is that we cannot. Muck happens. Nietzsche goes on to add, "And I rather think in themselves they never are." But this is no caveat, only a mark of the hard work involved in transformation. His answer is that we should become "the poets of our life": don't look too closely, look through tinted glass, abstract from the details.[17] Whatever this strategy is, it is not the creative containment of dread, but more like its denial.

This is not really Nietzsche, you might reply. Nietzsche idealizes the strength of the truly autonomous man who bears his suffering with noble grace. Exactly the problem! To idealize suffering requires that we reject the last man in each of us, who would give anything to slip into the herd if only he could, because life is so very painful. The pleasure in slapping some particularly distasteful specimen of the last man isn't simple and clean at all, a burst of righteous indignation which purifies us of resentment. It is about rejecting the last man in each of us. Or rather, rejecting him while becoming him, as we slap the last man in ourselves. The psychology is not obvious, but it is not all that complicated either.

Even when one considers that Nietzsche is writing about cruelty, not practicing it, it is interesting to consider whether *Thus Spoke Zarathustra* or Michel Foucault's *Discipline and Punish* are externalizations or internalizations of cruelty—interesting, because the very question shows how simplistic this formulation is. They are both, and neither. Above all they are texts, a fact that does not solve the problem either. In these texts, sadism is the scalpel. The knife that makes the *coupure*, the cut that literary theorists write about that separates signifier from signified, S/s. So that the letter will suffer in the author's stead. Intending to ennoble his suffering, Nietzsche would in the end escape it, alienating it in the text. The reluctant Nietzscheans come closer to the mark. Accept not merely that you will suffer but that you will necessarily inflict suffering on others in the course of living your life. And regret it.

Evil and Tragedy

What if we think about art a little differently? Not as a way to turn muck into gold but as a way to give form to our dread. It is what the ancient Greeks who Nietzsche celebrates in *The Birth of Tragedy* did, confronting the sheer terror of existence, their dread, with nothing but beauty, the beauty of their art and the graceful beauty of their lives. Perhaps Greek tragedy has more to teach us about evil, a perspective on evil which looks not to its sources but to its sheer mesmerizing presence.

Seen as a world historical force—not in terms of its sources but of its role in the human drama—evil has the quality of tragedy. The term "tragedy" is intended not to make evil beautiful but to capture the waste and loss that it represents. Greek tragedy is not about noble tragic heroes with a single fatal flaw. That is a Renaissance invention. *Hamartia*, the term frequently rendered as tragic flaw, means nothing more, and nothing less, than a big mistake, one with consequences disproportionate to the error. If, for example, Henry had known that his friend Tarik planned to blow up a market somewhere, but forgot, went shopping, and got himself killed, that forgetting would be *hamartia*.

It is false to contrast the tragic with the pathetic. The tragic *is* pathetic. The Greek term *pathos*, which may be translated as "suffering," connotes a sense of victimhood, a loss of control and agency.[18] It is this that so many interpreters of tragedy seek to escape. They seek, in other words, to escape man's doom. They are not evil, but the logic is the same: better, they say, that Oedipus be brought down by his own anger (or his own unconscious desires) than that terrible things should just happen to him. Better anything than that. This view, and much evil, arises from the mistaken belief that one can transform one's pathos into tragedy via action, even if that means inflicting doom on oneself and others, the only alternative to suffering it.

Tragedy is about waste: wasted potential, wasted youth, wasted lives, wasted possibilities. Tragedy is about the disproportion between cause and effect, how small failures lead to great disasters. Included here is the frequent disproportion between the smallness of the evildoer and the magnitude of the evil deed, though one should not call an evildoer such as Eichmann a small failure. As a human being he was a terrible failure, but there is nonetheless a terrifying disproportion between the ludicrous fool Eichmann and the suffering upon millions that he inflicted. Arendt is trying to get at precisely this idea with the "banality of evil," the awesome incongruity between man and deed that characterizes so much, but not all, evil.

The awesome incongruity works both ways. Seemingly evil men do not always commit evil deeds. Consider Mr. Roberts. Big, profane, abusive, he rarely neglects a chance to intimidate. Here is his Rorschach test.

That one there, that looks like a watermelon, you know with all that pink stuff inside, just waiting to explode when you smash it. . . . Man, I remember smashing this guy's head, his blood went everywhere, just like that picture there, a bloody pulp. It was great, except he got my clothes dirty. So I had to smash him for that too. . . . That one there, that looks like some woman who has just been cut open, you can see her tits there, and her guts spilling out of her [he smiles], and that one . . . looks like a cat, only someone shot a .357 magnum up its ass. Man, I love it.

Mr. Roberts is not a nice man. He has, however, done far less evil than most inmates. All his crimes have been against property, and all are small-scale and stupid, like stealing equipment from construction sites and trying to sell it back to the contractors. Not surprisingly, he got caught, and went out and did it again. In prison he has never been written up for assault, and only once for disobeying an order. (Prisoners commit lots of crimes for which they are never caught, but Mr. Roberts has no record of violent crime, even as a juvenile. His assaults, if true, evidently were bar fights.)

Most of the group members are quiet, gentlemanly (or gentlewomanly), respectful, contrite, and thoughtful. Among them they have killed fifteen people, including relatives and children, and raped several more. Their decency is not just an act. They really are decent gentlemen and women ninety-nine percent of the time. It is the other one percent that is hell. It does not add up: the evildoer seems so inadequate to his deed, the deed so heinous we must call it evil, even if we have to work like crazy to create an evil commensurable to its horror.

Mr. Roberts's insane rage is no joke, no bluff. I am careful not to push him into a corner. His reality testing, is, as they say, flawed. But somehow when he is overstressed he turns his violence toward himself, dooming himself to years in prison. One psychologist says that such men are actually a good bet for rehabilitation. Mr. Roberts acts out his aggression as well as his victimhood, and the split that divides him from himself is in some ways less profound than in the well-behaved murderer.

The explanation helps, but it does not satisfy. Psychology helps to explain the *origins* of evil, but it does very little to help us come to terms with it. The reality is that there is a disconnect between the selves we see and the evil that men do. Perhaps Mr. Roberts flaunts his evil as an alternative to doing it. In any case there is a disproportion between the man and the deed. Decent people do terrible things, and feel enormous regret. I have met them in prison. Mr. Roberts is neither decent nor regretful, yet manages to avoid doing evil. Go figure.

Alice Miller is a psychoanalyst who argues that childhood abuse is the one true source of mental illness—not the actual abuse, which may be emotional, physical, or sexual, but the inability to give it voice. Unacknowledged abuse gives rise to a destructive hatred, the impulse to fuse with the object one would destroy. No single theory has been more helpful to me in trying to make sense of the experience of inmates, all of whom were abused as children.

But Miller does not understand evil. Courage and honesty, she says, are useless as moral categories. Whether a person grows up honest depends on how much truth his parents could bear. Whether an individual is courageous depends on how much terror he had to endure as a child, and for how long.[19] Nietzsche would agree, arguing that "the complete unaccountability of man for his actions and his nature is the bitterest draught the man of knowledge has to swallow. . . . he may no longer praise, no longer censure, for it is absurd to praise and censure nature and necessity." [20]

Assume for a moment that Miller (and Nietzsche) are correct, that virtues such as courage, honesty, and decency are reflections of how our parents treated us, our biographical inheritance. This fact does not make these virtues morally irrelevant. It just makes the world unfair, out of moral balance. We do not earn our virtues, our morality. We may not be able to practice virtue even should we want to. Or perhaps it is the wanting that is passed from generation to generation. It does not matter. The fact that humans are not masters of their courage, honesty, and decency makes these virtues no less important or real. On the contrary, it makes these virtues more important, precisely because they are so fragile. These virtues are the only alternatives to evil: the courage and honesty to face it, and the decency to do something about it, living with one's doom. Miller has detected another great imbalance in the world, and another tragic irony. That is all. Is it not enough?

Tragedy is about generations, about how the sins of the fathers are visited upon the sons. And not just fathers, or sons. Michael T.'s accent suggests that he just arrived from the Deep South. In reality, he grew up in the distant suburbs of a mid-Atlantic state, his father the vice-president of a local department store. Michael is white; since fourth grade his best friend was black. Michael's parents are divorced, and his friend's family just about raised him.

When Michael is asked to define evil, he looks at the ceiling and sighs. "It's in the roots, you know. It's in my roots." Silent for what seems like forever, he acts as if he has just told me all there is to know about evil. Perhaps he has.

Mike's family is racist, no more than most in his area of the state, perhaps, but no less either. "For Grandma it's just a word, you know, 'nigger.' But for my uncle, man, he hates everyone: blacks, college students, you name it. My dad, he didn't like my spending all my time with George's family, but what could he do? He could barely keep it together after Mom left. I thought I'd overcome it, I really did. Man, I used to dream I was black. But now . . . now I'm just as racist as any of them."

Michael hasn't inherited just his family's racism. He has inherited its sadism, telling stories of uncles who locked him in the basement when he was little, whispering stories through the door about "Hatchet Harry." Years later, Michael hid in his dark house waiting for his father to come home from work, leaping out when his dad walked in the front door. Falling to the floor, his dad put his attaché case over his head, begging for his life before figuring out the attack was a joke. Mike seems pleased and embarrassed at his father's terror.

Michael hates his family, but he loves and needs them too, and so in his loneliness and alienation at a big university he turns to racism, his family's legacy, bonding with his family, while at the same time hating them and himself, a type of self-torture, masochism. It is the one thing his family seems really good at, torturing one another.

Michael believes that the evil of his family's racism has infected him despite his best effort. Racism is Michael's comfort as well as a burden, connecting him with them, but through values he despises, as though his roots were poisoned. But they are still roots. Recall the television series "Roots," about the way slavery displaced so many black Americans from their roots. Though he never mentioned the television show, I think Michael intends the irony. He is a young man trapped in history, a history he wants into as much as he wants out. That is tragedy.

Waste, the disproportion of man and deed, the weight of generations, and events that carry the actors with them like sticks in a river—these are hallmarks of evil too little discussed these days. In an earlier era, in which people were more accustomed to seeing evil as something that happens to humans, these dimensions of evil would not have seemed so odd. Consider what it means to live in a world in which not the Holocaust but the Lisbon earthquake is the paradigm of evil. It means that evil is not so much what man does as what he suffers, a view that Nietzsche, who died in 1900, understands, even as he flails against it.

If evil is a discourse, then what needs to be said about it will change over the course of history. Today there is a horror of passivity and powerlessness. Hardly new, it eclipses every other consideration regarding evil for many informants, who can more readily identify with Eichmann than with his victims: to be an evildoer is bad, to be the powerless victim of evil is simply unimaginable. Partly because many informants have no sense of history, they see being a victim as being lost to history forever. Better to be a vampire, more dead than alive, than to be powerless. If evil is a discourse, then the most important things to say are what are not being said: that evil is at least as much about what happens to us as what we do, and that we do what happens to us, so that it will seem as if we are doing it.

Evil Happens

The Holocaust was done. It did not just happen. Most people, though, even in Nazi Germany, and certainly today the world over, did not make the Holocaust. Yet it also happened to millions, the victims above all, and to all who live in its shadow. It happened in our world, we were born under the horizon of its history. If we do not come to terms with this aspect of evil, that it is something that happens to us, then we shall be forever secretly identifying with its persecutors instead of with its victims. We shall choose vampires over mere humanity, at least in our dreams. To live, to be human, is above all to be a victim: a victim of circumstances, a victim of fate. A victim of life.

For all its concern with disproportion, tragedy is ultimately about balance. There is a type of rough justice in the world, what the Greeks called *dike*. It is not human justice, "a wrong was done, and the wrong-doer is punished." It is more akin to natural law. For every action there is an equal and opposite reaction. If you live by the sword you will die by the sword, or someone you love will, even if quite innocent. Guilt and innocence are not at issue for tragic justice, action and reaction are. *Dike* is a fundamental balance in the universe, one that has very little to do with human justice but nonetheless dimly reflects a cosmic pattern whose outlines can be humanly glimpsed.

So say Aeschylus and Sophocles. Euripides is different, at least in his later works, the balance achieved with the help of the implausible *deus ex machina*, the outcome so ironic and incredible as to be unconvincing. As though Euripides said, "You want balance, I'll show you balance, everything worked out so perfectly you'll know it is a lie, even if you won't be able to say it. And just in case you don't say it, I'll make you wish it were a lie, giving you endings in which the noble and good die painful and pointless deaths, while fools and corrupt gods live forever in bliss and harmony."

Evil is about balance. It is our version of *dike*. Not a reverse version, just *dike*. *Dike* was never nice, never really about justice. Just balance. We want there to be evil in the world so that there can be some explanation or force adequate to the horror of our experience, our existence, our suffering. Because the world hurts and disappoints us so very much, we create the concept of evil in order to give dignity and meaning to our suffering, creating a cause for our suffering worthy of our pain.

One informant keeps referring to my study of good and evil.

No, I'm just studying evil, not good and evil.

"Yes, that's what I mean, your study of good and evil," the informant continues. He never got it. Or perhaps he did, their separation just too painful to acknowledge, a world without recompense. I take my stand with Adrian Leverkuehn. Of course one can study evil, as long as one is willing to accept that the only consolation prize is to give the truth its motto: "Thus it is." "Alas, it is not to be."

No wonder Arendt's thesis of the banality of evil is so threatening. It takes the proportion out of evil, making its cause unequal to its effect, making light of our suffering, revealing our tormentor to be not Satan but a ridiculous fool. As one of Robert Jay Lifton's informants puts it in *The Nazi Doctors*, "It is *demonic* that they were not *demonic*." Many evildoers are not fools as Eichmann was, but many are victims themselves—of fate, neglect, and all the rest. We want there to be evil so bad, for the same reason that the paranoid needs fiendishly clever enemies: to give dignity and meaning to his suffering. "Good is not the opposite of evil," says Mr. Leotine. "Indifference is." Better to be pursued by a vast conspiracy than for no one to care. Evil is a paranoid projection, the creation of a malevolent source to make human suffering meaningful. Which has nothing to do with whether evil exists.

Evil is created and maintained in discourse about it. It is a discourse worth continuing, for without evil the world becomes meaningless and inexplicable, out of balance. To create balance is a good reason to posit evil, and an equally good reason to be suspicious of the concept: that we need and want it too much.

In "The Unconscious Hums, 'Destroy!'" Lance Morrow writes about Thomas Hamilton, an "isolated, unwholesome smudge of a life," who took a semiautomatic weapon into an elementary school in Dunblane, Scotland, and murdered more than a dozen children before killing himself. After devaluing the murderer, Morrow has a problem: how could such a miserable wretch cause so much suffering? His answer is "evil": "Tiny cause, titanic effect—this is the social equivalent of splitting the atom. When Nonentity massacres Innocence, an especially horrible fission occurs."[21] Had Morrow put himself in the shoes of the Nonentity just a moment, he would not have needed the category of evil so desperately. It arose from his worry that "sometimes a crime as disturbing as Dunblane calls forth a line of universalizing nonsense," the nonsense of universal guilt, which would somehow exonerate the killer. It did not. Recognizing not universal guilt but universal humanity, one that understands that even the evillest one shares something with us all, is the proper perspective. This view has nothing to do with letting the evildoer off the hook, as I argue below in reference to another terrible crime.

The problem of imbalance does not disappear no matter how we formulate the issue. It is, dare one say it, built into the structure of reality. But we make the imbalance worse when we both trivialize and demonize the evildoer, idealizing the victim's "spotless innocence and hope," while rejecting any attempt at understanding as "a line of universalizing nonsense." Otherwise expressed, a little evil goes a long ways, and there is more than enough to go around.

Breaking the Circle of Evil

"In a message to [citizens] that he is tough on violent crime, [the Governor] said yesterday he will deny parole for practically all prisoners serving life sentences."[22] So reads a 1995 newspaper article.

Mr. Redeux is in a single cell, about eight by three feet. There is a black-and-white TV on the end of his bunk, a metal shelf covered with a mattress the shape of a mummy, no dangerous corners. A couple of sword-and-sorcery board games are on the floor, and a pack of cigarettes on the cardboard box that is his nightstand. We talk through the bars.

Yesterday morning, Mr. Redeux went to what he thought was a yearly review of his progress, only to find himself out of the prison's treatment program in which he had participated for fifteen years. He is serving a life sentence, and because he has no possibility of parole the program no longer has a place for him. Regarded as a suicide risk, he was taken from the hearing room, manacled, stripped, placed in various holding cells, and finally removed to a new cell in administrative segregation. The staff does not want him to commit suicide, but everything they require seems designed to increase his despair: manacles, no goodbys, no clothes, no contact with other human beings.

"My greatest fear," he had said earlier, "is dying alone." In all likelihood he will, an embittered old man with no friends and no family, serving out his life term. In a sense we all die alone, but he already has, if by dying alone we mean living in such isolation and alienation that one dies inside a little bit every day. Today is more than a little bit.

He sits on the end of his bed, next to his TV, which has the sound turned off. The flickering black-and-white image it casts on his chest makes it look as though he is seated behind a fluoroscope, his shattered insides pulsing to some beat the rest of the world no longer hears. "I wish they had executed me twenty years ago," he says. "I wish they had just killed me and gotten it over with. Now they're just torturing me."

The guard who pushes his food through the bars wears rubber gloves. Some of the men in "ad seg" wear handcuffs when they take a shower. Mr. Redeux wonders if that is his fate. His mind is still reeling. "It's like I've been run over by a truck, and I'm still in shock." Could this be what his victims felt, the young girl he shot in the head, the middle-aged man whom he hogtied and executed during a robbery? The man had a young daughter.

I say that I appreciate his contribution to the group, that he took some chances, that he tried to be honest. As I say these things a mental image of his victims hovering over his cell comes to me, like the dead children who hover over the House of Atreus in Aeschylus' *Oresteia*, setting the stage for all that follows. Mr. Redeux seems to become almost transparent, fading into the flickering glow of his TV.

Here is the problem of evil stripped to its bare essentials, the victimizer as victim. How is it possible to know both at the same time, to appreciate both? Mr. Redeux committed terrible, terrible crimes, about as evil as it gets. At the same time he is a victim—of parents who beat, molested, and abandoned him, and now of a system that cares, it seems, only that he not kill himself on its watch.

How can we know both: that the man who has done unspeakable evil is a desperately failed human being who needs nothing so much as some caring human contact? Can we flicker back and forth between these two incompatible realities fast enough to blur them just a little, enough so that we preserve the afterimage of one as we confront the other, for a second knowing both: the victimizer as victim, one who can find no alternative to evil to speak how bad he feels.

Asked why he murdered, Mr. Redeux had said at the time of his arrest that he wanted "to make someone feel as bad as I did." Recall the modal image of evil, a young man going down into the scary basement, saying afterward, "I felt evil." Mr. Redeux says, "I felt bad." In both cases it is precategorical dread speaking—feeling bad, being bad, and doing bad not well distinguished. Only Mr. Redeux could not live with the ambiguity, becoming bad—evil—in order to be free of feeling so damn bad, if only for a moment. A moment that cost him a lifetime of hell. And his victims each a lifetime.

He deserves it, you might say. An evildoer has forfeited his right to human compassion. Many on the outside say this. The prison staff, at least the professional staff, tends to respond differently, distinguishing between the sadistic psychopath with no regrets and no remorse and the remainder of the prison population. Only the former is evil, and he is rare. One psychiatrist who has seen thousands of inmates said he has met only a half dozen truly evil men, psychopaths without an ounce of conscience or remorse. It is an answer not so different from Marvin L.'s; he defined evil in such radical and extreme terms that he could think of no instances. A version of this answer is to distinguish between killers who seem relatively normal and those like Mr. Redeux who are neither normal nor psychopaths. It is only the apparently normal ones who are evil. Like Milgram, like Zimbardo, the staff does not want to find most prisoners evil.

We should be skeptical about these distinctions, just as we should be skeptical about the distinction between doing evil and being evil, another popular division of the problem. Recall the fork, leading image of evil among prisoners, connoting all the ways we might cleave evil. Making distinctions is a favorite activity among all informants, and it is not a bad one: big evils versus little evils, evils of the heart versus evils of the mind, an evil life versus an explosive act of evil. Many of these divisions reflect genuine puzzlement over the nature of evil, particularly the disproportion between man and deed, cause and effect (a moment's uncontrolled rage leads to a lifetime of suffering and regret). Recall Henry's puzzlement over how a good man like Tarik might kill you, a bad man not give you a second thought.

Call these metaphysical mysteries. Or call them simply the way of the world, their mystery stemming from nothing more than our misguided insistence on balance. In either case they will not be solved by parsing evil. It is more useful to distinguish "now" from "then": Mr. Redeux was evil once; he no longer appears to be evil. The trouble is, this distinction neglects the presence of evil over time. Even if Mr. Redeux is no longer evil, his evil act echoes into the future, a future in which no just or adequate recompense is possible for the past.

For this reason Mr. Redeux's continued imprisonment is just—not just from the perspective of justice but from the perspective of evil. We would trivialize the gravity of evil, its terrible destructive weight on the future, if evildoers were not punished in a way that reflects the gravity of their crime unfolded in time. "Life sides with life" says one prison staffer, reflecting the belief that our concern must ultimately be for the prisoner, the one who lives. He is not all wrong, as long as we remember that we side with life by taking evil seriously. Evil is a crime against life, and against that fundamental reality of life which is death. Evil is an attempt to impose the doom that each of us must face alone (though not necessarily all alone) upon another.

Mr. Redeux's continued imprisonment is just, a recognition of the gravity of evil. Mr. Redeux is also a suffering human who deserves our compassion. More than this, he deserves—as Socrates says about justice —not to be made a less excellent (*arete*) human being than he already is. If justice is a man's excellence, says Socrates, then it is hardly right that he use his excellence to make others less excellent, less human, less just (*Republic* 335b-e). The state is about to do just that, subjecting one man's vulnerable humanity to further insult and injury.

That is just what he did to his victims, you reply. Absolutely, which is why we should not do it to him. The problem of evil is at its core a problem of circles and cycles, what the East calls karma—not just the evil that runs through generations of family members but the evil that runs through our institutions, making ourselves and our children less excellent human beings than we might be. The first and best thing we can do about evil is to break the cycle. Humane treatment—and punishment—of evildoers is a good place to start. It is also the single most important reason that we should try to understand the sources of evil, so that we might find better ways to break the cycle and make the world a little less evil.

Recall Walsh's article about the bombing of the Federal Building in Oklahoma City, the article with which this book began: "The search for explanations is the search only for excuses. Evil itself cannot be explained, and the attempt to do so is both a denial of its reality and a cheapening of the suffering of its victims." My explanation has been psychological, but it might just as well have been sociological or political. The point for Walsh, and for so many, is that explanation is irrelevant to evil. Evil is not about why. Evil just is. We fail to respect evil when we mix judgment with explanation.

Walsh is far from wrong. But he is wrong in the unqualified way he states it. Evil is not the same thing as its explanation, but it is crucial not to make them separate categories, lest we stand mute and fascinated before evil. It is no accident that the snake transfixing its prey with a gaze, extorting fascination and wonder, is a leading image of evil. We should be careful lest we reproduce this image with our thought.

To call evil a tragedy is both revealing and misleading. The ways in which it is revealing were explored above. It is misleading insofar as it suggests there is nothing to be done about it. For Greek tragedy, everything is nature. Social injustice is a category virtually unknown to classical thought, completely absent in Greek tragedy. Individuals may be crazy with rage, as Heracles and Medea were in their eponymous tragedies, or noble in their suffering, as Prometheus and Hippolytus were in theirs. How they got that way does not matter. They are types, forces of nature embodied in persons.

If, however, we want to lessen the amount of evil in the world, then how people get to be the way they are matters. To explain evil is not the whole story, but to abandon explanation is to reify evil, making evil a more-than-human character, like a Greek god. Evil is not that either. Evil is human, all too human, the poisoned gift we pass among ourselves, and down the generations.

NINE   *Scales of Evil*

I told a graduate student I was taking a semester off to study evil. "Do you have a sabbatical to hell?" he asked with a devilish grin. But one does not have to go to hell to study evil. Evil is everywhere, and everyday, the thesis of this book. In this sense, at least, evil is banal.

What is the connection between everyday evil and large-scale historical evil, the radical evil that people so often refer to these days, such as the slaughters of the Holocaust, Cambodia, and Rwanda, to mention just a few infamies? Is there a connection? Though asking people about it is not the only way to proceed, it is an approach too little employed. People are often smarter than they, and we, know. Several questions (numbers 7, 10, 11) are about scale: how can a cutting remark and cutting off someone's head both be evil? The informant who referred to dropping his books while walking across the crowded campus gave the answer. When he retrieved them he glanced up and saw the look of "cold joy" in the eyes of another student about to step on his hand. "He had an excuse to hurt me and he did. I could never call him on it. That's evil."

If you call that evil, how can you also call a man like Eichmann evil, one who orchestrated the murder of millions?

"If Eichmann couldn't have murdered millions he'd have stepped on their hands. And if the guy who stepped on my hand could have, he'd have stepped on a million hands. Right then, anyway. Maybe not when he got home and thought about it. But right then, for that moment, there was no difference between him and that guy you keep referring to, what was his name . . . yeah, Eichmann."

What we call evil is the impulse to malevolent destruction. Deep down in the mind (or maybe not even so deep down) there is no difference between the desire to squash someone's hand and the desire to murder millions. Desires like this, primitive, destructive, malicious desires are by their very nature unmodulated. The hand-stepper does not say, "I don't really want to do a lot of evil, or hurt someone very much, just a little bit. . . ." He might say it to himself, but he does not feel it. What he feels —for just a moment—is total, unremitting malicious destructiveness. It is the maliciousness that Klein writes about, and the Bible too, the wickedness of man's heart from his youth (Genesis 8.21). If you do not believe it, catch the look in the eye of the next person who does you harm in one of the thousand socially acceptable ways we hurt others, such as cruel remarks that pass as witticisms.

This is not to say that we are all potential Eichmanns. Most can, and all should, contain the evil impulse within symbolic frames. Nasty jokes are one such frame. Not the presence of the malicious destructive impulse, but the capacity to contain it, marks the difference between humans, cultures, and good and evil. Most of Milgram's informants shocked the victim, but a number did not. That is important too, and worthy of explanation.

Large-scale evil, the terrible destruction of innocents which humans are capable of, is explained by the conjunction of human maliciousness with the failure of cultural containment, as well as by the ability of society to draw upon and use people deficient in symbolic resources of their own but not so crazy as to be unable to use the culture's scapegoats as their own.

About Josef Mengele, "Dr. Auschwitz," one of Robert Jay Lifton's informants, said that "in ordinary times he could have been a slightly sadistic German professor."[1] In ordinary times, Mengele would still have been Mengele, sadistic as hell, eager to evacuate his doom into others, more eager than many, more willing than most. But the culture of Weimar Germany would have channeled the expression of that sadism into the victimization of students, colleagues, wives, and children in all the ordinary ways. Colleagues and students might have noticed his "dead eyes," but only the most sensitive would have gotten the creeps, and some of them would have dismissed their feeling as a touch of the flu.

What turned Mengele into "Dr. Auschwitz" was the conjunction of his uncontained dread with a culture that was no longer able to contain it either, a culture regressed to providing directions for the obliteration of scapegoats under the ideology of a medical procedure. But why in Germany? When then? Perhaps these questions are unanswerable. If they are answerable, they are the topic not of disciplines, but of human knowledge.

In *The Politics of Cultural Despair*, Fritz Stern writes that Germans were haunted by dread and despair from the last half of the nineteenth century. Coming on top of this cultural tradition, if that is what it was, World War I resulted in an atmosphere "oppressive with doom, almost eschatological," dominated by death and "last things," as another historian has put it.[2] Add Daniel Goldhagen's account of the long history of German demonological anti-Semitism, and the Holocaust becomes conceivable. Not necessary, just conceivable, and only if we know and appreciate the malevolence of the human heart, its eagerness to externalize its doom, stealing the life of others as simulacrum of its own.

"Radical evil" is everyday evil. Kant helps us to understand it insofar as he calls attention to the way morality may become corrupted by desire (and, we should add, dread), so that the good becomes whatever mitigates dread, including the destruction of scapegoats. "This evil is *radical*, because it corrupts the ground of all [moral] maxims" and so cannot be corrected by others, every moral maxim being corrupted to serve desire.[3]

But Kant is not very helpful insofar as he fails to appreciate the destructiveness and maliciousness at the heart of evil. In fact, he excludes them from possibility from the beginning: man cannot be destructively malignant because that would make him diabolical, "a thoroughly evil will, . . . and thus the subject would be made a *devilish* being. Neither of these designations is applicable to man."[4]

Kant seems to argue that it is impossible for anyone to repudiate the moral law totally. "The law, rather, forces itself upon him irresistibly by virtue of his moral predisposition."[5] What's missing is a vision of human complexity, of human parts, of moments of pure destructiveness alternating with moments of universalizing love. Kant's is a strange type of splitting into willful desire and desiring will, with nothing left over for ambivalence.

How to know and live with this malicious destructiveness in oneself, one's friends, one's lovers, and the world around? In the end that is the problem of evil brought close to home. It is a complex question, concerned not just with why people are like this, but with why we live in a world with people like this, people like you and me and those we love and care about. The question goes beyond psychology, sociology, and history to metaphysics and theology, the realms of "why in the world" questions.

The answer, if that it can be called, is to find stories to tell about evil, sharing them with others. This book is one such story, but there are millions. Not all stories are in words, but the best use symbols instead of bodies, while not forgetting the body that lives beneath and beyond the symbol.

Some people are better than others in making up such stories, which, *ceteris paribus*, means they will live a little more easily with evil and be a little less likely to do it. But much is glossed, and lost, in a Latin phrase. While some people are better than others at telling stories, the real variable (at least as far as large-scale evil is concerned) is the culture, and whether it supplies individuals the narrative and symbolic resources to make sense of their doom. There is much to worry about in our culture, which is far more likely to provide imitations of doom than stories about it.

APPENDIX 1

Asking about Evil

Asking about a concept is asking about a concept. It is not asking about the thing-in-itself. In Chapter 8, evil is defined as a discourse about the meaning of suffering, malevolence, and loss. The questions asked about evil are not "What are suffering and malevolence, and are they truly evil?" Put like this, they could be answered only by a god. Nor is the question properly framed as "Does the term 'evil' apply to this or that in the world?"—a question assuming the picture theory of language discredited by Wittgenstein. Evil is a relational concept, but the relationships are all internal, about the relationships between concept and experience: the internal experience of those who use the term and the interpersonal experience of those who speak the term with others.

Chapter 1 argues that one understands the concept "evil" not just by what people say about it but by what they do not, particularly in their discrepancies between definitions and examples. It is the discrepancy that is key, the example as important as the definition—more important, as it tells us how the concept is used in practice, in life.

"Evil is just a name," says Sally L. "Once I took a writing class. I was trying to write about a dead friend, but I couldn't. The teacher understood. 'Sometimes it's better not to freeze things into words,' he said. 'Sometimes words substitute for real experiences.' Sometimes, when it really counts, words don't mean anything. They're just words."

Sam T. holds a similar view about words, but his reasoning is different.

For Sam, abstractions like evil are so big and grand as to be virtually meaningless. "I know the Holocaust is evil, but I just can't feel it like I feel my dad's death. I hope this doesn't make me evil too." What is most real for Sam is immediate experience, like his father's death when he was sixteen. It is from intensely personal experiences like these that Sam, and the rest of us, make terms like "evil" meaningful by giving them feelingful content.

"Evil is like a net," Sam continues in a quieter and more thoughtful vein. "We use it to catch the world, but it's always just our net." Our concepts are woven with our lives, and we cast them into the world. If we're lucky, if they do not have too many holes, we catch something, a historical experience such as the Holocaust made meaningful only because we can connect it with our own holocausts. Some, like Christopher Lasch, argue this personalization must trivialize the historical Holocaust.[1] My study reveals quite the opposite. Only if one can invest the historical Holocaust with the terror and tragedy of one's life can it become a meaningful moral category.

Consider Picasso's famous painting *Guernica*, which represents the carnage caused by Franco's bombing of the Spanish village. While some have argued that Picasso was inspired by photographs of the bombed village, Mary Gedo argues that he was inspired by quite another event, a devastating earthquake that Picasso had experienced when he was three, an earthquake that accompanied the birth of his baby sister. Believing that he was the "earthshaker," Picasso took the earthquake to be a mark of his rage at her birth, a rage that had been rekindled in his complex domestic life in the months before he painted *Guernica*.[2]

Assume for the sake of argument that this interpretation is correct. Would one argue that it renders Picasso's painting any less significant, any less adequate and faithful to the horrors of the bombing? On the contrary, *Guernica* becomes an even richer work, gaining its power from the way it combines the private and public. Into the village that was Guernica (a village that was already a symbol), Picasso poured his own earthshaking Guernica, creating the painting *Guernica*. This is how symbols become meaningful, including the symbols that are powerful words like "evil": we fill them with ourselves. Only the artist takes the process a step further, transforming the conjunction of personal and social into a new cultural symbol. Or rather, only the artist does so publicly. But we all do it. If, that is, we are to feel what we know and say and do.

For Wittgenstein, meaning equals use. The meaning of a term means no more, and no less, than how it is used in language. If you want to know the meaning of "evil" investigate how people use the term. There are as many meanings of "evil" as there are language games in which it is used.[3] If Sam is right, Wittgenstein is wrong, or at least he is not telling the whole story, not even the most important part.

Even within a particular language game, people only appear to be using the term in the same way. Or rather, it is difficult, though not impossible, to know whether they are. Certainly we cannot tell just by observing the *use* of terms. We must know the experiences of the speakers. Consider the statement "The Holocaust was evil." Sam would agree, imagining the Holocaust as an instance of terrible loss, terrible waste, and terrible bitterness. For Sam, the experience of his father's death doesn't give the term "evil" just its nimbus, but its core. Everything he knows and feels about evil is affected by this experience of sudden, total, and irredeemable loss.

For Rachel B., a Jew, the evil of the Holocaust evokes a loss of control, the same powerlessness she felt as a child when her friends conspired to ignore her—an experience so humiliating because she knew she would do anything to belong. It is the same loss of control she fears every day, and every night in her nightmares about robots with red eyes.

Sam and Rachel are using the same terms, and an observer might think that they are talking about the same thing when each says that "the Holocaust was evil." But they are not, though both would agree that evil involves a loss of control. For Sam, however, the loss of control, while galling, is secondary. The primary loss is of his beloved father, and all the opportunities to share they will never have. For Rachel the loss of control is primary, a threat to her existence as a person, power the only alternative to a living death, her own.

There is no private language, it is said. If language is private, then it is not a language. True enough, but there are dialects of cloistered meaning, inflections of a term so private the language user may be unaware of their influence—not just because she has forgotten the experiences that give the term its guts, but because she is resonating with the emotions of those who have talked about evil, or whatever the term, with her. We do not learn just words and concepts. We learn emotions to go with them, though that statement could be misleading, suggesting the emotion and the term are two. They are one, and the combinations are endless.

Judith K. is shocked at the things she finds herself saying about evil, defining it as looking possessed, a wild gleam in the eyes. Not until the interview is almost over does she remember where her definition comes from, from the Christian elementary school she attended. Until she remembers, we may say that the term "evil" spoke her, its use defined by emotional experiences she had forgotten. Now she has a chance to speak "evil" herself, to make it her own term.

Wittgenstein says that the world of language is divorced from the world of fact. Both exist, but there is no connection, language no picture of the facts, just its own reality. I am concerned about how language gets divorced from mental fact, from inner reality, from feeling. Because it is feelings that give the words their power. It is feelings that account for much of the discrepancy between example and definition. In focusing on this discrepancy, one is allowing a gulf to emerge, a gulf defined by the alienation of language from experience. It is the most interesting place to be if one is to understand a term.

Wittgenstein is a grammatical behaviorist. Your language use is all we can know of your inner world, the distance between inner world and language the same distance as that between language and the world of fact: infinity. "If I listened to the words of my mouth, I might say that someone else was speaking out of my mouth," Wittgenstein says.[4] He says this not just because he is dissociated from his feelings but because for him the inner world cannot be known and said—not in any way that adds anything to the meaning of the words.

Wittgenstein impoverishes words. They are more real and powerful than he knew. Words are the form of feeling, the building blocks of narrative form. Each individual holds a concept like evil in a unique way —which does not mean that there is no common experience, no common meaning. All have experienced terrible loss and a terrible desire to hurt, dominate, and control. (Though older informants did not always believe it, younger informants' experiences were as rich as those of older informants, though perhaps less varied.) It is out of these experiences that we build a common world, using terms like "evil" as a bridge between us. Wittgenstein is about this bridge, not about the experience.

This book is concerned with our islands of experienced meaning which we connect by bridges of words. But words are also a bridge within ourselves, between our terms and our experiences. Some people do this bridge-building better than others. Those whose use of the term "evil" resonates more deeply with feeling are better able to connect the outer world with inner experience from the inside out. They are able to connect their own private holocausts with the Holocaust, to invest the latter with personal meaning. They hold their concepts more deeply, although their views are not necessarily more likely to accord with a more universalistic and admirable view of evil. Sam and Rachel both make a deep connection to evil. The way Rachel does it is troublesome, but because her understanding comes from within there is much to work with. The next step for her would to be experience her holocaust in light of the Holocaust, so that the magnitude and scope of the latter could set limits on her own experience, highlighting the differences, not just the similarities. That is what moral education is about, but it can work only on felt experience, not on empty terms. The potential for moral development is best grounded in some feeling about evil, even if this feeling is troublesome.

My language of evil may not be a picture of the external world, but it is a picture of my inner world, one that can be compared and contrasted with yours, but only if neither of us assumes that our pictures are either identical or incommensurable. To know that we differ I have to enter your world. That takes lots of work, but I don't have to crawl into your head. The process is more like solving an algebraic equation: X is your concept of evil, revealed not just by what you say about it but by the values it takes on in your examples and stories. In an older and richer philosophical tradition this approach used to be called *verstehen*, imaginative understanding.

Nothing is more contrary to my experience than the idea that only a member of the same race, religion, and sex can truly know the experiences of another informant, that others "just don't get it." And can't. This view tacitly assumes an identity of experience among some, an unbridgeable gulf among others. Neither assumption is true. I struggled to understand people whose views of evil were very different from my own. Yet many of my informants seemed to feel I did; at least they said so. The fundamental barriers seemed not so much racial or sexual or ethnic as personal. I could not always find in my experiences of evil something to resonate with theirs, perhaps because these informants did not resonate deeply enough. More likely this failure—or limit—was in me, or rather within the relationship of understanding.

Understanding is an act of terrible and terrifying intimacy. Informants use the term "evil" with a variety and richness that would only be devalued by saying "Catholics believe this, Asians that"—not because such generalizations are meaningless, but because they are misleading, capturing what is often a fugitive similarity, ignoring subtle differences. Individuals are as different as the groups to which they belong. Listening for another's reality is the best path to understanding.

APPENDIX 2

Informants and Questions

Free Informants

Among free informants, 20 men and 20 women were interviewed, ranging in age from 18 to 80 years. Ten prison staff members were also interviewed; about the aspects of evil discussed here their answers were so similar to those of the other free informants that their responses were totaled.

Age Distribution   18–25: 24; 26–50: 18; 51–80: 8. With only a couple of exceptions the youngest informants were undergraduates, a few more from science and engineering than from liberal arts.

Ethnicity   10 Asian; 1 Indian (Eastern); 3 black; 36 white. Asian informants (20 percent) were asked why they thought so many Asians responded; none had a clue. All were self-identified Asians, four from ethnically mixed marriages.

Religion   14 Catholic; 3 Lutheran; 16 other Protestant denominations; 1 Jehovah's Witness; 1 Hindu; 2 Buddhist; 4 Evangelical Christian; 6 Jewish; 2 atheist/agnostic; 1 "born again pagan."

Like ethnicity, religion is not easily identified. Some informants were raised Catholic but no longer consider themselves Catholic; several had become strongly anti-Catholic. I categorized them as Catholic, however, because of the influence of Catholicism on their beliefs.

Names of informants, as well as those they refer to (unless these are public figures), have been changed, as have most identifiers, such as college major. Age and sex have not been changed. Changed identifiers reflect the spirit of the original: a professor of physics may have become a chemistry professor, not a professor of art history. None is a composite. All quotes are verbatim.

All signed a standard consent form approved by the graduate school of my university.

Because of the small number of informants, I made no attempt to conclude that "blacks believe this, whites that." This book is about the vicissitudes of a concept, not about those who hold it.

Diversity and Self-Selection If "diversity" means that a category of individuals is represented in proportion to its frequency in the general population, the informants are not a diverse group. On the other hand, each individual is actually quite infrequent in the population, appearing only once. The informants were a group of slightly quirky but by no means strange or alienated individuals, many deeply attuned to the contemporary culture. Ideas similar to theirs can be found in the popular literature to which many refer, such as *The Screwtape Letters*, by C. S. Lewis, *People of the Lie: The Hope for Healing Human Evil*, by M. Scott Peck, and *Interview with the Vampire*, by Anne Rice.

Not truly diverse, they were nonetheless a remarkably heterogeneous group, with ethnic and family roots all over the globe. Over two-thirds were born out of state, a number abroad. "Cosmopolitan" is perhaps the best term to describe them.

Informants were self-selected: those who took the trouble to call, make an appointment, show up, and be interviewed about evil. In this regard they were perhaps more troubled than average about evil, else they would not have come to talk about the topic, frequently to struggle with it. "Troubled," it should be noted, is not a clinical category but a philosophical one, a compliment not a diagnosis.

One might, however, at least speculate that free citizens who responded were more troubled about the intensity of their precategorical experiences of evil than those who did not respond. If so, then the truly average citizen, if there is such a thing, is perhaps not so likely to experience evil as an overwhelming, boundary-shattering experience of dread. This possibility does not, however, challenge the main point: the difference between inmates and average citizens regarding the ability to symbolize evil and its influence on violent acting-out. Instead, the contrast between inmates and free citizens is heightened, as the free citizens are possibly more concerned and in tune with experiences of dread than those who did not volunteer.

I spent over two hours with most informants. Only two struck me as "disturbed" in the clinical sense. Many struck me as more sensitive and reflective than the average citizen, though that difference is hard to determine.

Quantity into Quality   Unless otherwise specified, these terms when applied to informants have the following meaning:

> *Almost all* = 45 or more free informants, 12 or more inmates.
> *Most* = 30 or more free informants, 10 or more inmates.
> *Many* = 20 or more free informants, 7 or more inmates.
> *Some* = 12 or more free informants, 5 or more inmates.
> *Few* = 5 or more free informants, 3 or more inmates.
> *Very few* = 4 or fewer free informants, 2 or fewer inmates.
> The categories *all* and *none* are also employed.

When the response of both free informants and inmates falls within the same category, only one category will be given, as in "many hold that . . ." When there is a difference in categories, the response will be summarized as "many free informants, but only a few inmates hold that. . . ."

About many questions the response totals of free citizens and inmates were similar. The differences were in the reasoning and the tone. These differences in tone and logic are important differences (perhaps the most important) that numbers alone cannot capture. The numbers aim to give a feel for how a fairly large group of people responded. What is as interesting, and at least as important, is the tone of the informants' response, and this is not always adequately represented by numbers. It is often better represented by quotations from the informants.

Interview Strategy Each informant was asked if he or she would like to make an opening statement. A number did, and several took almost an hour! At the end of the interview I put down my notepad, asking if the informant wanted to chat a bit in an informal way. Sometimes this invitation opened new doors, but generally not, perhaps because the entire interview was conducted in as relaxed and conversational way as possible. I interrupted frequently, along the lines of "Let me see if I get what you're saying. I think you are saying. . . . Is that right? Or maybe I've got it wrong." Only then did I enter a statement in my notes.

I scribbled throughout the interview, always reserving at least an hour after the interview to organize my notes thematically. For each hour spent interviewing, two were spent organizing my notes. I did not use a tape recorder. Among the questions were ones asking informants what evil they had done or wished to do. A tape recorder would have made the interview resemble a police interrogation.

Several of the retirees were interviewed in their homes, one in the factory he still owned. Prison staff members were interviewed in an administrative office at the prison. The rest were interviewed in my office. It is not especially cozy, but it has a rug, large windows, and some plants. On the table opposite the informant were photos of my wife and grandchildren, the intended communication something like "Evil's a scary topic, but my office is a safe place to discuss it, and I'm a safe person to discuss it with." Many informants took long pauses, evidently a sign of thoughtfulness, as well as the fact that they were comfortable about being uncomfortable with the topic.

My interview strategy was twofold. The first was to listen for the image, the pause, the caesura. I tried to feel what was going on in the interview as well as to think about it. I tried to imagine what role I was playing in the informant's experience of the interview, what evil I might be representing. "Working the transference" it is called in psychoanalysis. I also tried to be aware of my own feelings toward the informant. Did he or she make me uncomfortable? Sad? Angry? Why? "Working the countertransference" it is called.

The second interview strategy was that of respectful confrontation, in which I challenged what informants said, but in a way that respected the experiences, recognizing their authority over their uses of the concept "evil." Although it might seem that these two strategies would not fit together very well, more often than not they seemed to mesh. Each interview was different, of course, and so was the balance between the strategies. A long interview is a journey, and I frequently had the experience that after a couple of hours each of us arrived somewhere neither of us expected.

The free informants were overall a young group. Several older informants were skeptical about the others: "What could such young people know about evil?" In fact, younger informants were at least as insightful, albeit in a different way. Referring frequently to childhood experiences and insights, the young seemed to see human experience more directly, less colored by hope and cynicism. Most will lose this immaculate perception shortly, a lucky few to regain it when they are old. Only then it will not be naive wonder but a mature and sadder insight. It takes a long time to recover what the Zen master calls beginner's mind.

The Prisoners

The prison inmates ranged in age from 19 to 48. Five were women (the largely male prison contains a small women's facility). A total of 18 inmates were members overall. Several others attended for only one or two sessions and are not included in the numbers. Dropouts, expulsions from the program, and one release reduced the group to such an extent that several new members were recruited. Of the original group of 13, 7 remained after a year. There were always more on the waiting list than could be accommodated.

Each was paid twenty dollars, the equivalent of a month's wages. (Inmates cannot have cash; the money was credited to their accounts in the prison store.) In addition, coffee, donuts, and cookies were provided at each session. In prison these are substantial rewards. For some the biggest reward seemed to be the chance to participate in a coed group. The inmates made a substantial commitment, two hours per week for a year. Many came early and stayed late. So did I, the unofficial group often running over the two hours.

Notices of the group "Popular Concepts of Evil" were posted on the tiers (cellblocks), the standard means of communication. The only peculiarity of the announcement was the following paragraph: "Dr. Alford does not believe that inmates are more, or less, evil than anyone else. He does, however, believe they have a unique perspective. Dr. Alford is particularly interested in hearing what inmates say among themselves, even if it is not always nice or proper. . . . Inmates with an immoral or moral perspective are welcome." The staff suggested the phrasing, so that mine would not be mistaken for a seminar in religious or moral indoctrination.

Interested inmates wrote letters to a prison administrator, stating their interest and giving the reasons. The administrator and I reviewed the letters and together chose the participants. All participating inmates were required to be eligible for the prison's treatment program. This meant, in effect, that they were regarded as needful of, and able to benefit from, psychological treatment, but not crazy or psychopathic. It also meant that the crimes for which they were charged were more bizarre than those of an average group of inmates.

The prison administrators had a veto over any inmate participant, but it was never exercised. Administrators were concerned that the group be racially balanced, so that several black inmates were actively recruited for the group.

Though the prison has a treatment program, it is not a so-called country club prison but a maximum-security institution housing some of the most violent and predatory offenders in the state. It is physically intimidating. One day room has a concrete floor with two picnic tables with benches bolted to it and a television high up on the wall. In general the prison seems to be well run and orderly. Inmates seem not to suffer physical abuse from guards, and generally seem to feel safe from other inmates.

Like the free informants, inmates signed a standard consent form, one approved by the state Department of Corrections. The only difference was a caveat regarding confidentiality, and another about benefits.

Confidentiality: All information collected in the study is confidential, and my name will not be identified at any time to persons outside the [prison]. The researcher has an obligation to report any information that might involve a threat to an inmate or the [prison]. However, what I say in the group will not be disclosed to other treatment staff or administrative staff by Dr. Alford.

No one, inmate or staff, ever asked me to violate this clause. I never did, but on one or two occasions I was tempted. There was, however, a related problem of which I was unaware until several months had passed, although inmates were quite aware: should an inmate implicate himself in a crime for which he has not been charged, he could still be prosecuted for it. Most participants committed crimes of passion. Several were re-peat offenders, however, and on one or two occasions awareness of legal exposure may have inhibited discussion, at least of details.

> *Benefits:* No decision regarding my status in the [prison], including participation in [special programs], will be affected by my participation in the research.

The work with prisoners was conducted in a group because one can learn more (or at least differently) about a concept such as evil by seeing how the concept emerges in group discussion. Because a term such as "evil" is a social construct, its use will be influenced by the society of the group.

I was also concerned that prisoners might tell me what they thought they should and that I would not be able to tell the difference. Always a problem, the detection of artifice (not just lies, but the framing of a response in terms of what the questioner is presumed to want to hear) is more difficult across cultures, and prison is a unique culture. The society of inmates was a useful check, helping to keep one another honest. "Don't con the doc, man. You can fool him, but you can't fool an old-timer like me." The old-timers were not always right. Sometimes just their cynicism was talking. But it was a useful check.

Though a long interview with an individual informant may take on an intimate quality, it takes a long time to build up trust with prisoners. After six months I was just beginning to gain their trust, and they mine. Only after several months did I cease wearing the "administratively re-quired" little siren on my belt when I was alone with them. Not the group format itself, but the length of time I was able to work with the inmates—over a year—was the major gain of this approach.

As member, staff member, and consultant for the A. K. Rice Institute for the study of group psychology, associated with the Tavistock School in England, I have done much of my work with groups. The prisoners' group was not run as a study group, in which the group process is analyzed as it unfolds, though I paid attention to process for my own research purposes. Instead, specific questions about evil were posed to the prisoners, the same questions posed to free informants.

Who is "holding" or representing the evil in this group right now? At least several times a session I asked myself that question, probably the most important question from a group-process perspective. Frequently it was the man who murdered his parents, the primal crime. Sometimes it was me. Understanding group process was important, but not for its own sake, and not to educate the prisoners about it. It was important for a better understanding of what the prisoners might be feeling, or fantasizing, but not saying. Group therapy may not be more effective than individual therapy, but I have little doubt that I learned far more about prisoners and evil in a group than I would have in individual interviews.

Kevin McCamant, a prison psychologist, was my associate in the prison component of the research project. He was assigned by the prison to work with me, and I was given the choice of whether or not to include him in the group. It was not an easy decision. Although Dr. McCamant had a therapeutic relationship with only one inmate in the group, he was a member of a prison staff that had influence on important decisions over prisoners' lives. Though he did not make decisions regarding most of the group members, he carried with him the aura of prison authority. And though the consent form states that neither their participation nor anything they say will affect their status in the program or their release, clearly such an influence is a possibility that could not be erased from inmates' minds. In this regard, Dr. McCamant's participation posed a problem.

On the other hand, he was familiar with prison culture and folklore as well as with the circumstances of inmates' lives. The prison is known as a "hot" institution, meaning there is lots of gossip and lots of relationships to gossip about. That culture infiltrates the group. A prisoner who had a run-in with another and was written up, as it is called, may see the world as evil in a way he would not a couple of weeks later. It helped me to know. Not only is the concept of evil held in different ways by different people, but it changes as informants' lives change. The temporal transformation of fundamental concepts like evil is an important and little-studied phenomenon.

Frequently Dr. McCamant would run the group for an extended period while I watched and listened, a process that allowed me to see things in a new light and catch up with my notes. Most important, we became a team, and it was in the hour before group, and the hour after, that we spent talking about it that I began to put the experience together. Without him this would have been a different, and lesser, work.

Sometimes (about one-fifth of the meetings) Dr. McCamant was unavailable, and I met with the group alone. There was no apparent difference in how the group members talked or acted during the sessions Dr. McCamant was absent, and the prisoners knew all too well that I had no say over their fates. Several times he ran the group in my absence, and he reported no difference.

Though my access to inmates' records was limited, Dr. McCamant's was not. Frequently he would check something for me, particularly whether an inmate's statement about his crime fit the written record. In almost every case I was able to compare what an inmate said about his or her crime and background with the written record.

Crimes were freely discussed, for an inmate's true crime story is part of his or her identity in prison. At first such stories were fascinating. Later it seemed more fruitful to steer the group away from another recitation of the gruesome facts and toward a more general discussion of evil, quite the opposite problem faced with free informants, who often wanted to discuss evil in the abstract.

As the group developed, the inmates who remained tended to be ones who had murdered or raped a relative or loved one. At one point 9 of 13 members fell into this category. Such crimes made a difference in how they saw evil. These were men or women whose deadly thoughts had become acts for one horrible moment, acts for which they are still paying and in many cases grieving. Two inmates were imprisoned for relatively minor, nonviolent offenses. Ironically, they looked to be the toughest, meanest men. Decent, likable, and in many ways humane people do terrible, terrible things. After all my research on evil, this still boggles the mind.

Age Distribution   18–25: 6; 26–35: 7; 36–50: 5.

Sex   13 men, 5 women.

Ethnicity   10 black, 8 white.

Religion   The varieties of religious experience among inmates defy my attempt at categorization, largely because of the influence of the black Muslims within prison. Inmates entering as Christians frequently leave as Muslims (and not just black inmates), though it is hard to tell how many remain Muslims, or how deeply the conversion settles. Suffice to say that most inmates grew up in nominally Protestant homes. One was Jewish; several came from Catholic backgrounds, and two from mixed marriages in which one parent was Jewish. One was agnostic, two were atheists.

Two had college degrees, one an advanced degree. Many had some college experience. One or two could not read the consent form. Most seemed to be above average in intelligence; the few IQ scores reviewed support this inference.

The names of all prisoners have been changed, but not their sex, race, or age. For several, the details of the original crime have been altered, but not the offense. Murder remains murder. Several of the offenses that brought the inmates to prison were so bizarre and notorious that any long-time newspaper reader or TV viewer would be able to identify the inmate if some details were not changed.

My plan with the inmates was to go through a couple of items on the questionnaire every session. Eventually we did, but we covered much more besides. On those topics in which a count was needed (How many think that . . . ?) we went around the room, one inmate at a time.

*The Written Questionnaire (administered to all
informants, inmate and free)*

[Note: the written questionnaire is misleading if taken as a reflection of how the interviews were conducted. Though almost all questions were asked of each informant, much was discussed that is not included on the questionnaire. Many of the questions functioned as "probe" questions, eliciting a wide range of individual responses, many of which were followed up at length. The purposes of the questionnaire were to generate probe questions and to ensure comparability among responses—that all informants would have responded to at least these questions, among others. Informants did not read the questionnaire; every question was asked verbally.]

Before presenting the questions, I read an introductory statement: "The purpose of this research project is to understand how different people view evil. Some think it's a concept that's a bit dated, others that it's still very important. I think different people mean different things when they talk about evil, but since they are using the same term they don't always know it. These are some of the things I want to find out." The questions:

1. Does evil exist? How do you know?
2. What's your definition of evil?
3. Why do you think there is evil in the world? Has there always been? Will there always be? Where does it come from?
4. Have you ever experienced evil in your own life? How? Tell me in as much detail as you can. [Sometimes I postponed this question if the informant did not seemed warmed up.]
5. Are some *people* evil?
6. Is it evil to follow orders that hurt innocents? There was a famous study about obedience. [The Milgram experiment is briefly verbally summarized.] Were the so-called teachers doing evil?
7. Is evil always big, like rape, murder, assault? Can there be "little evils," like a cutting remark? Or is all evil the same?
   —How can we call things at such different ends of the scale of suffering "evil"? Isn't one word doing too much work?
8. Have you ever done evil? Tell me in as much detail as you can. [Sometimes I postponed this question until later in the interview.]
9. Is it evil to think evil?
10. Maybe we make a mistake when we call something like hurting another person evil. Maybe evil's not about that. Maybe evil is about a bad feeling, a creepy experience. Is that true? Have you experienced evil like this?
11. Consider two examples. A "good German" [I said "quote good German unquote"] during World War Two works hard at his desk, helping to keep the trains running on time, making sure there are always enough boxcars available to transport Jews to the concentration camps. The officer knows what happens at the camps. He doesn't like to think about it though. He just likes to do his job well.
    —Another German officer leads a platoon that rounds up Jews

and shoots them in the neck. He has shot his share of Jews, mostly to set a good example to his men. Is either of these men evil? Is one more evil than another?

—What about a third officer, drafted into this murderous platoon. He uses every excuse he can to avoid the shooting, hates it, it makes him sick to his stomach, gives him ulcers, and nightmares. But when his commander says shoot, or you go to the Russian front, he shoots? Is he evil? As evil?

12. How does your religion help you understand evil? Does your family help you deal with evil? What did they teach you about it?

13. People often seem embarrassed to talk about evil. You're not, you're here. But why do you think this is? Do you talk about evil with your friends? Your teachers? Others?

14. There's an old saying, "evil spelled backward is live." What do you think it means? Is it true?

15. What is the best or most powerful story you have ever read about evil? The best book? The best movie?

16. In Milton's *Paradise Lost*, Satan says he would rather rule in hell than serve in heaven. Does this make any sense to you? Could evil be about disobedience?

17. What is the single most important thing about evil?

18. Let me tell you about the Faust legend [I did: a simplified, contemporary version]. Would you sell your soul? For what? Could it be worth it? What would this mean if you didn't believe in the devil?

19. Can animals be evil? Are they?

20. Is one sex more evil than the other?

21. Any questions for me?

With subjects who seemed particularly religious, a question about theodicy was also asked: "If God is all good and all powerful, why do innocents suffer? Is it evil that they suffer?"

Notes

Chapter 1. "I Felt Evil"

1. It is called Plato's doctrine of anamnesis; or recollection. Plato, *Phaedo* 73–76; *Meno* 82b–85e. I assume nothing about the soul but only that people preach too much and listen too little.

2. Paul Ricoeur, *The Symbolism of Evil*, trans. Emerson Buchanan (Boston: Beacon Press, 1969). Elaine Pagels, *The Gnostic Gospels* (New York: Random House, 1979), pp. 143–46.

3. "Simplicity is the key to effective scientific inquiry," says Stanley Milgram in *Obedience to Authority: An Experimental View* (New York: Harper and Row, 1974), p. 13. If one wants to know what people think about evil, ask them.

4. David Walsh, "No Excuses," *Washington Post*, May 5, 1995: A21. Walsh is a professor of political science.

5. Thomas H. Ogden, *The Primitive Edge of Experience* (Northvale, N.J.: Jason Aronson, 1989), pp. 47–82.

6. Otto Rank, *Will Therapy and Truth and Reality*, 1 vol. ed. (New York: Knopf, 1945), p. 130. Ernest Becker, *The Denial of Death* (New York: Free Press, 1973). Becker applies his theory to evil in *The Structure of Evil* (New York: Free Press, 1968) and *Escape from Evil* (New York: Free Press, 1975).

7. Ogden, *The Primitive Edge of Experience*, p. 75.

8. Alasdair MacIntyre, *After Virtue* (Notre Dame, Ind.: University of Notre Dame Press, 1981).

9. Richard Cohen, "War Criminals like Us," *Washington Post Magazine*, September 22, 1996: 6.

10. "Evil's Back," *New York Times Magazine*, June 4, 1995. The article by Ron Rosenbaum is serious, the cover is not.

11. Karl Popper, *The Open Society and Its Enemies*, 5th ed. rev. (Princeton: Princeton University Press, 1966), 1: 157–68. Judith N. Shklar, "The Liberalism of Fear," in *Liberalism and the Moral Life*, ed. Nancy Rosenblum (Cambridge: Harvard University Press, 1989), p. 29.

12. Anthony Storr, *Human Destructiveness* (New York: Grove Weidenfeld, 1991).

13. Martin Southwold, "Buddhism and Evil," in *The Anthropology of Evil*, ed. David Parkin (Cambridge, Mass.: Basil Blackwell, 1985), 128–41. J. W. Boyd, *Satan and Mara: Christian and Buddhist Symbols of Evil* (Leiden: E. J. Brill, 1975).

14. Southwold, "Buddhism and Evil," p. 132.

15. Peter Winch, a philosopher deeply influenced by Ludwig Wittgenstein, makes this argument in "Understanding a Primitive Society," *American Philosophical Quarterly* 1 (1964): 307–24.

16. Immanuel Kant, *Religion within the Limits of Reason Alone*, trans. Theodore H. Greene and Hoyt Hudson (New York: Harper and Row, 1960), p. 32.

Chapter 2. Evil Is Pleasure in Hurting and Lack of Remorse

1. J. Reid Meloy, *The Psychopathic Mind: Origins, Dynamics, and Treatment* (Northvale, N.J.: Jason Aronson, 1988), p. 71. More on this follows in the next chapter.

2. M. Scott Peck, *People of the Lie: The Hope for Healing Human Evil* (New York: Simon and Schuster, 1983), pp. 120–30.

3. Reinhold Niebuhr, *The Nature and Destiny of Man*, on Kant, quoted in Lionel Trilling, *The Liberal Imagination* (New York: Harcourt Brace Jovanovich, 1979), p. 259. In Chapters 4 and 9, I argue that Kant's radical evil is not radical enough, excluding in advance even the possibility of human malevolence. "A *malignant reason* as it were (a thoroughly evil will), comprises too much . . ." Kant, *Religion within the Limits of Reason Alone*, p. 30.

4. *Journal of Social Issues* 51 (Fall, 1995). In different experimental runs the level of compliance varied, depending primarily on the proximity of the subject to the victim. Milgram, *Obedience to Authority*, Table 2, p. 35.

5. Arnold Cooper and Michael Sacks, "Sadism and Masochism in Character Disorder and Resistance," *Journal of the American Psychoanalytic Association* 39 (1991): 218, referring to Maleson, who argues that much sadomasochism appears to lack a sexual component, as no sexual fantasy is involved. Sydney Pulver and Salman Akhtar, "Sadomasochism in the Perversions," *Journal of the American Psychoanalytic Association* 39 (1991): 751–52.

6. William Grossman, "Pain, Aggression, Fantasy, and Concepts of Sadomasochism," *Psychoanalytic Quarterly* 60 (1991): 47–48. John MacGregor, "Identification with the Victim," *Psychoanalytic Quarterly* 60 (1991): 52–72.

7. Sigmund Freud, *Beyond the Pleasure Principle*, in *The Standard Edition of the Complete Psychological Works of Sigmund Freud*, ed. J. Strachey (London: Hogarth Press, 1953–1974), 18: 24–43.

8. Philip Meyer, "If Hitler Asked You to Electrocute a Stranger, Would You? Probably," in *Down to Earth Sociology*, ed. James M. Henslin (New York: Free Press, 1993), pp. 165–71.

9. Craig Haney, Curtis Banks, and Philip Zimbardo, "Interpersonal Dynamics in a Simulated Prison," *International Journal of Criminology and Penology* 1 (1973): 90.

10. Ibid.

11. Norbert Elias, *The Civilizing Process*, trans. Edmund Jephcott (Oxford: Blackwell, 1994) [2 vols. in 1]. Elias argues that civilization is not about people becoming better, nicer, or more decent. Becoming civilized is about shifting powerful and disturbing emotions and experiences, such as sadism and violence, from the public to the private sphere. There they are not lessened or mitigated, but contained and stored up behind the scenes, in military barracks, police stations, and prisons, ready to be called upon in times of unrest and

exerting a continuous threat to those who would challenge the regime. "A continuous, uniform pressure is exerted on individual life by the physical violence stored behind the scenes of everyday life, a pressure totally familiar and hardly perceived" (p. 450).

It is this that explains the apparent paradox that the modern state, in which day-to-day violence has disappeared from large areas of life (but not from all; the "inner cities," as they are called, remind us of that), is capable of unleashing massive violence on a scale unprecedented in history. It is not just a matter of new technologies but of the capacity of the state to "store" its violence and rationally channel it. Michel Foucault has made a similar argument in his works.

12. Daniel Jonah Goldhagen, *Hitler's Willing Executioners: Ordinary Germans and the Holocaust* (New York: Knopf, 1996), p. 339.

13. Raul Hilberg's *The Destruction of the European Jews*, 3 vols. (New York: Holmes & Meier, 1985), exemplifies the structuralist approach, as does Zygmunt Bauman's *Modernity and the Holocaust* (Ithaca: Cornell University Press, 1989). See Chapter 5, note 4, for a quote from Bauman exemplifying this approach.

14. Colin M. Turnbull, *The Mountain People* (New York: Simon and Schuster, 1972).

15. See Otto Kernberg, "Hatred as a Core Affect of Aggression," in *Birth of Hatred: Developmental, Clinical, and Technical Aspects of Intense Aggression*, ed. Salman Akhtar, Selma Kramer, and Henri Parens (Northvale, N.J.: Jason Aronson, 1995), pp. 53–82. See too Akhtar's response, pp. 83–101.

Chapter 3. The Ground of Evil Is Dread

1. See Ronald Siegel, *Fire in the Brain* (New York: Dutton, 1992), on sleep paralysis. In *The Assault on Truth: Freud's Suppression of the Seduction Theory* (New York: Farrar, Straus & Giroux, 1984), psychoanalyst Jeffrey Masson accuses Freud of downplaying the reality of sexual abuse by falsely turning it into hysterical fantasy.

2. Erich Heller, *The Importance of Nietzsche* (Chicago: University of Chicago Press, 1988), p. 173. Nietzsche quoted in Heller.

3. D. W. Winnicott, *Playing and Reality* (New York: Basic Books, 1971), pp. 95–103.

4. Thomas Ogden, *The Primitive Edge of Experience*, p. 35.

5. Ibid., p. 39.

6. Melanie Klein, "Notes on Some Schizoid Mechanisms," *"Envy and Gratitude" and Other Works*, vol. 3 of *The Writings of Melanie Klein*, ed. R. E. Money-Kyrle (New York: Free Press, 1975), 1–24. "A Contribution to the Psychogenesis of Manic-Depressive States," *"Love, Guilt and Reparation" and Other Works*, vol. 1 of *The Writings of Melanie Klein*, ed. R. E. Money-Kyrle, 262–89. See also Chapter 2 of my *Melanie Klein and Critical Social Theory* (New Haven: Yale University Press, 1989), for a summary of Klein's theory, which stresses the power of love and reparation in her thinking.

7. Hanna Segal, "Notes on Symbol Formation," *International Journal of Psycho-Analysis* 38 (1957): 391–97.

8. Ogden, *Primitive Edge of Experience*, p. 46.

9. Becker, *The Denial of Death*, p. 59.

10. Edmund Husserl, *The Crisis of European Sciences and Transcendental Phenomenology*, trans. David Carr (Evanston, Ill.: Northwestern University Press, 1970), pp. 219–20. Husserl's term "prepredicative" is being used loosely to talk about an experience of the world that is prior to the natural attitude of wide-awake, everyday life, but which makes it possible. The concept is developed most fully in Husserl's *Experience and Judgment*, trans.

James Churchill and Karl Ameriks (Evanston, Ill.: Northwestern University Press, 1973). Its clearest statement (cleansed of Husserl's transcendental idealism) is by Alfred Schutz, "Choosing among Projects of Action," in *Collected Papers*, 3 vols., ed. Maurice Natanson (The Hague: Martinus Nijhoff, 1973), 1: 79–82.

11. Kant, *Groundwork of the Metaphysics of Morals*, 4: 421/88.

12. See especially Margaret Mahler's subphase of separation-individuation, described as "on the road to object constancy," in *On Human Symbiosis and the Vicissitudes of Individuation* (New York: International Universities Press, 1968). Heinz Hartmann, *Essays on Ego Psychology* (New York: International Universities Press, 1964), p. 181.

13. *New York Times*, July 21, 1995: A10.

14. Søren Kierkegaard, *The Concept of Dread*, trans. Walter Lowrie (Princeton: Princeton University Press, 1957), p. 38.

15. Whitehead, quoted in Becker, *The Structure of Evil*, p. 379.

16. Ricoeur, *The Symbolism of Evil*, pp. 30, 347.

17. Charles Baudelaire, *Les Fleurs du Mal*, trans. Richard Howard (Boston: David R. Godine, 1982). "To the Reader" is the first poem.

18. Nel Noddings, *Women and Evil* (Berkeley: University of California Press, 1989), p. 95.

19. Ibid., p. 94.

20. Terril T. Gagnier and Richard Robertiello, "Sado-Masochism as a Defense against Merging: Six Case Studies," *Journal of Contemporary Psychotherapy* 23 (1993): 183–92. Arnold Rothstein, "Sadomasochism in the Neuroses Conceived of as a Pathological Compromise Formation," *Journal of the American Psychoanalytic Association* 39 (1991): 363–75. Rothstein stresses such compromises as that between wish and defense; I am taking slight liberty with the title.

21. H. G. Gough, "A Sociological Theory of Psychopathy," *American Journal of Sociology* 53 (1948): 359–66. H. J. Eysenck, *Crime and Personality* (London: Methuen, 1964). R. D. Hare, *Psychopathy: Theory and Research* (New York: Wiley, 1970). H. Cleckley, *The Mask of Sanity*, 4th ed. (St. Louis: Mosby, 1964).

22. Denis Doren, *Understanding and Treating the Psychopath* (Northvale, N.J.: Jason Aronson, 1996).

23. Meloy, *The Psychopathic Mind*, pp. 44–48.

24. W. R. D. Fairbairn, *An Object-Relations Theory of the Personality* (New York: Basic Books, 1954). "Internal saboteur" is a term Fairbairn used earlier.

25. Meloy, *The Psychopathic Mind*, p. 44.

26. Anna Freud, *The Ego and the Mechanisms of Defense*, rev. ed., trans. Cecil Baines (New York: International Universities Press, 1966), pp. 109–21.

27. Meloy, *The Psychopathic Mind*, p. 71.

28. Quoted in Robert Ressler, *Whoever Fights Monsters* (New York: St. Martin's Press, 1992), p. 97.

Chapter 4. Suffering Evil, Doing Evil

1. Joanna Overing, "There Is No End of Evil," in *The Anthropology of Evil*, ed. David Parkin, pp. 244–78, 275.

2. Ricoeur, *The Symbolism of Evil*, p. 27.

3. Hannah Arendt, *Eichmann in Jerusalem: A Report on the Banality of Evil*, rev. and enl. ed. (New York: Viking, 1965), pp. 286–88.

4. Ibid., p. 229.

5. I would not want my methodological concerns regarding the prison's psychological treatment program to obscure a more basic point: the prison staff (and many prisoners) are doing brave and important work. Every day it gets braver and more important, as public opinion finds in prisons and prisoners the perfect scapegoat for a failing culture.

6. Carroll Dale Short, "A True Thing," *Oxford American*, Spring 1996: 31–35. Short cites Andrew Delbanco's *The Death of Satan: How Americans Have Lost Their Sense of Evil* (New York: Farrar, Straus and Giroux, 1995), p. 32. Delbanco does not hold evil to be a presence. His view is captured in his statement that "the idea of evil is not just a metaphor that 'some people find . . . useful'; it is a metaphor upon which the health of society depends" (p. 227).

7. Quoted in Jack Katz, *Seductions of Crime* (New York: Basic Books, 1988), p. 101.

8. *Gospel of Truth* 17.10–11 (*Nag Hammadi Codex* 38). Elaine Pagels, *The Gnostic Gospels*, pp. 143–46.

9. See William Chase Greene, *Moira: Fate, Good, and Evil in Greek Thought* (New York: Harper and Row, 1944), pp. 3–9.

10. My *Psychoanalytic Theory of Greek Tragedy* (New Haven: Yale University Press, 1994) has more on the morality of powerlessness. See especially Chapter 6, "Pity as the Foundation of Civilization."

11. Elaine Pagels, *The Origin of Satan* (New York: Random House, 1995), p. 184.

12. Ibid.

13. See Brent Shaw, review of *The Origin of Satan*, *New Republic*, July 10, 1995: 32–33. *The Dictionary of Quotations from the Bible*, ed. Margaret Miner and Hugh Rawson (New York: Penguin, 1988), lists thirty-seven entries under the category "evil." All refer to the evil of the human heart, beginning with the most famous: "And God saw that the wickedness of man was great in the earth, and that every imagination of the thoughts of his heart was only evil continually" (Gen. 6.5). In the New Testament the best known is probably Matthew 6.23, Christ's Sermon on the Mount, which refers to the darkness of the evil heart. Other well-known references to the evil of the heart not included in the Penguin *Dictionary of Quotations from the Bible* include Genesis 8.21; Job 1.1, 28.28; Psalms 34.13–14; Apocrypha (Eccles.) 3.25–26; Romans 2.16–17, 7.19; 2 Corinthians 6.8. In the Bible, evil, sin, and wickedness are almost always a problem of the heart, not of the "other."

14. Klein, "Envy and Gratitude," in *"Envy and Gratitude" and Other Works*, vol. 3 of *The Writings of Melanie Klein*, ed. R. E. Money-Kyrle, p. 189. I discuss Klein's view of envy in my *Melanie Klein and Critical Social Theory*, pp. 37–38.

15. Kant, *Religion within the Limits of Reason Alone*, pp. 30–32. Howard Caygill, *A Kant Dictionary* (Cambridge, Mass.: Blackwell, 1995), pp. 179–82.

16. Nietzsche, "Why I Am So Clever," in *Ecce Homo*, trans. R. J. Hollingdale (New York: Penguin, 1992), p. 68. About the Eternal Recurrence, implied above, Nietzsche says, "Live in such a way that you desire nothing more than to live this very same life again and again!" in "Notes from the time of *Zarathustra*," quoted in Heller, *Importance of Nietzsche*, p. 13. But Nietzsche does not mean it, at least for himself, confiding to his diary that "I do not wish to live *again*. How have I borne life? By creating. What has made me endure? The vision of the *Uebermensch* who affirms life. I have tried to affirm life *myself—but* ah!" Quoted in Heller, *Importance of Nietzsche*, p. 14. What if the trick to life, if there were such a thing, is not affirmation at all, but submission? Or acceptance? How different are the later pair anyway?

Chapter 5. Identifying with Eichmann

1. Arendt, *Eichmann in Jerusalem*, p. 91.

2. Herbert Marcuse, *One-Dimensional Man* (Boston: Beacon Press, 1964). Arthur Mitzman, *The Iron Cage: An Historical Interpretation of Max Weber*, with new intro. (New Brunswick, N.J.: Transaction, 1985).

3. The structuralist approach is captured in the following statement by Bauman in *Modernity and the Holocaust*, referring to Raul Hilberg's *The Destruction of the European Jews:* "Hilberg has suggested that the moment the first German official had written the first rule of Jewish exclusion, the fate of the European Jews was sealed. There is a most profound and terrifying truth in this comment. What bureaucracy needed was the definition of its task. Rational and efficient as it was, it could be trusted to see the task to its end" (pp. 105–6).

4. Max Horkheimer and Theodor Adorno, *Dialectic of Enlightenment*, trans. J. Cumming (New York: Herder and Herder, 1972).

5. See James Glass, *Mass Murder*, forthcoming.

Chapter 6. Splatter Movies or Shiva? A Culture of Vampires

1. Christopher Lasch, *The Culture of Narcissism* (New York: Warner, 1979), pp. 301–12.

2. Paul Barber, *Vampires, Burial, and Death: Folklore and Reality* (New Haven: Yale University Press, 1988), p. 4.

3. Ibid., pp. 2, 57, 68.

4. See Robert Jay Lifton, *The Broken Connection: On Death and the Continuity of Life* (New York: Basic Books, 1983), p. 95.

5. Anne Rice, *Interview with the Vampire* (New York: Ballantine Books, 1976), pp. 338–42. Like many informants, the fictional interviewer is so bewitched by Louis's power that he can't know the suffering of the undead. Or is it vice-versa?

6. Katz, *Seductions of Crime*, pp. 233–34.

7. Quotations are from Goethe, *Faust*, Part 1, trans. David Luke (Oxford: Oxford University Press, 1987).

8. See Mike Baxter, "Flesh and Blood: Does Pornography Lead to Sexual Violence?" *New Scientist*, May 5, 1990: 37–41. The article summarizes a dozen studies.

Chapter 7. "Evil Spelled Backward Is Live"

1. Simone Weil, "Criteria of Wisdom," and Lewis, quoted in Peck, *People of the Lie*, pp. 263–64.

2. Ogden, *The Primitive Edge of Experience*, p. 52.

3. Saul Friedlander, *Memory, History, and the Extermination of the Jews of Europe.* (Bloomington: Indiana University Press, 1993), pp. 110–11.

4. Hanna Segal, "A Psycho-Analytical Approach to Aesthetics," *New Directions in Psycho-Analysis*, ed. M. Klein, P. Heimann, and R. E. Money-Kyrle (London: Tavistock, 1955).

5. I discuss Kleinian art theory in *Melanie Klein and Critical Social Theory*, pp. 104–36.

Also in "Art and Reparation: or, Poetry after Auschwitz?" *Art Criticism* 5, no. 3 (1989): 16–32. Gilbert Rose, *The Power of Form: A Psychoanalytic Approach to Aesthetic Form*, expanded ed. (Madison, Conn.: International Universities Press, 1992), captures well the role of the body, including what Ogden calls autistic-contiguous experience, in art (pp. 97–109).

6. Nietzsche, *Human, All Too Human*, trans. M. Faber, with S. Lehmann (Lincoln: University of Nebraska Press, 1984), sec. 108.

7. See Elaine Scarry, *The Body in Pain: The Making and Unmaking of the World* (New York: Oxford University Press, 1985), p. 28. I follow her argument closely in the next two paragraphs.

8. Klein, "Envy and Gratitude," In *"Envy and Gratitude" and Other Works*, pp. 193, 216.

9. Quoted in Melanie Thernstrom, "Diary of a Murder," *New Yorker,* June 3, 1996: 62.

10. Jean-Paul Sartre, *Saint Genet*, trans. Bernard Frechtman (New York: George Braziller, 1963), pp. 50–51, 337, 353. Much of what Sartre writes about Genet's view of evil sounds more like a representation of Genet's confusion rather than reversal. See especially "The Evil of Consciousness and Consciousness of Evil," p. 337.

11. C. S. Lewis, *A Grief Observed* (New York: Bantam Books, 1961), pp. 37, 80–81. The debates in *Encountering Evil: Live Options in Theodicy*, ed. Stephen Davis (Atlanta, Ga.: John Knox Press, 1981), reveal by contrast what it is to think rigorously about these issues from a religious perspective. What Lewis gets right is the closeness of grief to fear (p. 1), which is why loss can lead to dread and be experienced as evil.

12. Thomas Mann, *Doctor Faustus*, trans. H. T. Lowe-Porter (New York: Modern Library, 1992), pp. 639, 641–42.

13. Theodor Adorno, *Philosophie der neuen Musik* (Frankfurt am Main: Suhrkamp, 1978), p. 28, quoted and trans. by Michael Beddow, *Thomas Mann: Doctor Faustus* (Cambridge: Cambridge University Press, 1994), p. 54.

14. Mann, *Doctor Faustus*, pp. 639–40.

15. Mr. Albright was in the program for evaluation. His high score on the psychopathy checklist, among others things, led to his being denied permanent status in the program.

16. Klein, "The Importance of Symbol-Formation in the Development of the Ego," in *The Writings of Melanie Klein*, 1: 227.

17. Bruno Bettelheim, *The Uses of Enchantment: The Meaning and Importance of Fairy Tales* (New York: Vintage, 1977). See too Appendix 1, this book, for a discussion of private meaning and public language.

18. Janine Chasseguet-Smirgel, "Brief Reflections on the Disappearance in Nazi Racial Theory of the Capacity to Create Symbols," in *The Spectrum of Psychoanalysis*, ed. A. K. Richards and A. Richards, p. 235 (Madison, Conn.: International Universities Press, 1994).

19. J. LaPlanche and J.-B. Pontalis, *The Language of Psychoanalysis*, trans. D. Nicholson-Smith (New York: W. W. Norton, 1973), p. 433. Sigmund Freud, "Leonardo da Vinci and a Memory of His Childhood," in *The Standard Edition of the Complete Psychological Works of Sigmund Freud*, ed. J. Strachey (London: Hogarth Press, 1953–1974), 11: 59–137.

20. Paul Ricoeur, *Freud and Philosophy: An Essay on Interpretation*, trans. D. Savage (New Haven: Yale University Press), p. 484. Joel Whitebook, "Sublimation—a Frontier Concept," in *The Spectrum of Psychoanalysis*, ed. A. K. Richards and A. D. Richards (Madison, Conn.: International Universities Press, 1994), pp. 321–36.

21. Ricoeur, *Freud and Philosophy*, p. 317. Whitebook, "Sublimation—a Frontier Concept," p. 330.

22. Roy Schafer, *Retelling a Life: Narration and Dialogue in Psychoanalysis* (New York: Basic Books), pp. 29–31.

Chapter 8. Evil Is No-thing

1. See David Parkin, "Introduction," in *The Anthropology of Evil*, ed. Parkin, pp. 10–11.

2. Freud, *Civilization and Its Discontents*, pp. 11–12.

3. Quoted in Ron Rosenbaum, "Explaining Hitler," *New Yorker*, May 1, 1995: 50–53.

4. Nietzsche, *Beyond Good and Evil*, in *Basic Writings of Nietzsche*, trans. Walter Kaufmann (New York: Modern Library, 1966), part 4, no. 153, p. 280.

5. Theodor Adorno, *Minima Moralia*, trans. E. F. N. Jephcott (London: New Left Books, 1974), pp. 97–98. Nietzsche, *Ecce Homo*, pp. 65–66 ("Why I Am So Clever"), 110 ("Thus Spoke Zarathustra"). The book's title is what Pilate said when he presented Jesus with his crown of thorns to the crowd (John 19.5).

6. Nietzsche, *Thus Spoke Zarathustra*, in *The Portable Nietzsche*, trans. W. Kaufmann (Harmondsworth, England: Penguin, 1954), III, 2. James Miller quotes this passage in "Carnivals of Atrocity: Foucault, Nietzsche, Cruelty," in *Political Theory* 18 (1990): 474. Miller goes on to compare the comment in *Zarathustra* with Nietzsche's observation, in *Ecce Homo*, that "cruelty is here exposed for the first time as one of the most ancient and basic substrata of culture that simply cannot be imagined away" (*On the Genealogy of Morals: A Polemic*). Quite right, but there is a big difference between the primordial reality of cruelty and its idealization. It is this that seems so hard to grasp.

7. Rank, quoted in Robert Jay Lifton, *The Broken Connection: On Death and the Continuity of Life*, p. 180. The chorus in Euripides' *Hecuba* makes much the same point.
> And now you know:
> Life is held on loan.
> The price of life is death. (line 1028)

8. In Christopher Middleton, ed. and trans., *Selected Letters of Friedrich Nietzsche* (Chicago: University of Chicago Press, 1969), pp. 198–99. Passage in internal quotes is from the epigraph to the first edition of *The Gay Science*. It is derived from Emerson.

9. In Michael Tanner, *Nietzsche* (Oxford: Oxford University Press, 1994), p. 58. There is a poor reproduction of the photo in *Nietzsche for Beginners*, by Marc Sautet (New York: Writers and Readers Publishing, 1990), p. 121.

10. The psychoanalytic literature calls it sadomasochism, and that is just right. Unfortunately, too much attention is paid to masochism, too little to sadism. Perhaps masochists go into analysis, while sadists send them there. In "Sadomasochism in the Psychoanalytic Process," a review article in the *Journal of the American Psychoanalytic Association* 39 (1991): 431–50, Harold Blum devotes one paragraph (p. 446) to sadism, the rest to masochism.

11. Nietzsche, *On the Genealogy of Morals*, in *Basic Writings of Nietzsche*, trans. Kaufmann, Essay 2, sec. 5. "Of doing evil for the pleasure of doing it" is in French in Nietzsche's original.

12. Ibid., Essay 2, sec. 6.

13. Miller, "Carnivals of Atrocity," p. 485. The internal quotes refer to categories developed by Gilles Deleuze, *Nietzsche and Philosophy*, trans. H. Tomlinson (New York: Columbia University Press, 1983), especially pp. 129–30.

14. Miller, "Carnivals of Atrocity," p. 485.

15. Ibid., p. 486.

16. Janine Chasseguet-Smirgel, "Sadomasochism in the Perversions: Some Thoughts on the Destruction of Reality," *Journal of the American Psychoanalytic Association* 39 (1991): 399–415.

17. Nietzsche, *The Gay Science*, trans. Walter Kaufmann (New York: Vintage, 1974),

book 4, no. 299: 239. Nietzsche is nothing if not subtle. But perhaps he is too subtle about evil in a way that is common among academics. When he was a boy of thirteen, he says in the Preface to *On the Genealogy of Morals*, he devoted his "first philosophical effort" to the question of the origin of evil: "A certain amount of historical and philological schooling, together with an inborn fastidiousness of taste in respect to psychological questions in general, soon transformed my problem into another one: under what conditions did man devise these value judgments good and evil? *and what value do they themselves possess?*" No matter how intellectually justifiable (I too have reformulated the question of evil), the turn from the origin of evil to its value and meaning is not without costs, transforming the deeply pressing problem of how to come to terms with the experience of evil in self and world into a more abstract intellectual one. Perhaps it is not just a question of age, but the costs of philosophical training. (Why should philosophy, like everything else in life, not have costs as well as benefits?) Almost all informants see the problem of evil as Nietzsche did at thirteen—where does it come from? Theirs is the power of the beginner's mind.

18. Aristotle, *Poetics*, c. 13. *Hamartia* means literally "to miss the mark," as when an arrow misses its target. For more see my *Psychoanalytic Theory of Greek Tragedy*, p. 197 n. 3. There I also discuss the meaning of tragedy, including its connection to pathos, pp. 59–61, 130, 147–49.

19. Alice Miller, *Thou Shalt Not Be Aware: Society's Betrayal of the Child*, trans. H. and H. Hannum (New York: Meridian, 1984), p. 82.

20. Nietzsche, *Human, All Too Human*, sec. 107.

21. Lance Morrow, "The Unconscious Hums, 'Destroy!'" *Time*, March 25, 1996: 78.

22. *Baltimore Sun*, September 22, 1995: A1.

Chapter 9. *Scales of Evil*

1. Robert Jay Lifton, *The Nazi Doctors: Medical Killing and the Psychology of Genocide* (New York: Basic Books, 1986), p. 377.

2. Fritz Stern, *The Politics of Cultural Despair: A Study in the Rise of Germanic Ideology* (Berkeley: University of California Press, 1961). Robert C. Cecil, *The Myth of the Master Race: Alfred Rosenberg and Nazi Ideology* (New York: Dodd, Mead, 1972), p. 93.

3. Kant, *Religion within the Limits of Reason Alone*, p. 32.

4. Ibid., p. 30.

5. Ibid., p. 31.

Appendix 1: *Asking about Evil*

1. Christopher Lasch, *The Minimal Self* (New York: W. W. Norton, 1984), pp. 126–29.

2. Whitebook, "Sublimation—a Frontier Concept," discusses Mary Gedo's *Picasso: Art as Autobiography* at some length, pp. 332–35.

3. On meaning equals use, see Ludwig Wittgenstein, *Philosophical Investigations*, 3d ed., trans. G. E. M. Anscombe (New York: Macmillan, 1953), secs. 1, 26–32. See also his *Blue and Brown Books* (Oxford: Blackwell, 1958), pp. 1–5, and *Philosophical Grammar*, ed. R. Rhees, trans. A. Kenny (Oxford: Blackwell, 1969), secs. 6–8, 10–13. On no private language see *Philosophical Investigations*, pp. 243–314.

4. Wittgenstein, *Philosophical Investigations*, part 2, sec. 10.

Works Cited

Note: classical sources cited in the text in the form that is customary in classical studies are not repeated here.

Adorno, Theodor. "Commitment." In *The Essential Frankfurt School Reader*, 300–18. Ed. A. Arato and E. Gebhardt. New York: Urizen Books, 1978.
——. *Minima Moralia*. Trans. E. F. N. Jephcott. London: New Left Books, 1974.
——. *Philosophie der neuen Musik*. Frankfurt a.M.: Suhrkamp, 1978.
Alford, C. Fred. "Art and Reparation: or, Poetry after Auschwitz?" *Art Criticism* 5, no. 3 (1989): 16–32.
——. *Melanie Klein and Critical Social Theory*. New Haven: Yale University Press, 1989.
——. *Narcissism: Socrates, the Frankfurt School, and Psychoanalytic Theory*. New Haven: Yale University Press, 1988.
——. *The Psychoanalytic Theory of Greek Tragedy*. New Haven: Yale University Press, 1994.
Arendt, Hannah. *Eichmann in Jerusalem: A Report on the Banality of Evil*, rev. and enl. ed. New York: Viking Press, 1965.
Barber, Paul. *Vampires, Burial, and Death: Folklore and Reality*. New Haven: Yale University Press, 1988.
Baudelaire, Charles. *Les Fleurs du Mal*. Trans. Richard Howard. Boston: David R. Godine, 1982.
Bauman, Zygmunt. *Modernity and the Holocaust*. Ithaca: Cornell University Press, 1989.
Baxter, Mike. "Flesh and Blood: Does Pornography Lead to Sexual Violence?" *New Scientist*, May 5, 1990: 37–41.

Becker, Ernest. *The Denial of Death.* New York: Free Press, 1973.

———. *Escape from Evil.* New York: Free Press, 1975.

———. *The Structure of Evil.* New York: Free Press, 1968.

Beddow, Michael. *Thomas Mann: Doctor Faustus.* Cambridge: Cambridge University Press, 1994.

Bettelheim, Bruno. *The Uses of Enchantment: The Meaning and Importance of Fairy Tales.* New York: Vintage Books, 1977.

Blum, Harold. "Sadomasochism in the Psychoanalytic Process." In *Journal of the American Psychoanalytic Association* 39 (1991): 431–50.

Boyd, J. W. *Satan and Mara: Christian and Buddhist Symbols of Evil.* Leiden: E. J. Brill, 1975.

Caygill, Howard. *A Kant Dictionary.* Cambridge, Mass.: Blackwell, 1995.

Cecil, Robert C. *The Myth of the Master Race: Alfred Rosenberg and Nazi Ideology.* New York: Dodd, Mead, 1972.

Chasseguet-Smirgel, Janine. "Brief Reflections on the Disappearance in Nazi Racial Theory of the Capacity to Create Symbols." *The Spectrum of Psychoanalysis: Essays in Honor of Martin S. Bergmann,* pp. 233–42. Ed. A. K. Richards and Arnold Richards. Madison, Conn.: International Universities Press, 1994.

———. "Sadomasochism in the Perversions: Some Thoughts on the Destruction of Reality." *Journal of the American Psychoanalytic Association* 39 (1991): 399–415.

Cleckley, H. *The Mask of Sanity,* 4th ed. St. Louis: Mosby, 1964.

Cohen, Richard. "War Criminals like Us." *Washington Post Magazine,* September 22, 1996: 6.

Cooper, Arnold, and Michael Sacks. "Sadism and Masochism in Character Disorder and Resistance." *Journal of the American Psychoanalytic Association* 39 (1991): 215–26.

Davis, Stephen, ed. *Encountering Evil: Live Options in Theodicy.* Atlanta: John Knox Press, 1981.

Delbanco, Andrew. *The Death of Satan: How Americans Have Lost Their Sense of Evil.* New York: Farrar, Straus and Giroux, 1995.

Deleuze, Gilles. *Nietzsche and Philosophy.* Trans. H. Tomlinson. New York: Columbia University Press, 1983.

Doren, Denis. *Understanding and Treating the Psychopath.* Northvale, N.J.: Jason Aronson, 1996.

Elias, Norbert. *The Civilizing Process.* [1 vol. ed.] Trans. Edmund Jephcott. Oxford: Blackwell, 1994.

Eysenck, Hans J. *Crime and Personality.* London: Methuen, 1964.

Fairbairn, W. R. D. *An Object-Relations Theory of the Personality.* New York: Basic Books, 1954.

Freud, Anna. *The Ego and the Mechanisms of Defense.* Rev. ed. Trans. Cecil Baines. Vol. 2 of *The Writings of Anna Freud.* New York: International Universities Press, 1966.

Freud, Sigmund. *Beyond the Pleasure Principle.* Vol. 18 of *The Standard Edition of the Complete Psychological Works of Sigmund Freud,* 3–65. Ed. James Strachey. London: Hogarth Press, 1953–1974.

——. *Leonardo da Vinci and a Memory of His Childhood.* Vol. 11 of *The Standard Edition of the Complete Psychological Works of Sigmund Freud,* 59–137.

Friedlander, Saul. *Memory, History, and the Extermination of the Jews of Europe.* Bloomington: Indiana University Press, 1993.

Gagnier, Terril, and Richard Robertiello. "Sado-Masochism as a Defense against Merging: Six Case Studies." *Journal of Contemporary Psychotherapy* 23 (1993): 183–92.

Glass, James. *Mass Murder.* [Forthcoming.]

Goethe, Johann Wolfgang. *Faust,* Part 1. Trans. David Luke. Oxford: Oxford University Press, 1987.

Goldhagen, Daniel Jonah. *Hitler's Willing Executioners: Ordinary Germans and the Holocaust.* New York: Knopf, 1996.

Gough, Harrison G. "A Sociological Theory of Psychopathy." *American Journal of Sociology* 53 (1948): 359–66.

Greene, William Chase. *Moira: Fate, Good, and Evil in Greek Thought.* New York: Harper and Row, 1944.

Grossman, William. "Pain, Aggression, Fantasy, and Concepts of Sadomasochism." *Psychoanalytic Quarterly* 60 (1991): 22–52.

Haney, Craig, Curtis Banks, and Philip Zimbardo. "Interpersonal Dynamics in a Simulated Prison." *International Journal of Criminology and Penology* 1 (1973): 69–97.

Hare, Robert D. *Psychopathy: Theory and Research.* New York: Wiley, 1970.

Hartmann, Heinz. *Essays on Ego Psychology.* New York: International Universities Press, 1964.

Heller, Erich. *The Importance of Nietzsche.* Chicago: University of Chicago Press, 1988.

Hilberg, Raul. *The Destruction of the European Jews.* 3 vols. New York: Holmes & Meier, 1985.

Horkheimer, Max, and Theodor Adorno. *Dialectic of Enlightenment.* Trans. J. Cumming. New York: Herder and Herder, 1972.

Husserl, Edmund. *The Crisis of European Sciences and Transcendental Phenomenology.* Trans. David Carr. Evanston, Ill.: Northwestern University Press, 1970.

——. *Experience and Judgment.* Trans. J. Churchill and K. Americs. Evanston, Ill.: Northwestern University Press, 1973.

Kant, Immanuel. *The Metaphysics of Morals.* Trans. Mary J. Gregor. Cambridge: Cambridge University Press, 1991.

——. *Religion within the Limits of Reason Alone.* Trans. T. H. Greene and H. Hudson. New York: Harper and Row, 1960.

Katz, Jack. *The Seductions of Crime.* New York: Basic Books, 1988.

Kernberg, Otto. "Hatred as a Core Affect of Aggression." In *The Birth of Hatred: Developmental, Clinical, and Technical Aspects of Intense Aggression,* 53–82. Ed. Salman Akhtar, Selma Kramer, and Henri Parens. Northvale, N.J.: Jason Aronson, 1995.

Kierkegaard, Søren. *The Concept of Dread.* Trans. Walter Lowrie. Princeton: Princeton University Press, 1957.

Klein, Melanie. "A Contribution to the Psychogenesis of Manic-Depressive States." In *"Love, Guilt and Reparation" and Other Works*, vol. 1 of *The Writings of Melanie Klein*, 262–89. Ed. R. E. Money-Kyrle. New York: Free Press, 1975.

———. "Envy and Gratitude." In *"Envy and Gratitude" and Other Works*, vol. 3 of *The Writings of Melanie Klein*, 176–235. Ed. R. E. Money-Kyrle. New York: Free Press, 1975.

———. "The Importance of Symbol-Formation in the Development of the Ego." In *"Love, Guilt and Reparation" and Other Works*, vol. 1 of *The Writings of Melanie Klein*, 219–32. Ed. R. E. Money-Kyrle. New York: Free Press, 1975.

———. "Notes on Some Schizoid Mechanisms." In *"Envy and Gratitude" and Other Works*, vol. 3 of *The Writings of Melanie Klein*, 1–24. Ed. R. E. Money-Kyrle. New York: Free Press, 1975.

LaPlanche, J., and J.-P. Pontalis. *The Language of Psychoanalysis*. Trans. D. Nicholson-Smith. New York: W. W. Norton, 1973.

Lasch, Christopher. *The Culture of Narcissism*. New York: Warner Books, 1979.

———. *The Minimal Self*. New York: W. W. Norton, 1984.

Lewis, C. W. *A Grief Observed*. New York: Bantam Books, 1961.

Lifton, Robert Jay. *The Broken Connection: On Death and the Continuity of Life*. New York: Basic Books, 1983.

———. *The Nazi Doctors: Medical Killing and the Psychology of Genocide*. New York: Basic Books, 1986.

MacGregor, John. "Identification with the Victim." *Psychoanalytic Quarterly* 60 (1991): 52–72.

MacIntyre, Alasdair. *After Virtue*. Notre Dame, Ind.: University of Notre Dame Press, 1981.

Mahler, Margaret. *On Human Symbiosis and the Vicissitudes of Individuation*. New York: International Universities Press, 1968.

Mann, Thomas. *Doctor Faustus*. Trans. H. T. Lowe-Porter. New York: Modern Library, 1992.

Marcuse, Herbert. *One-Dimensional Man*. Boston: Beacon Press, 1964.

Marrow, Lance. "The Unconscious Hums, 'Destroy!' " *Time*, March 25, 1996: 78.

Masson, Jeffrey. *The Assault on Truth: Freud's Suppression of the Seduction Theory*. New York: Farrar, Straus & Giroux, 1984.

Meloy, J. Reid. *The Psychopathic Mind: Origins, Dynamics and Treatment*. Northvale, N.J.: Jason Aronson, 1988.

Meyer, Philip. "If Hitler Asked You to Electrocute a Stranger, Would You? Probably." In *Down to Earth Sociology*, 165–71. Ed. James M. Henslin. New York: The Free Press, 1993.

Middleton, Christopher, ed. and trans. *Selected Letters of Friedrich Nietzsche*. Chicago: University of Chicago Press, 1969.

Milgram, Stanley. *Obedience to Authority: An Experimental View*. New York: Harper and Row, 1974.

Miller, Alice. *Thou Shalt Not Be Aware: Society's Betrayal of the Child*. Trans. H. Hannum and H. Hannum. New York: Meridian Books, 1984.

Miller, James. "Carnivals of Atrocity: Foucault, Nietzsche, Cruelty." *Political Theory* 18 (1990): 470–91.

Miner, Margaret, and Hugh Rawson, eds. *The Dictionary of Quotations from the Bible*. New York: Penguin Books, 1988.

Mitzman, Arthur. *The Iron Cage: An Historical Interpretation of Max Weber*, with new intro. New Brunswick, NJ.: Transaction Books, 1985.

Nietzsche, Friedrich. *Beyond Good and Evil*. In *Basic Writings of Nietzsche*, 181–438. Trans. Walter Kaufmann. New York: Modern Library, 1966.

——. *Ecce Homo*. Trans. R. J. Hollingdale. New York: Penguin Books, 1992.

——. *The Gay Science*. Trans. Walter Kaufmann. New York: Vintage Books, 1974.

——. *Human, All Too Human*. Trans. M. Faber, with S. Lehmann. Lincoln: University of Nebraska Press, 1984.

——. *On the Geneology of Morals*. In *Basic Writings of Nietzsche*, 439–602. Trans. Walter Kaufmann. New York: Modern Library, 1966.

——. *Thus Spoke Zarathustra*. In *The Portable Nietzsche*, 103–349. Trans. Walter Kaufmann. Harmondsworth, England: Penguin Books, 1954.

Noddings, Nel. *Women and Evil*. Berkeley: University of California Press, 1989.

Ogden, Thomas. *The Primitive Edge of Experience*. Northvale, N.J.: Jason Aronson, 1989.

Overing, Joanna. "There Is No End of Evil." In *The Anthropology of Evil*, 244–78. Ed. David Parkin. Cambridge, Mass.: Basil Blackwell, 1985.

Pagels, Elaine. *The Gnostic Gospels*. New York: Random House, 1979.

——. *The Origin of Satan*. New York: Random House, 1995.

Parkin, David. "Introduction." In *The Anthropology of Evil*, 1–25. Ed. Parkin. Cambridge, Mass.: Basil Blackwell, 1985.

Peck, M. Scott. *People of the Lie: The Hope for Healing Human Evil*. New York: Simon and Schuster, 1983.

Popper, Karl. *The Open Society and Its Enemies*, 5th ed. rev. 2 vols. Princeton: Princeton University Press, 1966.

Pulver, Sydney, and Salman Akhtar. "Sadomasochism in the Perversions." *Journal of the American Psychoanalytic Association* 39 (1991): 741–55.

Rank, Otto. *Will Therapy and Truth and Reality*. [1 vol. ed.] New York: Knopf, 1945.

Ressler, Robert. *Whoever Fights Monsters*. New York: St. Martin's Press, 1992.

Rice, Anne. *Interview with the Vampire*. New York: Ballantine Books, 1976.

Ricoeur, Paul. *Freud and Philosophy: An Essay on Interpretation*. Trans. D. Savage. New Haven: Yale University Press, 1970.

——. *The Symbolism of Evil*. Trans. Emerson Buchanan. Boston: Beacon Press, 1969.

Rose, Gilbert. *The Power of Form: A Psychoanalytical Approach to Aesthetic Form*, expanded ed. Madison, Conn.: International Universities Press, 1992.

Rosenbaum, Ron. "Evil's Back." *New York Times Magazine*, June 4, 1995: 36–63.

——. "Explaining Hitler." *New Yorker*, May 1, 1995: 50–73.

Rothstein, Arnold. "Sadomasochism in the Neuroses Conceived of as a Pathological Compromise Formation." *Journal of the American Psychoanalytic Association* 39 (1991): 363–75.

Sartre, Jean-Paul. *Saint Genet.* Trans. Bernard Frechtman. New York: George Braziller, 1963.

Sautet, Marc. *Nietzsche for Beginners.* New York: Writers and Readers Publishing, 1990.

Scarry, Elaine. *The Body in Pain: The Making and Unmaking of the World.* New York: Oxford University Press, 1985.

Schafer, Roy. *Retelling a Life: Narration and Dialogue in Psychoanalysis.* New York: Basic Books, 1992.

Schutz, Alfred. "Choosing among Projects of Action." In *Collected Papers*, 3 vols., 1: 67–96. Ed. Maurice Natanson. The Hague: Martinus Nijoff, 1973.

Segal, Hanna. "Notes on Symbol Formation." *International Journal of Psycho-Analysis* 38 (1957): 391–97.

———. "A Psycho-Analytical Approach to Aesthetics." In *New Directions in Psycho-Analysis*, 384–405. Ed. M. Klein, P. Heimann, and R. E. Money-Kyrle. London: Tavistock, 1955.

Shaw, Brent. "Review of *The Origin of Satan.*" *New Republic*, July 10, 1995: 32–33.

Shklar, Judith N. "The Liberalism of Fear." In *Liberalism and the Moral Life*, 21–38. Ed. Nancy Rosenblum. Cambridge: Harvard University Press, 1989.

Short, Carroll Dale. "A True Thing." *The Oxford American*, Spring, 1966: 31–35.

Siegel, Ronald. *Fire in the Brain.* New York: Dutton, 1992.

Southwold, Martin. "Buddhism and Evil." In *The Anthropology of Evil*, 128–41. Ed. David Parkin. Cambridge, Mass.: Basil Blackwell, 1985.

Stern, Fritz. *The Politics of Cultural Despair: A Study in the Rise of Germanic Ideology.* Berkeley: University of California Press, 1961.

Storr, Anthony. *Human Destructiveness.* New York: Grove Weidenfeld, 1991.

Tanner, Michael. *Nietzsche.* Oxford: Oxford University Press, 1994.

Thernstrom, Melanie. "Diary of a Murder." *New Yorker*, June 3, 1996: 62–71.

Trilling, Lionel. *The Liberal Imagination.* New York: Harcourt Brace Jovanovich, 1979.

Turnbull, Colin M. *The Mountain People.* New York: Simon and Schuster, 1972.

Walsh, David. "No Excuses." *Washington Post*, May 5, 1995: A21.

Whitebook, Joel. "Sublimation—a Frontier Concept." In *The Spectrum of Psychoanalysis: Essays in Honor of Martin S. Bergmann*, 321–36. Ed. Arlene K. Richards and Arnold D. Richards. Madison, Conn.: International Universities Press, 1994.

Winch, Peter. "Understanding a Primitive Society." *American Philosophical Quarterly* 1 (1964): 307–24.

Winnicott, D. W. *Playing and Reality.* New York: Basic Books, 1971.

Wittgenstein, Ludwig. *Blue and Brown Books.* Oxford: Blackwell, 1958.

———. *Philosophical Grammar.* Ed. R. Rhees. Trans. A. Kenny. Oxford: Blackwell, 1969.

———. *Philosophical Investigations.* 3d ed. Trans. G. E. M. Anscombe. New York: Macmillan, 1953.

Index

cheating, 45, 124
child abuse, 131
Christianity, 17–18, 67, 70, 77. *See also* Bible
civilization: changes in, 109–10; critique of, 77; definition of, 164–65n. 11; good and evil in, 85–86, 121–29; and violence, 30–31, 75–76. *See also* culture; humanity
Cleckley, H., 54
Cohen, Richard, 15, 16
confusion, 105–7
consolation, 107–10
crackpot realism, 81
creativity: and body, 103–4, 110, 168–69n. 5; and consolation, 107–10; function of, 22, 102–3, 129; limits in, 101–4; and symbolism, 146–47; torture as, 111; and vampires, 91–95
crimes: appeal of, 92; control inherent in, 21, 28; definition of, 30–31; distinctions among, 33–34; doing versus telling of, 12–13; fantasies about, 97–98; by inmates, 4, 6, 33, 75, 105, 130–31, 137, 159–60; responsibility for, 63–65. *See also* abuse; bombings; motives; victimhood; violence
cruelty, 123–24, 126–29. *See also* sadomasochism
culture: challenges to, 14, 16; dread contained by, 112–16, 142–44; as frame for dread, 86–87; lack of regret in, 64; meaningful victimhood in, 17, 79–80, 115; narrative form provided by, 15; portrayals of evil in, 13, 17–19, 32–33, 138, 140, 148; role of, 24, 109–10; totalizing tendency in, 77; of vampires, 87–91. *See also* media
cutting, self versus other, 100–101

Dahmer, Jeffrey, 96
Dante, 22, 52–53
death: acceptance of, 72–73; aloneness in, 137; attempt to cheat, 124; chagrin of, 84–85; versus evil, 49; fear of, 10, 50; of loved ones, 67–70, 146–47; and meaning of life, 87; mourning for, 72, 90–91, 107; personification of, 35; vampires as messengers of, 89–90; in war, 60–61. *See also* dread; loss; suicide

Delbanco, Andrew, 66
depressive position: acceptance of doom in, 72; and creativity, 103; description of, 41–45; and responsibility, 122
desire: denial of, 123–24; and maliciousness, 142; and sublimation, 114, 116; as threat, 70–71
devil. *See* Satan
dike, 134–36
doom. *See* death; dread
Doren, Dennis, 54
dread: of being human, 50–53, 80; containment of, 13, 44–45, 110–16, 142–44; defense against, 37, 65; definition of, 10–11, 40, 50, 66, 118; denial of, 10, 128; escape from, 51–53, 58–59, 91–95, 129–30; ethical, 50, 93, 118; experience of, ix, 2–3, 51–53; as formless, 39–40, 43; function of, 3, 9–10, 13, 19, 45, 50, 67; giving form to, 43–45, 49–50, 59, 86–87, 97, 100; inflicted on others, 95, 100–101, 113–14, 119–21, 125–26, 130, 138, 143; personification of, 35–36; proximity to, 4, 75–76; versus reason, 80–83; sources of, 10, 43, 102; striving that stems from, 93–95; sublimation of, 114–16; unboundedness of, 17–18; unreachability of, 57–58. *See also* death; loss; precategorical experiences; narratives
dreams, evil in, 35–36
dukkha, 17–18
Dunblane, Scotland, shootings in, 135–36

earthquakes, as evil, 17, 62, 133, 146
Eichmann, Adolf: attitudes toward, 4–5, 74–78, 82–83; characterization of, 62, 130, 141–42; identification with, 17, 77–79, 133
electric shock experiments, 9, 25–29, 79
Elias, Norbert, 31
Eliot, T. S., 86
Enlightenment, 80, 82
envy, 70–71
ethics, 14, 46–48, 50
Euripides, 68–69, 134, 170n. 7
evil: appearance of, 21–24, 56–57; approaches to, 14–19; attraction of, 99–101; breaking circle of, 136–40; claimed

as one's own, 121–29; as discourse, 66–69, 118–19, 133–35; distinctions in, 32–34, 138–40; experimenting with, 24–31; explanations of, ix–x, 14–15, 117–21, 135–36, 140; function of, 3–4, 9–10, 12–13, 86; images of, 13, 17–19, 32–33, 138, 140, 148; limits in, 101–4; natural versus moral, 2, 62–63, 65; as performance, 104–5; playing at, 115–16; prehistory of, 60–62; questions about, 2–5, 145–50, 160–62; scales of, 141–43; sources of, 50, 62–65, 70–71, 73, 89, 96–97, 119, 131–33; spelled backward, 86, 93, 100, 104, 121; understanding of, 7–9, 18–19, 24, 34, 36, 77–80, 85–86, 105, 149–50. *See also* dread; motives; precategorical experiences; radical evil
Eysenck, Hans, 54

Fairbairn, W. R. D., 56
Foucault, Michel, 126–27, 129, 164–65n. 11
Franco, Francisco, 146
Frankfurt School of Critical Theory, 77, 80
free informants: attitudes of, 6, 84–85; characteristics of, 151–52; dread contained by, 110–11; on Eichmann, 4, 74–75, 77–79; imaginations of, 97; interviews of, 152–55; and rules, 76. *See also* informants
Freud, Anna, 56
Freud, Sigmund, ix, 5, 27, 114, 119
Friedlander, Saul, 102, 121

Gagnier, Terril T., 52
Gedo, Mary, 146
Genet, Jean, 169n. 10
Germany, culture of, 142–43. *See also* Holocaust
God, 91, 94, 107. *See also* religion
Goethe, Johann Wolfgang, ix, 93–95, 99
Goldhagen, Daniel Jonah, 27, 31–32, 79, 143
Gomes, Peter, 106
Gough, Harrison, 54
Grabbe, Christian, 119
Grotstein, James, 55

hamartia, 129
Hamilton, Thomas, 135–36

Hare, Robert, 54
Hare Psychopathy Checklist (PCL-R), 23–24, 54, 169n. 15
Hartmann, Heinz, 47
hatred, 33–34
Heller, Erich, 37
helplessness. *See* powerlessness; terror/helplessness
Herodotus, 72
Hilberg, Raul, 168n. 3
Hinduism, 85–86
Hitler, Adolf, 10. *See also* Holocaust
Ho, Trang, 106
Hobbes, Thomas, 40–41, 75
Holocaust: aftermath of, 11, 60, 78–79; attitudes toward, 63–64, 78; bureaucratic nature of, 79, 81; and evil, 2, 17, 62, 133; explanations for, 24, 74, 81, 120, 146–49; identification with victims of, 79; participation in, 27, 31–32, 134–35, 142–43; and transgressed limits, 102. *See also* Eichmann, Adolf
Holocaust Museum, 81
Homer, 41
honesty, 131–32
Horkheimer, Max, 80–81, 90
humanity: and balance, 134–36; categorical imperative for, 46–48; characteristics of, 45, 51–52, 69, 71; and compassion, 137–40; and complexity, 105–7; connections among, 22–24; dread of being part of, 50–53, 80; and language, 147–50; meaning of, 108, 134; nature feared by, 81; original experiences of, 46–50; responsibility and regret of, 63–65. *See also* civilization; free informants; inmates; others; self; suffering
Husserl, Edmund, 46

identity, 10–11, 17, 21, 28. *See also* self
Ik (tribe), 32
illness, 51–52
imagination: and evil, 12–13; and playing evil, 115–16; role of, 97–98; in understanding, 149–50. *See also* narratives; symbolism
informants: attitudes of, 1–3; characteristics of, 4–6, 24; and iron cage, 77–80; and Milgram's experiment, 28; precategorical experiences of, 49–50,

informants: attitudes of (*continued*)
110; questionnaire for, 2–4, 160–62;
recruitment of, 5–7; responses by, 153–
54; vampires mentioned by, 87–88. *See
also* free informants; inmates
inmates: attitudes of, 6–7, 75–77, 110;
characteristics of, 4, 12, 30–31, 138,
155–56, 159–60; crimes of, 4, 6, 33, 75,
105, 130–31, 137, 159–60; dread
contained by, 113–16; on Eichmann, 4–
5, 74–76; evil done by, 110–11; images
of evil by, 32–33; interviews of, 156–59;
motives of, 8–9; responsibility of, 63–
65; treatment for, 136–37; on vampires,
13, 95–96. *See also* informants
internal saboteur, 56
iron cage, 77–80

James, William, 60
Jews, 70, 78. *See also* Holocaust
justice, 134–36, 139

kakía (evil in New Testament), 3, 67,
70
Kant, Immanuel: on categorical
imperative, 10, 46–48, 103; on radical
evil, 2, 18, 24, 69, 71, 143–44
Karadzic, Radovan, 15
Katz, Jack, 92
Kierkegaard, Søren, 50, 118
Klein, Melanie: art theory of, 103; on
depressive position, 41–42, 45, 64, 72,
122; on envy, 70–71; influence by, 15,
40; on maliciousness, 142; patients of,
112; on splitting, 105
Kosinski, Jerzy, 52

language, 145–50. *See also* narratives;
symbolism
Lasch, Christopher, 89, 146
Levi, Primo, 52, 80, 120
Lewis, C. S., 95, 99, 107, 152
Lifton, Robert Jay, 135, 142
Lisbon earthquake (1755), as evil, 17, 62,
133
loss: and dread, 118, 169n. 11; effects of,
147; as evil, 67–69; exposure of, 89;
meaning of, 69–70, 117; of self, 9, 43,
55, 66, 92, 119–20. *See also* death;
powerlessness

MacIntyre, Alasdair, 14, 80, 86–87, 114
Mahler, Margaret, 166n. 12
Mann, Thomas, 22, 107–9
Mara, meaning of, 18
Marcuse, Herbert, 77, 80
masochism, 133, 170n. 10. *See also* sadism;
sadomasochism
McCamant, Kevin, 158–59
McCarthy, Cormac, 66
Mead, George Herbert, 54
media, 6, 13, 64, 87, 90
Meloy, J. Reid, 23, 54–56
Mengele, Josef, 142–43
Micheels, Louis, 120
Milgram, Stanley: experiments by, 9,
25–28, 29, 79; on scientific inquiry,
163n. 3
Miller, Alice, 131–32
Miller, James, 126–27, 170n. 6
Mills, C. Wright, 81
Milton, John, 91–92, 99, 119
moira, 68
morality: Bible on, 70; components of, 10–
11, 48–49, 71; corruption of, 18, 24,
69, 101; and ethics, 14, 46–48, 50;
influences on, 81–83; of powerlessless,
68–69; and problem of evil, 15, 143–44;
and self/other distinctions, 46–49;
sources of, 132–33; and war, 60–61, 78.
See also precategorical experiences
Morrow, Lance, 135–36
motives: for bombings, 7–8, 82, 120–21,
139–40; evil versus good intent in, 120–
21, 138–39; as explanation versus
justification, 8–9; hatred as, 33–34;
pleasure as, 24–28, 30–32; social forces
as, 29; and threats to self, 11. *See also*
dread
mourning, 72, 90–91, 107–9. *See also* loss
murder, 4, 6, 33, 75, 105–6, 137. *See also*
Holocaust
music, role of, 107–9

narcissism, 23, 88–89, 91–92, 101
narratives: complex roles in, 114–16; dread
contained by, 112–16; role of, 97–98,
117, 144; sources of, 15. *See also*
symbolism
Nietzsche, Friedrich: on bad faith, 72; and
claiming evil, 121–29; doom experience

of, 37; on eternal recurrence, 167n. 16; on evil and dread, 15–16, 68, 118, 170–71n. 17; on good and evil actions, 103; on unaccountability, 132

Noddings, Nel, 51, 53

no-thing, ix, 117–18

nothingness, ix, 60–61

obedience: and Holocaust, 79, 102; role of, 26–28; and rules, 76; versus sadism, 30–31

Ockham's razor, 31–34

Ogden, Thomas: on anxiety, 53; on consolation, 108–9, 119–20; influence by, 15; patients of, 13, 43–44; on sensory floor, 113; on symbols, 39–40. *See also* autistic-contiguous position

Oklahoma City bombing, 7–8, 140

others: dread inflicted on, 95, 100, 113–14, 119–21, 125–26, 130, 138, 143; as evil, 70–73; and morality, 46–49; possession of, 95–98

Overing, Joanna, 61–62

Pagels, Elaine, 3, 16, 69–70

pain: function of, 51–52, 70; infliction of, 95, 100, 127; reduction of, 123–24; survival of, 126; in torture, 104. *See also* others, dread inflicted on

paranoid-schizoid position: and confusion, 105; and creativity, 103; and demonization, 71–73; description of, 40–45, 55

pathos, 129. *See also* suffering

Patuxent Institution: description of, 5, 137, 156; psychopathy-identification project at, 6–7, 23, 54, 169n. 15. *See also* inmates

PCL-R. *See* Hare Psychopathy Checklist.

Peck, M. Scott, 15, 23, 99, 152

phenomenological philosophy, 37, 45–50

Picasso, Pablo, 146–47

Plato, 1

pleasure, 24–28, 30–32

Popper, Karl, 16

Popular Concepts of Evil (group), 6–7, 155–56. *See also* inmates

positions of experience. *See* autistic-contiguous position; depressive position; paranoid-schizoid position

power: and cruelty, 126–27; versus dread, 80; quest for, 91–95; in torture, 104. *See also* vampires

powerlessness: and dread, 169n. 11; exposure of, 89; fear of, 133–34, 147; meaning of, 68–70. *See also* loss

precategorical experiences: and categorical imperative, 46–48; definition of, 11, 36–45; dread carried in, 48–49, 57; example of, 66–67; and Holocaust, 81; of informants, 49–50, 110; and morality, 47–48, 82; and need for definition, 118; positions of, 40–45; and vampires, 90. *See also* dread; dreams

prepredicative experiences, 46

prisoners. *See* inmates

prisons: as iron cage, 77–80; role of, 30, 75–76, 113, 167n. 5. *See also* Patuxent Institution

psychoanalytic theory: and precategorical experiences, 37–45; role of, 14–15; on sadism, 27–28. *See also names of specific theorists*

psychopathic moment, 52, 58–59

psychopaths: characteristics of, 23–24, 56–57, 97, 138; role of, 6–7, 54; and stranger selfobject, 55–56, 65; study and theories on, 42, 54–55; victims possessed by, 58, 100

ra (evil in Old Testament), 17–18, 60, 63, 66–67

racism, 132–33

radical evil: approach to, 2, 25; definition of, 18, 24, 143; implications of, 18, 69, 71; scales of, 141–44; shortcomings of, 164n. 3

Rank, Otto, 10, 124

Rausch, 102, 121

reason versus dread, 80–83

Rée, Paul, 124–25

regret/remorse, 41, 64–65, 122, 124

relativism, 9

religion: evil considered in, 169n. 11; of informants, 151–52, 160; and understanding evil, 36, 85–86, 105. *See also* Buddhism; Christianity; Hinduism

responsibility: versus confusion, 106; for evil, 121–29; and knowledge, 77; for violence, 29–30, 63–65